W9-AXD-297

THE DESIGNER'S GUIDE TO
BUSINESS
AND CAREERS

how to succeed on the job or on your own

WITHDRAWN

Peg Faimon

HOW
BOOKS
Cincinnati, Ohio
www.howdesign.com

SCHAUMBURG TOWNSHIP DISTRICT LIBRARY
130 SOUTH ROSELLE ROAD
SCHAUMBURG, ILLINOIS 60193

331.129
FAIMON, P

3 1257 01873 3112

THE DESIGNER'S GUIDE TO BUSINESS AND CAREERS. Copyright © 2009 by Peg Faimon. Manufactured in the United States of America. All rights reserved. No other part of this book may be reproduced in any form or by any electronic or mechanical means including information storage and retrieval systems without permission in writing from the publisher, except by a reviewer, who may quote brief passages in a review. Published by HOW Books, an imprint of F+W Media, Inc., 4700 East Galbraith Road, Cincinnati, Ohio 45236. (800) 289-0963. First edition.

For more excellent books and resources for designers, visit www.howdesign.com.

13 12 11 10 09 5 4 3 2 1

Distributed in Canada by Fraser Direct, 100 Armstrong Avenue, Georgetown, Ontario, Canada L7G 5S4, Tel: (905) 877-4411. Distributed in the U.K. and Europe by David & Charles, Brunel House, Newton Abbot, Devon, TQ12 4PU, England, Tel: (+44) 1626 323200, Fax: (+44) 1626 323319, E-mail: postmaster@davidandcharles.co.uk. Distributed in Australia by Capricorn Link, P.O. Box 704, Windsor, NSW 2756 Australia, Tel: (02) 4577-3555.

Library of Congress Cataloging-in-Publication Data

Faimon, Peg, 1962-
  The designer's guide to business and careers / by Peg Faimon. -- 1st ed.
    p. cm.
  ISBN 978-1-60061-156-8 (pbk. : alk. paper)
  1. Graphic arts--Vocational guidance. 2. Commercial art--Vocational guidance. I. Title.
  NC1001.F35 2009
  741.6023--dc22

                                                            2008048357

Edited by Melissa Hill
Designed by Grace Ring
Production coordinated by Greg Nock

DEDICATION

To my students. You've been my inspiration and joy throughout my years of teaching.

And to my family. You've been my support and passion throughout my life.

ACKNOWLEDGMENTS

This book is the result of many years of experience as a design professional and educator. At Miami University I've had the privilege of graduating seventeen classes of design students and witnessing their continued growth and development into seasoned professionals. The idea for this book actually arose from a course I teach at Miami called The Business of Design.

Thanks to everyone at HOW Books for giving me another opportunity to work with them. Special thanks go to several individuals at HOW who have shared their knowledge, skill and advice: Megan Patrick, Acquisitions Editor; Amy Schell and Melissa Hill, my project editors; Grace Ring, the HOW Books Art Director, and Jane Friedman, Editorial Director.

I'm also grateful to those that have contributed their ideas and knowledge to the book by responding to my inquiries and questions: Rita Armstrong, Todd H. Bailey, Erin Beckloff, Barbara Berne, Erik Borreson, Ken Bullock, Eileen Corey, Kim Cornwall Malseed, James Coyle, Juliet D'Ambrosio, Deidre Evans, Tammy Fink, Jeff Fisher, Jez Frampton, Bryan Gaffin, John Garofalo III, Steff Geissbuhler, Paul Ghiz, Thomas H. Gilmore, Nikki Glibert, Anne Haag, Mark Hamilton, Jim Hardy, Bennett Holzworth, Cindy J. Hurley, Joan F. Insel, Cole Johnston, Amanda Kohnen, Lisa Kuhn, Bob Konold, Jenny LaNicca, Jennifer Laino, Jennifer Merchant, Bridgid McCarren, Howard McIlvain, Jeni Moore, Hollis Oberlies, Nancy Owyang, Samantha Perkins, Ellen Petty, Cynthia Pinsonnault, Glenn Platt, Kevin Potts, Steve Reist, Grace Ring, Katie Rundell, Bruce Shaffer,

Jim Sharp, Jennifer Specker, Brian Sooy, Sara Syms, Vance V. VanDrake III and Mike Zender.

At Miami, I'd like to thank all those who have supported me in this and related endeavors, especially Jeffrey Herbst, Provost; James Lentini, Dean, School of Fine Arts; Dele Jegede, Chair, Department of Art; Glenn Platt, Director, Armstrong Institute for Interactive Media Studies, and John Weigand, Chair, Department of Architecture and Interior Design. Special thanks go to Tom Effler, my long-time colleague in Graphic Design; Samantha Perkins, visiting design faculty; and Howard Obenchain and Thomas Gilmore, adjunct faculty; for helping maintain a great design program in the midst of writing this book.

Lastly, and closest to my heart, I am especially thankful to God for His grace and blessings and to my husband Don, and children Anna and Noah, for their love, encouragement and support throughout this process and life.

ABOUT THE AUTHOR

 **Peg Faimon** received a Bachelor of Fine Arts from Indiana University and a Master of Fine Arts from Yale University. Her academic honors include membership in Phi Beta Kappa and Summa Cum Laude honors from Indiana University, and the Yale University Norman Ives Memorial Award. Ms. Faimon has worked as a designer for corporate and small firm offices. She is currently a Professor of Graphic Design, the Director of Miami Design Collaborative, a program in collaborative design studies, and an affiliate faculty member of Armstrong Institute for Interactive Media Studies and the Department of Architecture and Interior Design at Miami University in Oxford, Ohio. Her teaching responsibilities include a wide variety of undergraduate courses in design, including studio, history and interdisciplinary coursework. She was named the Miami University School of Fine Arts Crossan Hayes Curry Distinguished Educator in 2000, and the Naus Family Faculty Scholar in 2008. In addition to teaching, Faimon maintains a design consultancy. She has received national and international recognition for her design work.

Peg Faimon is also the author and designer of *Design Alliance: Uniting Print and Web Design to Create a Total Brand Presence,* and the co-author, with John Weigand, of *The Nature of Design: How the Principles of Design Shape Our World—from Graphics and Architecture to Interiors and Products*, both published in 2003 by HOW Design Books. *The Designer's Guide to Business and Careers* is her third book.

At home, Peg shares her life with her wonderful family: Don, Anna, and Noah. They love to travel and spend time together.

CONTENTS

ABOUT THE BOOK

Design is certainly about aesthetics, but there is much more to being a successful designer than understanding color and composition. If you are like most design students, you realize this during the last year of college, while busily looking for that magical first job. How do you create an effective résumé? How do you correspond with prospective employers? What is good interview etiquette? Then during the first five years in the profession, you come to the realization that there are many aspects to business practice that you have to learn on the job. How do you develop a strategy? What are the best practices for working with vendors like photographers and printers? How do you communicate with marketers and other business people? What about clients?

The Designer's Guide to Business and Careers is a comprehensive guide to basic business issues for designers in today's competitive marketplace. It is for students who are newly entering the world of design and for young professionals who are trying to figure out all the details of day-to-day living as designers in business today. Additionally, individuals who are interested in venturing out on their own, whether through freelancing or officially starting their own firm, will find this information beneficial.

The book is written in an interactive format to provide you with case studies, tips, examples and exercises that will help make new careers and businesses successful. The book is divided into eight parts from choosing a career path to staying fresh as a "creative" to understanding production basics. Each part is divided into more specific topic areas that include exercises to help you put the information into practice.

It is increasingly important that young professionals understand the larger context in which they work, as more and more, designers are called upon to work in a multidisciplinary business environment. Long gone are the days of working alone in an isolated studio on a simple logo job. As the world and its problems become more complex, experts who are also broad in their contextual understanding are highly sought after for their skills and knowledge, as well as their abilities to communicate and connect with others. Even if you are working in a one-person studio, you are going to be collaborating more and more with individuals whose expertise is outside the specific world of graphic design. To be a leader in tomorrow's economy, it is key to have depth and breadth—to have the specialized knowledge of a professional graphic designer, along with a general understanding of related fields and their vocabularies. This ensures that collaboration and communication are efficient and effective. This book will help you gain a better understanding of the language of business and the communication skills to connect with colleagues in related disciplines.

The following pages spotlight those sometimes intangible skills that set a person apart in today's marketplace. Unfortunately, in many design schools, these skills are not taught and are rarely even discussed. As a university professor, I believe it's my responsibility to teach and share this important information. You shouldn't have to learn it through trial and error—the field of design should not be the school of "hard knocks." By being immersed in the information and inspirational ideas of the contributing designers on the following pages, I hope to motivate and educate you about how to be a more effective professional in this fast-paced field—from day one.

Enjoy!

Peg

PART ONE

KNOWING YOUR CAREER OPTIONS

Knowing and understanding the breadth and depth of the graphic design discipline will help you make more educated choices about your career and your future. Many people find themselves moving from one specialty to another at least once, if not multiple times, throughout their career. It's important to understand and be aware of the connections and relationships between these various specialties so you might better plan your path. Being intentional about your career is important. Don't just drift from one job to another—rather, carefully and thoughtfully build your portfolio, experience and reputation of excellence.

The following section will give you a snapshot of the many options available in today's design world. There are many resources available online or in print if you want to get more detailed information about any particular specialty or perspective. The real world advice within this section will give you a sense of that personal perspective. If you want more advice, I encourage you to seek out a professional who is working in that particular corner of design—show interest, ask questions and keep your eyes open for new and exciting opportunities.

CHAPTER 1
DESIGN SPECIALTIES

NUMBERS AND TITLES

It's interesting to look at the actual size of the graphic design profession. We aren't going to take over the world, but we are a formidable force with a strong impact and professional voice. According to AIGA, the professional association for design, as of May 2008, they had approximately 22,000 members. Additionally, the U.S. Bureau of Labor Statistics notes that "Graphic designers held about 261,000 jobs in 2006," with the projected number for 2016 being 286,000. This may sound like a large number, but when you consider the tremendous impact that the "product" of graphic designers has on the general public, it puts that number in better context. You probably come in contact with some form of graphic design, whether it is a newspaper, signage, packaging, advertising or web site, during every hour of your waking day.

Those 260,000 plus graphic designers are involved in all kinds of businesses, institutions, organizations and industries. Companies vary greatly in size and scope. Some are quite small, one to five persons, and the designers are required to take on a wide variety of tasks since there aren't very many of them. On the other end of the spectrum, there are international firms with thousands of employees. The larger the firm, the more distinct the job functions and designations tend to be. Multidisciplinary design firms clustering several design disciplines (architectural, industrial, interior and/or graphic design) under one roof are becoming more and more common and are a wonderful opportunity for graphic designers who like to connect with other design professions.

Of course, salaries also range substantially. The highs and lows vary not only with experience level, as would be expected, but with the location and the type of company as well. Additionally, the size of the company and the level of clientele walking in the front door can affect what the company can pay its employees. Generally speaking, larger firms in major metropolitan areas pay on a higher scale. (But the cost of living must also be taken into account.) Additionally, management and executive positions with greater responsibility and oversight also come with greater pay. (Additional information is available on AIGA's web site: www. aiga.org/content.cfm/salary-survey)

The standard job titles and levels within the design field can be rather confusing since they aren't consistently applied throughout the profession. Most young designers start off at entry level as a junior/assistant designer or a production artist. There are also firms that hire new graduates in intern or freelance positions. (This is a short-term commitment that allows the company and the designer to "try out" the relationship.) The next level, with more responsibility, includes designers and assistant or associate art directors. Above that level are senior designers and art directors. (The term "art director" is commonly used in advertising agencies whereas the term "designer" is used in design firms.) The managerial level involves creative/design directors and managers. Owners/partners/principles are at the top of the list.

MAJOR DESIGN SPECIALTIES

Early in your career, it's useful to be fluent in as many design specialties as possible to broaden your future career options. Generally speaking, design firms offer the broadest range of activities and client types. More specialized firms, such as those focusing on packaging or publishing, can give you great depth, but can pigeonhole you early in your career. If you find you don't want to continue in packaging after several years, once your portfolio is made up of packaging samples and experience, you might find it difficult, for instance, to move over to magazine design, since you can show no experience in page layout. For this reason, it's important to continually expand your knowledge base so you can show a growing breadth and depth of experience. Ultimately, many designers choose some type of specialty and become an expert in that area. The discipline is so vast that it's essentially impossible to keep up with all aspects. Keep in mind that every job is unique and every company has its own corporate culture. Even within a specific category, such as interactive design, there are a wide variety of options. Begin thinking now about what kind of specialties and work environments you want to pursue. Planning and solid research will help you find the job that's the best fit for you.

Magazine and Newspaper Design

Even in this day of online communication, there are a vast number of printed magazines and newspapers at the local, regional and national levels. Additionally, many print publications have online formats and need designers in both the web and print worlds. Some magazines and newspapers are highly specialized in their content and focus on specific topics, such as the arts, science or sports. This gives you a great opportunity to connect your design work with another personal passion or interest.

Both the creation of the actual newspaper or magazine and its promotion need to be designed. Larger publications may divide these functions into editorial and promotional offices that each employs their own design staff. Additionally, there might be a separate staff for the online companion. Online newspapers and magazines normally repeat print content, as well as offer unique interactive features that work best in a web format, such as interactive charts or maps.

Editorial design of magazines and newspapers can be intense, constant work, due to the fact that there is a strict publication schedule that is unyielding. Missing a deadline is not an option. Newspapers come out on a daily or weekly basis and magazines on a weekly, monthly or quarterly basis. A designer or art director, who manages the overall design, working with the design staff and coordinating photographers and illustrators, leads this work. The designer must tightly partner with the editorial staff to make sure the overall visual solution is consistent with the verbal messages being presented. Words and images must work together.

REAL WORLD ADVICE: MAGAZINE DESIGN

BRIDGID MCCARREN, ART DIRECTOR, *HOW* MAGAZINE

HOW Magazine's goal is to help designers—whether they work for a design firm, for an in-house design department or for themselves—run successful, creative, profitable studios. *HOW* Magazine strives to serve the business, technological and creative needs of graphic-design professionals. Our working environment is creative, inquisitive, respectful, supportive and fun, so that each of our individual talents can flourish. If you want to be a part of the magazine industry, get in the know and keep abreast of news, issues, challenges and developments in the design profession by reading books and publications, web sites and listening to radio shows. Get involved by attending industry events and maintaining contact with other creative professionals.

Many young designers are naturally drawn to magazine design, due to years of interaction with exciting and visually stimulating publications. Magazine design can appear to be quite a glamorous profession. Newspaper design, on the other hand, often suffers the opposite impression—all that text! But keep in mind that newspapers are becoming more visually engaging with increased use of photography and illustration. Larger papers have soft news sections, such as lifestyle and home, that have many exciting page design opportunities. Better printing technology also allows for higher quality imagery and use of full-color. Additionally, most larger newspapers have a weekend magazine that offers designers a great deal of creativity. These lifestyle magazines are normally a different size than the normal newspaper and are close to traditional magazines in style and format.

So, you can see that even within what seems to be the narrow category of editorial design, there are many different opportunities and directions.

Consider these questions:

- Does the intense and consistent pace required by editorial design match my personality and working style?
- Do I enjoy working with photographers and illustrators?
- Do I enjoy working with editors and writers?
- Is page design—working with text and imagery—my strength and passion?

Book Design

The publishing industry is a major employer of graphic design talent. Just like with magazine and newspapers, publishers need designers to design books, but they also need to create promotional and marketing materials to sell the books. Book design is divided into two basic categories: book interior and book cover/jacket. These are traditionally separate, but can intersect or be done by the same designer. The book cover/jacket design is closely tied to the sales and marketing strategies, while the book interior design requires especially strong typographic skills.

Publishers can be grouped into several categories. One of the largest and most creative is the trade or commercial publishers who produce both fiction and nonfiction books with a general audience in mind. When people think of books, they generally think of trade books that can be purchased at the national bookstore chains like Barnes & Noble or Borders. Another large category is mass-market paperback—everything from romance novels to travel series. There are also reference books, which are traditionally books, like encyclopedias and dictionaries. Textbook publishers focus on educational books, where the main market is college students; scholarly or academic book publishers work with university faculty to disseminate their research findings. And lastly, there are professional publishers that cater to a specific professional group to meet their disciplinary needs. Designers can be found working in any of these publishing environments.

REAL WORLD ADVICE: BOOK DESIGN

**GRACE RING, MANAGING DESIGNER,
HOW BOOKS AND WRITER'S DIGEST BOOKS**

The work environment in a publishing company is very different from a design firm. In our company, designers sit in close proximity to editors, who require much more quiet for their work than we designers might prefer. But it also serves to create a highly collaborative work environment. You can frequently find editors and designers sitting shoulder to shoulder at one computer, reviewing the finer points of a page together. The editors are always looking at designs to ensure that the text is legible and the hierarchy is clear—things that we should remember as designers, but which we sometimes forget in the throes of our creativity. And it's not uncommon for us to remind an editor that while yes, that ten-word chapter title sounds nice, it really looks long and ridiculous. In the end, the collaboration makes for a better book.

Each of these work environments is quite unique so it's important to do your homework if you are interested in pursuing this industry. For instance, you may think that working for a textbook publisher or university press would be less creative, due to the academic nature of the content. This may be the case with some publishers, but many put out visually engaging materials. Look through the shelves of your neighborhood, university or chain bookstore and pay attention to the publishers that keep coming up again and again as you browse. Which publishers are putting out books that connect with you?

Consider these questions:

- Do I enjoy page design? Would I prefer cover and interior book design? Do I want to work with a publisher that will allow me to do both?
- Do I mind working on longer, larger projects, as opposed to ones that are short and quick?
- Would I enjoy working with an author to make their vision come to life?
- Would I enjoy working hand-in-hand with an editor to make sure that the author's message is being effectively communicated?
- Do I have a particular strength and passion for typography?

Design for Corporations

Many large and some medium-sized corporations have in-house corporate design departments—sometimes referred to as design centers—that are normally managed by a design director who supervises all the work being done by the senior and junior designers and interns. This design team may create work both for internal functions and external promotions. They may also supervise the work of freelance designers who are brought in during particularly busy times or develop relationships with outside firms or agencies that take on specific promotional or advertising campaign work for the corporation. In-house corporate design can be one of the best-paid specialties, as many designers move from design positions up through management, where they transition into related or new areas of the company or directly manage other designers.

Much of the work carried out by these corporate designers focuses on the brand and corporate identity of the company. Early in the twentieth century, Peter Behrens created the concept of corporate design through his outstanding work for the German electrical company, AEG. Along with the company logo, Behrens created a consistent system of typefaces, colors and applications that became a "design standards manual." The control of a consistent brand image is key to a company's successful connection with consumers.

REAL WORLD ADVICE: CORPORATE DESIGN

JENNIFER MERCHANT, PRINCIPLE DESIGN MANAGER, P&G

I decided to get into corporate design for a number of reasons. I have always had a personal passion for design, but also find myself most content when thinking about and contributing to the bigger picture. Beginning my career as a graphic designer, I quickly wanted to influence the business and marketing decisions that were being made in my organization. I went back to graduate school to complete my master's of business administration so I could better understand business models and objectives of the organizations I would be working in (or for) as a designer. Once I was equipped with the right tools, corporate design seemed to be the perfect fit. As a Design Manager at P&G, I still have both feet firmly planted in creative development, however. I also work very closely with my Consumer Research and Business partners to truly understand what the consumer wants and how to build a strong business by connecting with them. In the end, my goal is to lead the External Design Agencies we work with to develop consumer-inspired design that will deliver upon consumer needs.

In a consumer goods corporation such as P&G, design plays the unique role of bringing the consumer experience to the product development process and then visually bringing to life the product and story that have been created by a broader multifunctional team for the consumer.

As a corporate designer, you could be involved in the creation of a company's design standards manual (often referred to as a brand identity manual) or its implementation and application, or both. These guidelines identify the dos and don'ts in applying the different graphic elements of the brand, including such elements as typefaces, color palette, patterns and photographical style. These elements are applied in items such as stationery, paper goods, web site, uniforms, vehicles, etc. Corporate designers often function as the "brand police" for the company, ensuring that these brand guidelines are followed by all internal departments and external vendors.

When looking at this specialty, it's important to think about the size of the company and what that offers you. A large corporation will normally have a variety of products or services with which you will have the opportunity to engage and interact. Smaller companies are generally more focused and less diverse. This will impact your day-to-day environment and the type of jobs on which you work.

Consider these questions:

- Will I enjoy focusing on one company and the consistent application of that company's brand?
- Is the company's business as a whole something that interests me?
- Am I interested in moving into corporate management someday?
- Does the company own many brands in which I might be involved? Is there a lot of variety? Are there particular brands that interest me?
- How large or small is the in-house design group?
- How large of a company am I interested in working with? Do I want international opportunities?

Design for the Music Industry

According to *Becoming a Graphic Designer* by Steven Heller and Teresa Fernandes, "Graphically designed album covers were not used by the recording industry until the late 1930s, but from that moment on, original cover art changed the courses of design and music history. The first record album designed by pioneer Alex Steinweiss for Columbia Records increased record sales by an incredible 800 percent over nondesigned covers." Like book jackets, a creative and visually stimulating design can help gain consumer attention on the shelf and in the store, resulting in greater sales overall. Additionally, great CD covers can add substantial attention, identity and brand equity to the recording artist, band or musical group. Think of how many cover images you remember, perhaps even better than the actual music on the CD. Many have even become iconic images over the generations. Think of the Beatles *White Album* or *Sgt. Pepper's Lonely Hearts Club Band*. Because of the nature of this industry, design for music can be highly creative and result in very innovative work, especially for certain genres.

Now that most music can be downloaded, it might seem that cover images have lost their power. But not with software like Apple iTunes, where you can view the imagery on your computer or mobile device. The covers become a quick visual cue for identifying different artists and their music without even having to read names or titles.

REAL WORLD ADVICE: MUSIC INDUSTRY DESIGN

SARA SYMS, FORMER DESIGNER FOR SONY BMG, INTERACTIVE DESIGNER, RAZORFISH

There are a lot of projects you can be on at any given time. The turnaround for CD packaging is very quick. A day in the life of a music project starts with the artist. First we have to determine if they have their own design team or if we are designing from scratch and working with the artist to discuss look and feel and what they would like to portray. Initial design comps are created and approved by the artist. Stylists and photographers are all hired and, depending on budget, the photo shoot for the album can either be very limited or super substantial. There is a lot of opportunity for creative packaging beyond your basic jewel case.

> It's easy to stay energized. Working for a large company such as Sony, the music artists are constantly in and out of the building, from Springsteen to the Osbourne family, rap artists, the Dixie Chicks, etc. I think it's enough in itself to see your product on billboards, in record stores, out on the streets and advertised on TV to know you are making a difference in music culture.

A creative director will oversee a design department within a record label, and in larger companies, there are sometimes divisions for the different genres of music managed by art directors. The record industry, somewhat like the publishing industry, has many independent labels. Within these smaller companies, there is less hierarchy and they may work with freelancers only. Freelance jobs can offer an up-and-coming designer a good opportunity to develop portfolio pieces, in hopes of getting a full-time job with a larger company. Within this industry, designers are responsible for cover designs, as well as the different promotional materials such as lyric booklets, packaging for special collector's pieces, displays and posters.

Consider these questions:

- Am I particularly strong with imagery, since CD covers commonly use imagery to communicate their message?
- Do I have a good balance of image and type skills since the lyric booklets and promotional materials can be text heavy?
- What size of company and genre would interest me most?
- Do I have a particular passion for music? Would I enjoy working with musicians to help them visually communicate their messages?

Design Within Advertising Agencies

Advertising agencies are one of the most common places that young designers end up working. Most people think of the mega-agencies with offices all around the world, like JWT or Leo Burnett, when they hear the words *advertising agency*, but there are many medium-sized and even smaller agencies that focus more on local and regional work. Midsized to smaller agencies might also focus on a specific category, such as the medical industry. Two or more partners, specialized in either the creative or the business side, normally head agencies. Pairs of art directors and copywriters usually form teams within the firm and these creatives are the heart of any agency. Account executives interface with the clients, manage the accounts and run the business side. Below the creative teams are production assistants that produce work and execute ideas with the team.

Given the importance of the copywriter/art director team, it's good for students who are interested in advertising to take copywriting courses to better understand how to work with their copywriting counterpart. Additionally, courses in narrative and storytelling are helpful, because advertising, especially television advertising, is about telling a very condensed tale. Today, television and radio are still important, but advertising and promotion through interactive media are steadily growing in use and influence. Additionally, consumer-generated advertising and media are quickly changing the face of the industry. It's important for young designers to say abreast of new developments in digital media, so they are ready to apply these ideas to new client needs. (See Chapter 24: Trends in Digital Marketing.)

REAL WORLD ADVICE: ADVERTISING DESIGN

BOB KONOLD, GROUP CREATIVE DIRECTOR, SPM: MARKETING & COMMUNICATIONS

Some agencies are account driven; some are creative driven. SPM is strategy and results driven. It's not creative unless it works. SPM is a marketing communications company. We do any form of communications related to marketing hospitals. For the most part, we are an advertising agency. Our work environment is fun, upbeat, creative, energetic, fast-paced. We're serious about what we do, but we always try to have fun. You can't be creative if you're too serious.

We specialize in healthcare, with hospitals all over the country as our sole focus. In fact, we're arguably the largest hospital ad agency in the country, with fifty employees and thirty-plus clients. So, working here is challenging, because the industry is complex, challenging to learn and ever-changing. Hospitals are highly complicated with different service lines that appeal to different target markets with different problems. However, the challenge is worth it. In the end, you feel good about working on a product that can improve someone's well-being or even save someone's life. It's a "feel good" industry. Literally.

To fit into our corporate culture, it's important to be a great designer: to have a cool-under-pressure, can-do personality; to be a strategic thinker, and not just a person who designs pretty stuff; to be hip on the latest, coolest trends in design, advertising and new media; and to be a pure creative person. Someone who might shoot videos, edit, paint, illustrate, play music and constantly ask "why not?"

Today, print work is still an important part of any advertising agency's portfolio. Graphic design is integral to developing an appropriate and compelling look and feel. The big idea is still important as a central driving force to any advertising campaign, but the overall mood and attitude that are driven and communicated by visuals are of growing influence, given the increased visual literacy and design sensitivity of the general public. Typical assignments for young designers within an advertising agency include projects such as promotional pieces, packaging designs and sales displays.

Full-service agencies or firms who work on all aspects of the brand are more and more common. These firms offer a cohesive vision for a client that includes logo and identity, advertising, packaging, point of purchase displays, in-store design and signage, internet advertising, etc. The line between advertising agencies of this sort and branding firms is becoming fuzzy. (See branding design below.)

Agency jobs can be energizing, yet high-pressure positions. The movement of client accounts in and out of a firm can change the dynamic and day-to-day workflow very quickly. There are many opportunities in larger agencies, even international work and connections. Midsize to smaller firms can be good places for young designers to get experience in order to break into the competitive larger agencies.

Consider these questions:

- Do I like a fast-paced environment?
- Do I like working closely with writers and marketers in an interdisciplinary environment?
- Am I interested in the type of clients the agency works with?
- What is the scope of the work being done? What are the various opportunities to build my portfolio?
- Am I especially good at generating unique approaches and creative ideas? Is there any wit or humor to my work?

Design Within Branding Firms

Branding firms focus on the brand development of a client in print, packaging and web environments. They can and will engage in advertising creation but are less focused on that aspect of the brand—that territory really belongs to advertising agencies. Traditionally, branding firms have done a great deal of identity and packaging development, especially related to placement in retail and consumer environments.

Jez Frampton, Global CEO from Interbrand, describes the importance of branding, "Brands have the power to change the world. It's a lofty statement, indeed, but brands are an important influence on our lives. They are central to commercial markets and democratic societies. They represent free choice. Global brands act as ambassadors for nations and capture the spirit of an age. Most importantly, strong brands bestow value far beyond the tangible performance of the products and services themselves. Brands that do this represent an idea worthy of consumer loyalty. And the more the consumer believes in the brand, the more value the brand returns to its owner."

REAL WORLD ADVICE: BRAND DESIGN

HOWARD MCILVAIN, EXECUTIVE VICE PRESIDENT/ CHIEF CREATIVE OFFICER AND BRUCE SHAFFER, VICE PRESIDENT/DIRECTOR OF CREATIVE SERVICES, LPK

Our vision is to be the best! LPK seeks long-term strategic partnerships with clients that stretch our capabilities.

We recommend that young designers build great relationships and that they get exposed to opportunities to be influential, learn something new, teach somebody what you know, make a positive difference and add value. In addition, it's important to act like it's your first day on the job. Be enthusiastic, eager to learn, ask lots of questions, listen really hard and take risks (and fail faster).

The creative portion of a branding firm is traditionally headed by creative or design director who oversees the work of the senior and junior designers. Many of these firms are quite large, with offices around the country and world. There is some opportunity for individuals to move from office to office and even internationally, but most offices abroad are staffed with local individuals. This gives the firm a truly global reach with expertise in various cultures and languages.

To pursue branding, it's critical to have great skills in logo and identity development. Additionally, it's important to demonstrate the flexibility of your branding solution by showing how this logo can be applied to a wide variety of applications, such as packaging, stationery, paper goods, uniforms and vehicles. Being able to show thoughtful process development is also key. This can be demonstrated through a process/sketch book that shows the development of ideas throughout the project.

Consider these questions:

- Do I like to create logo designs?
- Do I like packaging and other identity applications?
- Do I like to take a project through many steps and through different types of applications?
- Would I enjoy working on a comprehensive team of individuals?

Environmental Design

Environmental design started as sign painting way back in the 1800s. Today, this category includes a breadth of activities from wayfinding (signage systems), to billboards, to interactive kiosks, to exhibition design, to experience design within a retail setting. Environmental designers can be involved with almost any aspect that deals with the physical environment in which we live and interact, both interior and exterior. For this reason, graphic designers who specialize in environments normally work intensively with interior designers or architects, especially if new environments are being constructed. For those interested in all three of these fields, this is a wonderful point of intersection between them.

If you are interested in pursuing environmental design, it's important to have strong three-dimensional design skills and to get as much experience as possible with working in environmental contexts and in handling the wide variety of materials that are used in this specialty. More than other areas within graphic design, environmental design has complex requirements in terms of structural and fabrication knowledge. Sign creation and construction, for instance, require very specific fabrication instructions that are similar to architectural blueprints. There must be clear understanding of materiality and function—the sign must stand up and cannot fall on someone's head. Additionally, there are building and zoning codes that need to be understood and followed in order to have your design approved for installation.

REAL WORLD ADVICE: ENVIRONMENTAL DESIGN

AMANDA KOHNEN, CREATIVE DIRECTOR, INTERBRAND DESIGN FORUM

The work environment at Interbrand Design Forum is incredibly fast-paced, collaborative and inspiring. It's an environment where every day is different, and we're continuously learning by working hand-in-hand with strategists, designers, planners, architects and engineers to bring a brand to life in a 3-D retail environment.

If you're interested in pursuing a career in environmental design, you have to have an interest in three-dimensional forms, in materials, and in the way pieces work together to create a space or object. You have to be interested in learning skills that are different than a traditional print design background. And most importantly, you have to think big: big graphics, big spaces, big ideas. If you come to the table with a passion to learn, you'll succeed.

Wayfinding is a common form of environmental design. It can be a focused project in itself or part of a larger design solution that encompasses many other parts. Wayfinding is certainly not a single sign that you would find over a retail store entrance. It's an integrated system of signs and graphics (letters, symbols and imagery) that guide, for instance, patrons in a museum or customers in a mall, throughout their visiting or buying experience and to their intended destinations. A wayfinding system needs to be highly functional and easy to understand, but at the same time, it should work to increase the brand identity of the company or organization and be aesthetically pleasing and visual engaging. Designers must study and understand traffic patterns and ADA (Americans with Disabilities Act) requirements in order to create a cohesive and efficient plan for all audiences.

Environmental designers also work to educate in many different settings. Wonderful examples are zoos, museums and historic districts. I'm sure you've visited many of these organizations and can even recall ones that had particularly effective systems of maps, charts and informational signs. Today, more and more institutions are incorporating interactive elements as well, such as screens and kiosks, to make the exhibitions even more engaging.

You can get involved with environmental design on various levels and in different work settings. There are large environmental and multidisciplinary design firms that employee different design disciplines. Additionally, some architecture firms have divisions for the design of environments that employ in-house designers. There are also general graphic design firms that engage in this type of work, along with their other projects. This may be a good place to get experience and build your portfolio for future work at a more focused firm.

Consider these questions:

- Do I have a strength and passion for three-dimensional design?
- Do I like the idea of building holistic, physical experiences for clients and their audiences?
- Do I like working on teams and am I interested in collaborating with other design disciplines since these projects are normally too large for one person or one discipline?
- Do I enjoy working on larger, more complex projects that require a longer commitment of time and energy?

Interactive Design

Interactive design is a growing field and it offers many diverse opportunities for graphic designers, especially younger designers who have been recently trained in new media applications. There are dedicated web design firms that focus on interactive development, in-house positions within larger corporations and web-focused positions within more generalized graphic design firms. Additionally, some positions offer the opportunity to combine both print and web, but this does require a breadth of both software and design skills. Due to its highly technical nature, interactive design requires designers to know, or at least understand, the applications and programming involved. Knowing one web-publishing package is not enough; knowing several, in addition to some programming basics, is essential. Designers will often be paired with a programmer, but it's still critical to be able to understand the parameters and potential of this environment in order to design for it.

REAL WORLD ADVICE: INTERACTIVE DESIGN

PAUL GHIZ, FOUNDING PARTNER, GLOBAL CLOUD

Through our innovative web software and services, Global Cloud improves people's lives by enhancing and continually evolving the way they communicate. We increase our customer's capacity to foster and develop relationships that drive success and deliver on their missions. Interactive and web software engineering is the focus of the firm. We provide full interactive design and marketing services as well as proprietary web software that empowers our clients to manage their own content. We have three core departments, which include creative, technology and marketing. Our work environment is extremely creative, collaborative and dynamic. You have the ability to bring ideas to the table at all times and learn new businesses. It is high energy, fast-paced and fun.

The various media are becoming more and more connected and interdependent. As previously mentioned, many magazines and newspapers have online counterparts. There are e-books. Television and radio commercials are now found on the web. The online environment enables traditional media to become more interactive, taking a simple idea and expanding on it. Additionally, user-generated content is becoming more and more influential.

Due to its complexity, the professional work environment for interactive media is highly collaborative. Designers work with programmers, writers, marketers, videographers, etc. The structure within these firms is similar to the other specialties—a design director leading senior and junior designers. Because there is only so much technical knowledge that can be fit into a four-year college education, internships and co-ops are an excellent way to get hands-on experience and more technical skills.

Consider these questions:

- Do I have the technical skills needed (or could I acquire them)?
- Do I like working with others in a highly technical environment?
- Do the limitations and opportunities of the online environment excite me?
- Would I enjoy a firm that does both print and web work, or does specializing interest me?

Motion Design for Television, Film and Video

Graphic designers are increasingly involved with motion graphics used in television, film or video environments, creating film titling, station identifiers and program branding. Designers work in live action or animation, while integrating motion typography. Due to the complexity of this type of work, like interactive design, this specialty normally requires a great deal of collaboration with other skill sets. Most larger film studios have their own creative and production departments where designers work in-house. There are also some independent design firms that specialize in this type of work, along with freelancers.

REAL WORLD ADVICE: TELEVISION DESIGN

JENNIFER SPECKER, DESIGNER, CNN

The work environment at CNN is completely different from one day to the next. For weeks, I might be working on the redesign of a show. Or I might have to crank out animated graphics for a last-minute special that's related to some breaking news. Most of my day is spent designing under an extremely short deadline. I'm lucky if I have several weeks to work on a project.

One aspect that is both good and bad is that you're always working with the same size rectangle. Of course now with some of our programming in HD, that allows us to work with a much larger canvas, which is fabulous. But at the same time, that's challenging, since for one animation we have to design for two different television sizes. Due to the nature of our business, for our daily graphics workload, we work with a lot of stock photography CDs. For those graphics, there just isn't time to schedule a photo shoot.

Just like any other field, you really have to be willing to start at the bottom and work your way up. When I was an entry-level designer, I think I begged my art directors for a side project every single day.

Designers interested in pursuing motion design should be versed in the basic techniques of filmmaking—understanding sequencing, movement and narrative. Experience with film editing software is also important. Many people gain experience through apprenticeships and internships, since this field is highly specialized and many universities do not cover this information in depth.

Designers focusing on motion graphics might also create the print promotional materials for the movie or program they are working on. These items might include posters, billboards, online graphics and press kits.

Consider these questions:

- Do I like working with others in a highly technical environment?
- Do I understand narrative and sequencing?
- What motion typography experience do I possess?
- Do I enjoy working with a diverse team of professionals?

Design Within a Generalist Design Firm

As mentioned previously, many young designers get their start in design firms that do a variety of work and do not necessarily specialize in one area of design practice. In these firms you might be designing a brochure, a web site and signage for three different clients all during the same day's work. In this way, you build a broader portfolio and can move into more specialized work as your career develops.

REAL WORLD ADVICE: GENERALIST DESIGN

KEN CARBONE, PRINCIPAL, CARBONE SMOLAN AGENCY (TAKEN FROM *DESIGN ALLIANCE: UNITING PRINT AND WEB DESIGN TO CREATE A TOTAL BRAND PRESENCE*)

We like the full palette of possibilities and challenges that can be presented to a designer in two dimensions, three dimensions and now in the digital realm. That has given us an opportunity to both build professional and personal careers enriched by a multitude of different kinds of experiences. [Philosophically, CSA is truly a creative think tank.] We pride ourselves on being thinking designers. Yes, we are interested in what it's going to look like in the end, but we're equally interested in the strategy that gets us there. So it's been a long time since someone gave us the typed brief that says, "We want a twenty-four-page brochure and here's a stack of photographs; put it together."

These firms often integrate other disciplines to increase the skill sets they can offer clients. This might include a business component to assist with strategy development, programmers to increase technical depth or project managers to oversee more complex solutions.

Consider these questions:

- Do I like to do a wide variety of work?
- Do I like to keep a lot of different balls in the air and have the ability to switch back and forth throughout the day?
- Do I enjoy working with other designers in a close-knit environment?
- Do I like working with a range of clients?

APPLICATION: DEFINING YOUR DIRECTION

Go to www.myersbriggs.org and take the Myers-Briggs Type Indicator (MBTI) personality inventory to establish your personality preferences. This can help establish possible directions within your professional career choices. The first step to figuring out what you want to do is to think about who you are.

Next, complete the following exercise. The goal is to consider your personality and different types of design specialties to end up with a more focused list of design specialties that you want to further investigate.

On the next page is a summary list of specialties we've discussed. In the second column, list your level of interest from 1–11 (most interested=1). For each specialty, consider how each aspect of your personality would affect your aptitude for that type of work and your job satisfaction.

In the third column, list any past experience in this area. Include in-depth experience, like internships, and smaller experiences, like a project you enjoyed for a class in college.

In the fourth column, mark if you want to gain future experience in or perform further research this area, and list where you'll go to get the information you need (job shadowing, online research, interviews, etc.).

SPECIALTY	CURRENT LEVEL OF INTEREST	PAST EXPERIENCE	FUTURE RESEARCH
SAMPLE			
Advertising	7	Internship	
Interactive	4	Class/workshops	job shadowing
Music	3	Freelance work for area bands	online research
Magazines			
Newspapers			
Books			
Corporate			
Music			
Advertising			
Branding			
Environmental			
Interactive			
Motion			
General			

From this chart, what are your top interests?

1.

2.

3.

CHAPTER 2
OTHER CAREER PATHS

Along with the various specialty areas mentioned in chapter one, there are many opportunities for designers in less traditional settings. Some of the paths and directions discussed below are more appropriate for an individual who has several years experience within the field. For instance, pursuing design management or becoming a professor requires a certain level of experience in order to guide and mentor others. As you think about your future, it's good to know about these options so you can determine if they are right for you.

WORKING IN A COLLABORATIVE ENVIRONMENT

Graphic design is a fuzzy term that doesn't always encompass every aspect of today's ever-changing design environment. A graphic designer's keys to longevity are flexibility, curiosity and adaptability. Keeping abreast of changes and developments within this profession is an exhausting, yet critical, component to any designer's success; however, there's too much to know. Incorporating a breadth of media, skills and knowledge into your portfolio and repertoire is key, but it's not possible for one person to do everything that is currently under the umbrella of graphic design. Medium to large clients are interested in one-stop shopping, where they can get a holistic and consistent approach to their problem solutions, and large clients have larger, more complex problems and projects that require a wide set of skills. The best way to cover it all is to partner with people whose skill sets vary from your own. Crossing disciplinary boundaries is no longer the exception: It's the rule.

Not long ago these types of partnerships were nearly nonexistent, and when they did exist, graphic designers were brought in late in the project to "polish" the already developed solution, not to assist with the actual conceptual creation. Today, in most cases, this has changed for the better. Graphic designers are now active participants on the team from the very beginning of the project, involved in the overarching planning and schematic design, along with their counterparts from the other disciplines.

You will find yourself on various types of teams, depending on the project and client needs. You may collaborate with other graphic designers who have different skill sets than your own—perhaps someone with more packaging or interactive expertise. You may be on a team with other design disciplines (architectural, interior or industrial design), especially if the project is related to environmental or product design. Many times, teams also have marketing, communication, technical communication, copywriting, programming or project management components. Depending on the project parameters, you might need other experts like musicians, composers or videographers, as design solutions today are multisensory, not just visual.

After working with and getting to know other disciplines, some graphic designers find that they are interested in transitioning into interior design or marketing, for instance. Depending on the situation, this may take additional schooling. Sometimes pursuing a graduate degree, such as an MBA or an MFA in the specific disciplinary area, is the best step to getting the knowledge, skills and experience necessary to shift into a new field. Always remember that there is never a hard line between disciplines. Look for the gray areas and enjoy the ambiguity. Many graphic designers do work that would be considered product or interior design, and vice versa. Does the title really make that much difference? I don't think so. What is important is to be doing the work that interests and inspires you, no matter what title you want to give it.

APPLICATION: CREATING THROUGH COLLABORATION

List three different disciplines (creative or otherwise) you are interested in working with.

1.

2.

3.

Think about a place or time where you might connect with these disciplines. For instance, musicians and their original music are often needed in an interactive environment.

1.

2.

3.

Think about your ideal team. What abilities/qualities do the other "players" possess? How do these skills link up with the disciplines you have previously listed?

1.

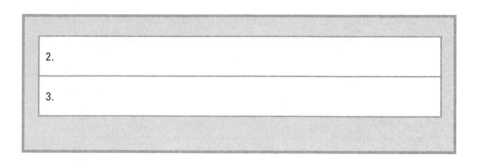

2.

3.

BECOMING A DESIGN ENTREPRENEUR

An entrepreneur is someone who manages, organizes and assumes re-sponsibilities and risks of a business. In the world of graphic design, this is someone who manages a more traditional design business and also creates and sells products. Many times, these products are available on the firm's website or are distributed through some sales channel, such as museum stores. Often, the products also serve as great promotion for the design firm, and if successful, this venture can spin off into its own business. De-pending on the complexity of the item(s), this endeavor can be a simple or complex undertaking. Much depends on how the item(s) will be produced and how expensive and time-consuming that process becomes.

One of the best-known design entrepreneurs was Tibor Kalman. His M&Co. watches came out in the early 1980s and are still popular today for their witty, sleek designs. Other items that are commonly marketed include clocks, posters, furniture, books, toys, magnets, screensavers and desktop screens, and clothing. Obviously, most of these items aren't directly related to graphic design work, but you can be sure that the suc-cessful ones have a design flair and a strong visual aesthetic to set them apart from everyday objects. That's why they are successful.

If becoming a design entrepreneur interests you, then start now by gaining the basic business skills necessary to run your own company. No matter how small, you should be aware of best practices so you don't misstep and make unnecessary mistakes that cost you time and money.

(See Part Six: Doing Your Own Thing for more information.) If you have an idea, run it by someone you trust who has experience; find a mentor and get some first-hand advice.

GETTING INVOLVED WITH NONPROFIT CLIENTS

Many designers are involved in design for nonprofit organizations, including museums, environmental institutions, organizations for the needy and performing, cultural and visual arts institutions. This gives designers the opportunity to donate their talents and services to causes in which they are personally passionate. Most nonprofit work is done by design firms, small and large, that give a portion of their time and effort back to the community through local, regional and national nonprofit work.

There are several different ways that designers work with nonprofit organizations; doing pro bono (or donated) work, working at a reduced design fee or working at a normal fee. As Jeff Fisher of Jeff Fisher LogoMotives explains, "Nonprofit design work does not necessarily mean only pro bono efforts. I do a great deal of paid work for nonprofit organizations as well. In the past, some have gotten grant funds to pay for my services, a few have lined up a specific sponsor to finance a project, others have put me on a monthly retainer for my work fees, and still others simply pay my invoiced charges."

Designers are interested in working with nonprofit organizations for various reasons. As Jeff continues, "The support for specific causes in which I am interested, public awareness of my efforts, involvement with highly regarded community Board of Directors members, creative freedom in many nonprofit situations and the establishment of long-time client relationships are all important elements in my continuing pro bono and nonprofit design work. I've had one long-standing relationship with a small nonprofit theater company for over eighteen years and have created nearly one hundred logo designs for them over that time." (See Chapter 11: Community Involvement.)

APPLICATION: GIVING BACK

List some nonprofits in your area that could benefit from your devoted time, energy and skills. Do some research online and link up your choices with your passions.

NAME OF ORGANIZATION	LINK BETWEEN MY PASSIONS AND THEIR NEEDS
Sample: Big Brothers Big Sisters	Love for kids and design skills match with their need for local promotional materials that highlight needs of children.
1.	
2.	
3.	

EVOLVING INTO A DESIGN MANAGER

Designers who are successful in the corporate environment often find themselves moving up the ladder away from day-to-day design work into management positions. There is no degree in design management specifically. It's the type of position that comes with years of experience and successful problem-solving. If becoming a design manager is your goal, it can be helpful to take courses in business and leadership. Some designers even pursue an MBA to better prepare themselves for a management role.

This job requires excellent organizational and communication skills, as well as experience with project management. In fact, the title for managers of design functions within a company can vary from design director, to project manager, to creative director, to brand manager. In any case, design managers support the designers working under them through mentoring their development, directing day-to-day activities, critiquing their design work and performance, fostering new ideas and creativity, facilitating collaboration and looking at design from the business perspective. It is very much a "forest *and* trees" position—a design manager must keep track of the details while seeing the overall direction.

Beyond guiding their design team, a design manager must connect, collaborate and communicate with the rest of the management team. Most of these individuals are not designers and may have little to no understanding of design process, so it's the design manager's job to promote the value of design and connect business strategy with design strategy. As a design leader, he or she must effectively demonstrate, persuade and inspire colleagues of the power of design to positively impact their organization and their consumers.

BECOMING A PROFESSOR OF DESIGN

Some young designers set their sights on eventually returning to academia as a design professor. Teaching is a wonderful way to give back to the profession and have an impact on the next generation of designers. There are several different ways to do this. While keeping your day job, you can connect with a local art school, college or university and see about teaching a course. You could also teach at an area art center if they offer design coursework. The next level of commitment is a visiting teaching position, which is full-time. At most institutions, this means teaching three or four courses per semester, plus some departmental committee work. Teaching as a part-time instructor or a full-time visiting faculty member may or may not require a graduate degree depending on the school. Some institutions allow professional experience to stand for graduate work if the teaching position isn't permanent.

A full-time tenure-track position is a more permanent situation that would require a terminal graduate degree at most institutions—a master of fine arts in graphic design or equivalent. Teaching full-time as a tenure-track faculty member requires the balancing of teaching a full load of courses (usually three per semester), plus departmental committee work and service and research within the field. For graphic designers, this research can be a variety of things from maintaining a practice in the field, to exhibiting and having design work in annuals and publications, to writing articles and books.

For me, teaching is all about the students. Professors should encourage their students to learn and explore for a lifetime, not just the short time they are in college. This is about learning to use their knowledge, passion and skills in ways that not only service them, but also help others in their community and beyond. I decided to teach because I saw the great opportunity to connect with people to positively impact their growth and development and to guide them into a profession that they would enjoy for a lifetime.

WORKING INTERNATIONALLY

If you are interested in working internationally, you will need to have determination and persistence. You will be dealing with a foreign language and different cultural customs, along with the normal job search issues. You need to develop a strategy and do your homework. Look at the design work of the country you are interested in, along with specific research on firms. You will also need to look into the specific work and visa guidelines for the country. Each country is different, and it's important to understand the various guidelines and restrictions even before you begin your search. For your research, there are various search engines and informational sites online that will assist you on the next page.

RESOURCES FOR YOUR
INTERNATIONAL JOB SEARCH

- Helpful online translator: http://babelfish.yahoo.com
- Global guide to web design and development firms: www.firmlist.com
- Worldwide business and marketing directory: www.kompass.com
- Monster's international section with helpful tips and articles: http://international.monster.com/workabroad/articles
- Job posting site with an international section: www.careerbuilder.com
- Job resource with overseas postings: www.aboutjobs.com
- U.S. Department of State homepage: www.state.gov
- Official list of embassies from the U.S. Department of State: www.usembassy.gov
- List of foreign embassies, with contact information, in Washington, DC: www.embassy.org/embassies
- Online community that assists people with moving abroad and finding jobs: www.expatforum.com
- Global career center for nonprofit jobs: www.idealist.org/en/career

International Job Search Strategies

I have several students who have worked abroad, and they have approached the problem of finding a job in these various ways:

• **Go now and get a job later:** You have to be a very adventurous and determined person to go this route, but it can work. You need a certain amount of preparation. For instance, it's good to go with a stack of résumés and samples of work because access to computers and printers may be unpredictable. This strategy is especially viable if you already have contacts abroad. Those people can form a ready-made network to jump-start your job search and give you advice on cultural issues. If your money and luck run out and you still don't have a job, at least you've had a great adventure.

• **Use your U.S. contacts:** Use your network in the United States to gather names and contacts abroad. Ask your professors, design colleagues and friends in the community about their networks. Let everyone know you are interested in going abroad and see how many people have connections that they can share with you.

• **Look to work for a company with offices abroad:** Even during your interview process, you can mention your interest in working abroad. Some employers are interested in people who are flexible and eager for relocation. Working for an American company in London, Frankfurt or Hong Kong can be a safer way to get an international experience without too much risk. You have your work colleagues as a ready-made community, along with the security of a paycheck and the knowledge that you can be transferred back to the States if things don't work out.

• **Work through the Internet:** Once you've established freelance contacts and clients in the U.S., it may be possible to move abroad and continue those working relationships through e-mail and the internet. Having a partner back in the States to do face-to-face meetings and cover production needs is the best situation, but you can do this on your own as long as your clients are understanding and independent. Once you've established an online freelance business, it might be possible to add local clients, depending on the governmental guidelines.

All of these strategies require you to be patient, open-minded and determined. Unless you are very fortunate, you will not find an international design job without an incredible amount of work. Plan for it to take time and effort and you won't be surprised when it does, but the challenge will be worth every risk. You will grow and be enriched in more personal and professional ways than you can imagine.

REAL WORLD ADVICE: WORKING ABROAD

**JENN LAINO, DESIGNER FROM NEW YORK CITY
WHO MOVED TO FLORENCE, ITALY**

• Learn the local language. English is an asset you can use to your advantage, but it is becoming more common that locals already know English, so now you'll be competing with bilingual natives.

• Learn the legal requirements for working in the desired country. You don't want to be breaking any laws or asking your employers to break laws.

• Prepare your best marketing materials (business cards, webpage, samples) before you go and have a translated version, too.

• Become active in a networking group abroad. Every relationship you create is another opportunity for you to find work (but don't be disappointed if it only leads to new friends to go to aperitivi [happy hour] with!).

• Learn what the principle market is in your desired city and try to use it to your creative advantage, which gets back to the being flexible lesson. You may have experience designing scientific manuals back home, but if you are moving to a fashion mecca like Milan, for example, maybe you should bone up on your fashion advertising skills instead.

• Remember that every experience (good/bad, moving away/returning home because it didn't work out) adds to your overall human experience and builds character. They are all relevant for a successful career wherever it may be. Sometimes opportunities will not fit in with your expectations or experience. You will be frustrated. You may feel lost. But, if you are persistent, creative and flexible, the pieces of the puzzle will click into place eventually. Your human experience will be even more fulfilling, and you will be living the "dolce vita" just like you imagined.

APPLICATION: LOOKING ABROAD

Do research about specific design firms abroad (or American firms that have offices abroad). What did you discover? Make some notes.

What cultural differences did you take note of? How could you adapt to these differences?

What firms interest you the most?

1.

2.

3.

PART TWO

SEARCHING FOR DESIGN JOBS

Looking for a job is much more than just sticking your work in a box and hitting the streets. You should take it as an opportunity to learn more about yourself—to figure out what you want to learn next. What are your strengths and weaknesses, your likes and dislikes? How can you better tailor the job search to the type of position that ultimately fits your career and personal goals?

Think carefully about how to effectively communicate who you are and what you have to offer. Competition is heavy, and there are many applicants for almost any job you apply for. How will you stand out? How will you communicate your professionalism, passion and potential?

The following section highlights the key skills for young designers searching for work. Think of the following pages as a toolbox of sorts. The tips and tools work well individually, but they are even more effective when taken together as a holistic approach to building a solid foundation for your job search. And you should take this toolbox with you as you develop and grow; these skills will serve you well throughout your career as a designer.

CHAPTER 3
JOB SEARCH STRATEGIES

A job search is a serious task that takes a great deal of time and commitment. It doesn't need to be frustrating or frightening; it can be rewarding and educational if approached with the proper attitude. Actually, securing a position is as much about job search strategies as it is about your specific qualifications. Unless you know how to connect with employers, you will not even have the opportunity to sell your credentials.

Your first position is very important and can set you up for a more successful future, but it's important to remember that you aren't married to this first job. Many young designers change positions after two to three years, and most designers have several different jobs over the course of their careers. It's the nature of the profession that there is a certain amount of movement from company to company, especially in the early years of your career. Keep that in mind, but remember your first job can impact the positions you have later in life, due to the mentors you will have and the network you develop. For this reason, you need to be targeted and serious in your search.

DOING YOUR HOMEWORK

Your first priority is to decide which specialty area of the profession you are best suited for, given your talents, skills and interests and which you feel would be the most fulfilling to you personally. As I noted in part one, this is a vast field. You need to focus your efforts. For instance, are you interested in staying general with a design firm, or do you want to focus on a specific field within design, like packaging or interactive? There are literally thousands of possible opportunities, so it's important to narrow your search to those positions most in sync with your interests and skills. Every bit of information you uncover in your research will help you.

Once you've identified your interests, then it's time to look for specific companies. Researching companies and their design work will give you a better understanding of the various opportunities and will help you narrow your choices. For this research, the web will be your best friend. You can find information about the field in general, narrow in on specific areas, look in-depth at company web sites, locate possible positions, etc., Printed resources at the library, bookstores, career service offices, etc. can also be helpful, especially for general information and strategy advice. Design annuals and AIGA resources are particularly helpful for researching specific companies. Paging through design magazines, such as *Print* Magazine, *HOW* Magazine and *Communication Arts*, is a good way to see a lot of great work and to identify firms that might interest you. This will tell you if the design work you have to show is compatible with the type of place you would like to work. If not, you have some work to do on your portfolio.

If your problem is that you don't know which area of the industry interests you, perhaps it would help if you consider your interests and try combining them with your career. For instance, if you are wild about music, perhaps you should look into design for the music industry. In the end, look for a job, whether full-time or freelance, that represents a good step forward in your career and one that will help you refine your goals and directions. (See Part One: Knowing Your Career Options.)

One way to start looking for a job is by deciding where you would like to live, whether in a city or the suburbs, on the East or the West Coast or somewhere in between. Naturally, there will be more jobs in major cities.

However, within many smaller towns and cities there are many opportunities. If you decide to work in a distant city, plan on visiting it for a week or two with your portfolio. Plan your trip well in advance; write to various art and design directors notifying them of your upcoming trip and requesting interviews. After a week or two of making rounds and showing your portfolio, you will have an idea of your potential and an indication of whether you would enjoy working and living in that particular city.

WEBSITES FOR YOUR JOB SEARCH

- AIGA the professional association for design: www.aiga.org
- Global guide to web design and development firms: www.firmlist.com
- Job search and career management resource: www.monster.com
- Job postings and search tools: www.careerbuilder.com
- Career guide and job search resources: www.rileyguide.com
- Search for internships, overseas and resort jobs: www.aboutjobs.com
- Online classifieds with job postings: www.craigslist.com
- Marketing and creative staffing agency: www.aquent.com
- Employment community for designers: www.coroflot.com
- *Communication Arts* job posting and portfolio builder: www.creativehotlist.com

PLACES TO START YOUR JOB RESEARCH

• **Friends:** Ask people you know, friends and relatives, to give you suggestions. Be sure to give these people your résumé so that they can speak more intelligently about your skills if they come across someone who is hiring.

• **Career Services Offices:** Check with your local career services office for advice on your job search. They not only have some good contacts, but can advise you on all aspects of employment.

• **Clubs or Organizations:** Art director's clubs, advertising clubs, graphic design clubs, interior design clubs and architecture clubs are valuable places for making contacts in a natural, informal way. It gives everyone the opportunity to get to know one another in a relaxed atmosphere. Contact the clubs in your area and ask about job listings, special programs, lectures, portfolio reviews and membership information. Many of these clubs offer special discounts for student members and new graduates.

• **Employment Agencies:** Although most employment agencies prefer to deal with experienced professionals, they will occasionally take on an inexperienced individual with strong potential. If you decide to try an agency, make sure it is one that specializes in placing designers. Agency services do not come free of charge. There is a fee, which is generally paid by the employer. You may also wish to check out your state and federal government employment agencies. The government is one of the biggest employers in the country.

• **Faculty:** Your instructors, current and former, will be a good source of general information, especially if they are working in the field and are well acquainted with the region.

• **Publications:** Every major industry publishes a trade magazine to inform the reader of news in the industry. While these publications do not specialize in listing jobs, they may be of help to anyone who is seeking a job. For example, if you are interested in book publishing, there is the Literary Market Place. This has a complete listing of publishers classified by field of activity and subject matter. Other titles are the Standard Rate & Data Service, for magazines; the Standard Directory of Advertising Agencies, for advertising; and The Black Book, which lists agencies, photographers and designers. These are generally large books and copies may be available in the library. Many of these publications also have corresponding web sites.

• **School alumni:** Most schools keep an up-to-date listing of their alumni along with their titles, company names, addresses and phone numbers.

You will find that alumni are generally fond of hiring people from their alma mater.

• **WWW:** The web is the best resource for researching companies. There are job banks, web sites of specific companies with information and design organizations like the AIGA.

A successful job search requires persistence, confidence and organization. You need to accept from the very beginning of the search that you will be rejected. Learn from each situation and move on with a positive attitude. Being positive, organized, energetic and passionate will get you the job. Remember that there are lots of paths to pursue to land a job.

APPLICATION: DESIGNING YOUR CAREER

MAKE LISTS AND TAKE NOTES

First, make a personal inventory.

	RELATED TO DESIGN	POSSIBLY RELATED TO DESIGN	UNRELATED TO DESIGN
Preference, interests, passions, motivations and dreams			
Strengths (including talents and skills)			

	RELATED TO DESIGN	POSSIBLY RELATED TO DESIGN	UNRELATED TO DESIGN
Weaknesses			

Next, prioritize the lists according to which characteristics are strongest or most important to you. A proven simple technique is an A/B/C rating of your priorities, such as with the Franklin Planner. As are high priority, Bs are less important, and Cs are the ones that are lowest priority. Now examine your lists again to reveal your personal profile.

Now that you've looked at yourself, write a description of the type of job you're looking for.

What part(s) of the industry am I most interested in and best suited for (considering my work and personality)?

What type of company would I like to work for? Large? Small? Corporate? Privately Owned?

Do I have some specific companies that I am interested in working for? Why? What type of work do they do?

Where do I want to live? Why?

How important is salary to me? What priority does it hold for me?

What are my interests/hobbies and how do those relate to my career?

What are my personal and career goals?

WRITING THE JOB SEARCH/CAREER PLAN

1. Goal Statements. Identify your main goals: Think about what you'd like to accomplish through your job search process. A specific sample goal would be to find a challenging, exciting design job in the music industry in Nashville. Try to limit your goals to two or three, with one goal probably being the primary goal over the others.

1.

2.

3.

2. Task List. Outline the specific tasks that you will need to do to achieve your goals. For instance, you should outline the research tasks you will need to perform. This list is a very detailed part of your plan. This can be in checklist form. For example, taking the goal from the previous page (Find a challenging, exciting design job in the music industry in Nashville), some tasks might include: researching specific music labels headquartered in Nashville, understanding how the companies differ from one another, building a portfolio that reflects that industry (which might include specifically creating new projects to show greater focus on this particular industry), etc.

GOAL 1 TASK LIST	GOAL 2 TASK LIST	GOAL 3 TASK LIST

3. Priorities. Next, prioritize the sequence of tasks. Just take your list of tasks and categorize them. Feel free to directly prioritize on the task list instead of wasting time recopying everything.

> **4. Action Plan/Timetable.** Finally, organize the prioritized list into a timetable/ calendar. The more specific it is, the more effective it will be. This will give you a specific schedule to follow for your job search process. Your future employer will ask you to work in a similar way so they can keep track of your work productivity.

SALARY NEGOTIATIONS

Some employers have set salaries for entry-level positions and others are negotiable. If the employer clearly indicates that the salary is nonnegotiable, it will be fruitless to attempt to negotiate; if it is negotiable, some salary negotiation is generally expected. It's okay to be straightforward and ask if there is room for negotiation.

Salary Research

It's best to go into this part of the process with a clear idea of appropriate salary ranges for your experience level and location within the country. Some research is in order. There are several resources available online to give you general salary information. This best specific resource for graphic designers is the AIGA | Aquent Survey of Design Salaries (www. designsalaries.com). This resource is updated yearly with accurate salary information on various job levels and geographical locations. There is also a PDF version available for download on the AIGA web site (www. aiga.org). If you know that most entry-level designers are making approximately $35,000, you will feel more comfortable entering into salary negotiations. In addition to online salary resources, it's always good to speak with local designers to get first-hand information about what they are making and what benefits to expect. (Alumni databases from your alma mater are particular good for this research task.) This will give you a sense of context for the geographical location in which you are looking. The main point is to do the proper research so you have reasonable expectations and aren't either caught off guard or embarrassed.

REAL WORLD ADVICE: SALARY NEGOTIATION

BRYAN GAFFIN, SENIOR VICE PRESIDENT AND GROUP CREATIVE DIRECTOR, RAPP COLLINS WORLDWIDE

Hands down, job negotiation is where people mess up the most. You *must* find out what the going rate is for your desired position before you start looking or go into interview. Otherwise, you are sure to undervalue yourself, and get less than you could, because you are desperate to get the job. Don't be afraid to ask for more than the going rate. It's a negotiation. No one will pass on you for asking for a little money. They will expect you to. They will negotiate down and you will find a fair and reasonable salary. The sure sign you've undervalued yourself is when you ask for a salary and they give it to you without negotiating. That means you asked for less than what they were willing to pay. The dirty secret about this business is that it's hard for companies to give you a big raise later, due to corporate policies on what percentage increase they can give in raises and holding company rules. If you undervalue yourself on the way in, you will stay undervalued, until you finally get tired and find a new job. Also, ask for the little things too—extra vacation, help with continuing education, state-of-the-art equipment, etc.

INTERNATIONAL JOB SEARCH TIPS

If you are interested in working abroad (also see Chapter 2: Other Career Paths), it's important to consider some strategies that are specific to an international search. Much of the general advice already covered will work for finding and securing positions abroad, but the following points will help guide you in the even more challenging environment of a foreign country.

• **Prepare a solid strategy and do your research:** The world is a big place so it's important to focus your search efforts as much as possible, otherwise you will be completely overwhelmed. Government (country and city) and tourist web sites offer valuable information on the locations that interest you. Try to get a hold of design magazines and publications, look at international design annuals both in print and online and look for information about specific firms that interest you. Also do research on the etiquette of the country so you can avoid cultural missteps.

• **Figure your budget:** Figuring your finances is particularly important before accepting a position or going abroad. Adjusting to a new economy can be challenging. Quantitative information like the U.S. State Departments per diem rates and cost of living indexes (found on the web) can help you anticipate the fiscal logistics of relocating to another country. Having a good sense of a budget and your spending priorities before going abroad is wise (even when you're just going to research jobs). Some cities, like London and Paris, are notoriously expensive, so be prepared.

• **Make connections:** As much as possible try to connect with people from your target country. This might mean joining online communities or social networks. Do some research and see if there are any international designers in your local community. Connecting with someone in the United States who is from your target country might yield some contacts abroad. According to Anne Haag, an international student who recently went through a search in Luxembourg, "Be friendly and have integrity; it opens a lot of doors."

• **Contact specific companies:** Unless you know for sure that e-mail is an accepted form of communication for job searches, traditional mailing of a formal résumé package with samples of work is preferred. (See Chapter 4: Persuasive Résumés and Business Correspondence.) Just as with domestic job searching, even if you do connect through e-mail, sending a hard copy of all your materials with a well-written cover letter is a nice touch and shows your attention to detail. If you can correspond with the prospective employer in their native language, it's a great opportunity to showcase that skill. Ensure that your spelling, grammar and phrasing are correct by having it proofread by a native speaker. Even if you have to pay for this service, it's well worth it.

REAL WORLD ADVICE: PERSONALITY AND ATTITUDE

STEFF GEISSBUHLER, C&G PARTNERS, NEW YORK CITY

We are looking for intelligence, true intelligence—someone who can under-stand and communicate. When we hire someone, we expect that person to assert himself and learn as much as he can. We like self-starters. If you have a question, stop to get the answer, and go on. Know when to ask and when to act. Become a part of us. We throw junior designers in a project and expect them to take on a lot of responsibility, much more than is usually offered at other design firms. We expect a lot from our people, and if they don't want the responsibility, they won't be happy here. We try to find people who accelerate beyond the bounds of their job description very quickly.

ETHICAL CONSIDERATIONS

There are certain ethical guidelines you should consider while perform-ing your job search:

• Interview only if you are interested in the job or if you are honestly look-ing for more information about the company. Some companies are OK with you interviewing for "practice," but try to judge if this is in fact the case. Don't waste the employer's time.

• In your résumé and correspondence provide only accurate and honest information about yourself, your experience and your work. Exaggerating your skills, especially computer skills, will only hurt you in the long run. When you actually can't perform that Photoshop trick, you'll be up a creek without a paddle.

• Any kind of reimbursement, for travel or meals during an interview, should be arranged in advance. Don't assume anything and keep all your receipts.

• Your acceptance of a job offer should be done in good faith. You should not accept an offer knowing that if another offer comes through you will turn around and dump the first. Reneging on an employment acceptance is a very serious ethical offence and it will come back to haunt you.

• You should quit interviewing once you have accepted a position. If you have interviews scheduled, you can call and inform them that you have already accepted an offer.

APPLICATION: DEMONSTRATING YOUR VALUE

Write a brief value proposition—a statement of what you have to offer a company. How will they benefit from your presence on their team? A company invests a lot of time and money into you, what is their return on that investment? Answer the question: "Tell me about yourself and tell me what you can offer my company." Use a specific company as an example.

CHAPTER 4
PERSUASIVE RÉSUMÉ AND BUSINESS CORRESPONDENCE

Your résumé is like that important first handshake. It should be firm and confident, not weak and limp. The résumé puts all the disconnected pieces of "your design life" into one concise, well-communicated page. It is an advertisement of your skills, accomplishments and capabilities. You need to make a strong connection with your prospective employer and the résumé package should be thought of as a clear and concise introduction of your strengths, knowledge, abilities, and to a degree, your personality.

The résumé should not be a disconnected piece, but a part of a package in which you "brand" yourself. This will make you and your work more memorable, as well as present you in a cohesive, unified fashion. This package should be made up of the résumé, corresponding envelope and letterhead with your cover letter, and a self-promotional piece of some sort. Later in the chapter, we'll look at each of these pieces individually, as well as discuss how to write effective thank you notes and other key business correspondence.

YOUR REFLECTION: THE RÉSUMÉ

In many ways, the résumé is the most important piece in this package. It will be the piece that is passed around the office, sent to other offices electronically, discussed and debated. You need to make sure that every aspect of your résumé is perfect—from the spelling to the typography, from the grammar to the design. This represents *you* on one piece of paper, synthesizing and summarizing all the aspects of your life that are important to communicate to a prospective employer. And you only have a few precious minutes of attention to get all that information across, so it's key to be concise.

There are generally two résumé formats. The chronological approach is the most common format and presents information in the various categories, such as "education" and "work experience" in reverse chronological order. The functional approach emphasizes qualifications, skills and accomplishments and is generally organized by broad categories like "leadership," "technical" or "interpersonal."

Key Advice for Résumé Content

• **Contact information:** Include your mailing address, phone number(s), e-mail address and web address (if you have a web site). If you are a traditional student, you will most likely have two addresses, one on-campus and one that is more permanent. Think about listing both your permanent and campus addresses, so that the employer can find you no matter where you are living. Your résumé might be on file for quite awhile before it gets any real attention, so you never know exactly when they might become interested and wish to contact you. Be careful to use more professional words like "permanent" and "current" rather than "school" or "campus" to describe which address is which.

List your landline(s), but also think about including your cell number. The cell can be the easiest way for a company to reach you. Do remember to check your voice mail greetings. Cute, comical, rowdy or rude greetings can be very unprofessional and embarrassing. You should have a professional and friendly greeting that reflects well on you.

• **Career objectives:** Many career service offices will tell you to put a career objective on your résumé. Additionally, if you look online at examples of business résumés you will probably see these objectives prominently displayed at the top of the page. It's my experience, with graphic design résumés specifically, that these objectives are usually so obvious that they are not necessary. Everyone's objectives sound alike, and they are normally a repetition of your cover letter. It's better to just spend the time to write a really effective cover letter with this information included. See cover letter writing advice on pages 61–62.

• **Education:** If you are newly graduated, you should list your educational information first, because this is the most important, and hopefully most impressive qualification that you have early in your career. Make sure to list your specific degree title, the institution and its location. If you had a good grade point average (3.5 or higher), then list it as an asset, but it is not necessary to list the GPA in most cases. If you do list the GPA, make sure to list the cumulative, not just the major GPA. Everyone will assume you have a good grade point in your chosen major. If you participated in any special programs, like international or honors programs, than make sure to list those as part of your educational experience. Once you have had one or two professional positions, the education listing can move down on the résumé.

• **Technical or related skills:** It's important to list the computer software with which you are familiar. It can be beneficial to generally list the level or proficiency: "familiar," "proficient," "expert." If you work on both Mac and PC platforms, you should also note that point. There may be other specialty skills to mention, such as illustration or photography abilities.

• **Work experience:** When you list your work experience, it's important to note the job title, company, job location and dates of employment in a consistent order and style. Additionally, it's important to be descriptive, yet concise, about the responsibilities of each job. Even a seemingly unrelated job, like a library assistant or waitress, might have some important responsibilities to communicate. Any communication or leadership skills that were developed should be noted. For design-related jobs, you should note responsibilities related to design skills, tasks and knowledge.

• **Related experience:** This is a good "catchall" for items that you want to include that don't fit into another category. The types of things that normally find their way into this category are unpaid design jobs, such as pro bono or volunteer work, and special design programs or projects.

• **Honors:** It's important to list any significant honors that you have received or honors programs in which you have participated.

• **Activities:** List your important activities, especially those related to the graphic design field. It's good to get involved in design organizations, like AIGA or regional groups, as a student or young professional. Many AIGA members will interview people if they have "AIGA" on their résumé. It's important to show that, even as a young professional, you are interested in and eager to support the profession through involvement in our national organization.

• **References:** It is most flexible to have a separate reference sheet that matches your résumé: that way you can include them or not depending on the situation and what the employer is requesting. List your references from most important to least important, as many people begin at the top of the list and may not call everyone. Ask a variety of people that know you from different perspectives, like former professors, employers, etc. Do not list personal references, such as relatives or friends—keep the list professional. Make sure your references have a résumé to refer to if an employer calls. Speaking from personal experience, it's very disconcerting to get a call from a prospective employer from out of the blue. Even if you give a glowing review of someone, it's not good to be caught off-guard.

Your résumé writing should be clear, concise and easy to read. Keep your tenses consistent. It usually makes most sense to put everything in past tense, such as "worked," "created" or "learned." Use strong verbs and an active voice to make the writing more interesting and energetic. Ask a trusted friend or colleague to proofread your résumé. Make sure there are no spelling or grammatical errors. I once had a boss that would toss a résumé if it had even one error. If you have errors in your résumé, it communicates that you are not careful and are not detail oriented.

Key Advice for Typography and Visual Organization

Since the résumé is essentially a typographic piece, it is extremely important that you pay close attention to the typographic details. Show your final résumé to other designers to get their feedback. If you know someone who is especially gifted with typography, ask him/her for advice.

The typographic and visual hierarchy of the résumé is especially important. You should be sure that your name and section headings are primary and that the other information is secondary. If all the information is on the same visual level, then it will be disorganized and difficult to read.

IMPORTANT TYPOGRAPHIC DETAILS

- Use only one space after periods, not two—typing rules aren't the same as typography rules.
- Use actual quotations and apostrophe marks—not inch and foot marks.
- Use an en dash between dates on your résumé—don't use a hyphen.
- Do not hyphenate words on your résumé—it's a short document.
- Use the proper special characters and accent marks
- Don't use the underline function—underlines look like web links.
- Rarely use all capital letters—they're difficult to read
- Double-check your kerning between letters, especially for headings.
- Don't use too many fonts and weights—don't overcomplicate it.
- Set your tabs in the software—don't use the space bar.

- Avoid widows (last word of a paragraph on its own line) and orphans (last word of a paragraph on the top of the next column).
- Flush left/ragged right text works best on a résumé—there are generally not enough words for justified text.
- Make sure your leading works well with your typeface choice—tight leading is difficult to read.

General Organization

Make sure to consistently list your entries from most recent to least recent. Additionally, early in your career, your résumé should be a very concise one page. There is no reason to go to two or more pages until you have several years of experience.

If you have just a little information in certain categories, it is visually stronger to combine these into one. Categories that make sense together include: honors and activities, education and computer skills, related skills and coursework, etc.

Print or Electronic

A well-designed, typographically sensitive résumé package printed on beautiful paper and received through the traditional mail can set you apart from the endless e-mail résumés received by art/design directors. Ultimately, designers, especially older ones, love to hold something in their hands. If a company is specifically asking for an electronic copy of the résumé, such as in an online application, please follow their instructions. But that doesn't mean that you can't also send along a hard copy to a specific design professional within the firm. Often both tactics, print and electronic, work well in tandem and connect with different targets and needs.

YOUR INTRODUCTION: THE LETTERHEAD AND ENVELOPE

If your résumé is sent through traditional mail, your envelope will be the first thing seen by your prospective employer. It's important that it sets a tone that is carried through to your cover letter and résumé. This set should reflect a consistent and well-organized theme from the design to the writing style.

Designing Your Envelope

With the design of the envelope, it's very important to check current postal standards. Generally speaking, you shouldn't have anything on the right half of the envelope (or at least any marks must be very light in value) so there is no interference with the bar coding and cancellation machinery. The last thing you want is to spend the time and money to send out a stack of résumés and have them all returned to you as undeliverable. It's worth the time to print a mock-up of your envelope and stop by your local post office to make sure all's well, especially if you are doing anything unusual.

There are some advantages with using a traditional #10 business-size envelope. There is no additional charge for an unusual size; it is easy to put through a laser or ink-jet printer and standard size envelopes are available in a wide variety of paper stocks and flap styles. There are other sizes available, but make sure you can easily fold the contents to get them in the envelope. An envelope that's too small can be problematic.

Writing Your Cover Letter

The cover letter and personal letterhead should resemble your résumé in typography and organization. Your name and address information can be in the same location on both pieces, for instance. The content of the cover letter is very important and should be carefully written. In the letter, you should do the following:

- Be brief and succinct.
- Assess employer's needs and match your skills to them.

- Start with a "standard letter" and then tailor it to each circumstance.
- Show some personality, but write in a mature, professional style.
- Don't get fancy or cute with the typography of the letter.
- Have perfect spelling and grammar!

It should include the following content in this specific order:

1. writer's return address (already designed into your letterhead)
2. date
3. employer's name and address
4. salutation
   - Ms. or Mr. unless you are familiar with the person
5. opening paragraph
   - state why you are writing
   - establish a point of contact, if appropriate
   - give a brief description of who you are
6. paragraph(s) 2–3
   - highlight a few salient points from your résumé
   - mention points that are likely to be important to the reader
   - show how your education and experience fit the position and organization
7. closing paragraph
   - politely request a review/interview/meeting with the employer
   - offer to provide additional information
   - thank the reader for his/her consideration
   - state that you will contact them in a certain time period.
8. writer's name and signature
9. enclosure notation (when appropriate)

YOUR FOLLOW-THROUGH: FURTHER CORRESPONDENCE

Many people stop short and miss many opportunities to communicate with their prospective employer in a consistent, responsible and effective manner. There are several points in the job search process where you should touch base in either a formal or informal way. This consistent correspondence shows your thoroughness, attention to detail and enthusiasm.

QUESTIONS TO GUIDE ALL BUSINESS CORRESPONDENCE

Who is my audience?

What is my objective?

What are the objectives and needs of my audience?

What benefits can I offer the audience?

What will grab attention and make my point(s) clear?

What examples and evidence can I present?

How can I show my interest and enthusiasm?

Have I spent sufficient time revising and proofing the letter?

Interview Confirmation

It's best to confirm your interview in writing. Today, this is normally done through a brief, yet professional, e-mail that restates the date and time of your interview and confirms any specific details that may have been discussed by phone. This is a great opportunity to grease the skids for your interview by expressing your appreciation and enthusiasm for the opportunity to interview. Sometimes employers will send a confirmation e-mail themselves. In that case, you can reply, acknowledging the e-mail and interview.

Post-Interview Thank You

Sending a thank you note following your interview will set you apart, as many people do not follow up in this way. Send the note promptly after the interview so your meeting is fresh in the interviewer's mind. Remind him or her who you are, since they may have interviewed many people in the same day, and briefly reiterate your strengths and experience. Show enthusiasm for the position and convey appreciation for the opportunity to interview. If the place is very informal, the thank you can be hand written (but not crafty), or you can use your letterhead. The thank you note will have more impact if it's sent by mail as opposed to e-mail.

Clarification of Job Offer

If you receive a job offer and you have questions, it's best to clarify and confirm everything with your main contact person at the company and/ or the HR department, if there is one. This can be done by phone or e-mail. You should indicate your interest in the company and position and ask specifically for the information you need. Always make sure to express your appreciation for their assistance and cooperation.

Acceptance Letter

Once you have clarified everything and your questions are answered, you should confirm all the details and your acceptance of the position in writing. Employers will send you a contract, but this letter is a good way to express you appreciation and enthusiasm for the position and at the same time, avoid any future miscommunication. In your letter, refer to the offer made by the employer and restate the terms of the employment, such as salary and vacation time. Confirm any preemployment details, such as the starting date. It's preferable to put this document on letter form as opposed to e-mail.

Letter of Declination

As a courtesy, if you officially decline an offer, you should write a polite and tactful letter informing the company of your acceptance of another position. The design world is small, and it's very important not to burn any bridges. You never know when you might interact with this company or these individuals again. Decline the offer, but there is no need to give a lot details. Simply inform them of the acceptance of another offer and express your appreciation for the interview with their company.

APPLICATION: KEEPING DETAILED RECORDS

It's very important to keep an organized file of your correspondence to and from each prospective employer (either an electronic or physical file). This is especially important if you are working with a number of companies. It's very easy to get confused and forget the particular details of each company. Erin Beckloff, a designer who recently went through a job search in a new city remarks that, "Both times I've searched for a job, I've tried to stay as organized as possible. Even in the age of electronic communication and with our career being very focused on the computer, I found the easiest way to stay organized was to make note cards, one for each company with their address, any contacts names, and date(s) and what was said when I communicated with them. For my Kansas City search, I did the same thing in an InDesign document, listing all the agencies and design firms and finding out ways to contact each, recording every time I contacted them via e-mail/mail/phone."

As you begin your job search, create records that include the information below. When you're making notes about the conversation and action items, try to write bulleted points about the important aspects of the conversation, such as details about the company or specific requests the company is making of you.

Company Name:	Main Address:	Main Phone Number:
Contact Names:	E-mail Addresses:	Extension Numbers:

RECORD OF CONTACT		
Date and Time:		
Conversation:		
Action Items:		

CHAPTER 5
EFFECTIVE PORTFOLIO AND SELF-PROMOTION STRATEGIES

There are entire books written on portfolio presentation. I'd like to briefly touch on the subject here, focusing mostly on organizational and strategic issues. Your portfolio, whether in traditional form, PDF or web site, will represent you through individual projects, and as an overall design presentation; it is a project in itself and should be thought of as such. There should be unity of presentation, clarity of purpose and thoughtful organization.

VARIOUS PORTFOLIO FORMS

Today the form of a portfolio can vary a great deal. It's important for you to create various portfolios to meet different needs and situations. Prospective employers may ask to see your portfolio web site, may request digital work sent via web upload or e-mail, or will want to see "real" work in hard copy (or a combination of these three). All of these forms need to be presented in a coherent and well-designed fashion, and there should be a consistent overall look and feel between them, creating your own brand identity. (See Chapter 4: Persuasive Résumés and Business Correspondence.)

REAL WORLD ADVICE: WEB PORTFOLIOS

**BRYAN GAFFIN, SENIOR VICE PRESIDENT AND
GROUP CREATIVE DIRECTOR, RAPP COLLINS WORLDWIDE**

You have to have a digital portfolio in addition to your actual portfolio. You want to send your book out to as many people as possible, and only an online portfolio can do the job. The best part is not having to hassle someone to get your book back. Send the URL and you're done. I remember in the predigital era, having to create five to ten mini books to pass out in the city, and then having to follow them around, bug people about the status, pick them up without anyone even seeing it because I had an interview elsewhere. It was difficult. With an online book, you can basically manage your career from a Starbucks with Wi-Fi. This online portfolio, however, is the reviewer's first introduction to you, so it must also be beautifully designed, as well as completely easy and graceful to use. I can't tell you how many designers I see who have terrible online portfolios. If you can't manage to design well for yourself, you'll never be able to do it for a client.

The traditional hard copy portfolio presentation can take various forms as well. There are many different types of portfolio cases that can be purchased at any art store. There are two different portfolio types that I recommend for different reasons and situations:

• **The first type of portfolio is a well-constructed portfolio box.** It can be opened flat on a desk, with the work on individual (not bound) black or gray foam core boards.

This type of presentation gives you the flexibility to swap boards in and out and change the order with ease. The boards can also be laid out for simultaneous viewing. These boxes generally come in standard sizes, such as 16" x 20", 14" x 17" and 11" x 14". With a larger case, you can show many of your pieces without reduction. A smaller case is excellent for travel and is convenient to carry and store.

• **The second type of portfolio is a book with bound pages.** This creates a very professional and holistic presentation of your work and becomes a true design project in itself, since it is a completely designed book. Your project images will need to be reduced in size and the order of presentation will be fixed, but the overall impression of this type of presentation is often quite impressive. Process work can still be incorporated into the page design to express the development of selected projects.

Whichever you choose, keep this in mind: Rita Armstrong, a recruiter with fifteen plus years of experience with graphic designers, notes that, "The biggest complaint I get about junior designers entering the market is that they have no polished communication skills. Be prepared to show your book in a manner that explains why you made certain choices. I am also getting more requests for backup sketches, so that designers can show the thinking behind their designs."

REAL WORLD ADVICE: PORTFOLIOS

ERIN BECKLOFF, ART DIRECTOR, RECENTLY WENT THROUGH A JOB SEARCH IN KANSAS CITY

I found that setting up my book with the strongest pieces first and last worked well. I found that it's best for your portfolio to be a manageable size for you, if you're comfortable with black boards, than go with that. This last time, I made my book in a lime green canvas album, it worked for me and matched my personal branding. I had both flats and comped brochures/three-dimensional pieces. The interviewers liked being able to hold the work in their hands, notice the craft and choice of paper.

ORGANIZING THE PORTFOLIO

Your portfolio should contain ten to fifteen pieces, depending on the number of projects requiring multiple boards or pages. You should count by projects, not by pages. A complex project with multiple parts (logo, stationery, packaging, signage, etc.) might take two or three pages of the portfolio, but it should still be counted as one project. Discussed below are several different ways to order the work.

Ordered by Strength of Work

Pick out your three best pieces and order them from one to three, one being the strongest. Open your portfolio with piece number one, close your portfolio with piece number two and put piece number three in the middle. Equally disperse the other strong pieces throughout the portfolio with the weaker pieces scattered throughout. The advantage of this strategy is that you are continually reminding the reviewer of the strength of your work. The disadvantage is that everything in your portfolio should be strong, so deciding on weak pieces could be difficult and subjective.

Ordered by Design Specialties

If you have a generalist background, with pieces from various specialties within design, you can organize the portfolio by category: branding, packaging, interactive, etc. This method points out the variety of your skills and emphasizes your flexibility. The disadvantage of this strategy is that many things don't fit into nice, neat categories. A branding project, for instance, might have packaging components. You should base your decision on what works best for the overall portfolio organization and not get too caught up in overly stiff categorization.

Ordered by Skill Sets

Instead of using categories such as branding, packaging and interactive, use skill categories, such as leadership, collaboration and communication. This is a more conceptual way to go and gives you greater flexibility and creativity in terms of ordering. You can even identify the categories using some type of divider pages/boards.

Ordered by Company Match
It will show that you've done your homework if you order your portfolio to emphasize how your work aligns with the interviewing company. For instance, if you are interviewing with a branding firm, showing several branding projects with prominent placement in your portfolio will communicate to the firm that you have the skills they need.

Other Portfolio Advice
• Your first piece shouldn't be too complex, but should have quick impact.

• You can end with a more complex piece, and perhaps one that's more personal.

• Have one "story" piece, perhaps in the middle or end. This is a piece that has an engaging and positive story (i.e., challenging project process, interesting content or complex client relationship).

• Mix up black/white and color pieces, horizontal and verticals.

• Three-dimensional work, such as packaging, should be professionally photographed. The photograph can be displayed on the same board with a full-size printout of the main labeling/identity.

• Show complex projects with several parts on multiple boards. Don't crowd images together.

• Showing team projects is good, but be able to intelligently explain what the project entailed and how the team worked.

• Do not use chronological order to organize the portfolio.

- Show fine art work within a design context, such as an illustration within a magazine layout.

- High quality craft is essential.

APPLICATION: PLANNING YOUR PORTFOLIO

In what kind of package do I want my portfolio?

What kind of message do I want to communicate with it?

How accurately does my portfolio portray me?

What kind of person would like my work? What kind of person wouldn't?

What are my strengths? My weaknesses?

What projects are my strongest? Which are my weakest? Why?

What about my portfolio will set me apart from the rest?

How many pieces will I have in my portfolio?

How many of those pieces already exist in a finished form? How many need to be reworked?

SELF-PROMOTION

A self-promotional piece can be almost any type of visual communication vehicle that says something about you and your work. It can attract prospective employers to connect with you by promoting your skills, knowledge or personality. If effective, it will set you apart from other designers and give your audience something to remember you by. For this reason, many self-promos are uniquely clever and engaging, both visually and verbally. For professionals, self-promos attract new clients and are a business development tool. They can increase your public image and reputation as a designer.

It's key with any self-promotional piece to carefully consider your audience. What are you trying to accomplish? Who are you trying to connect with? What types of things do they like? What will really catch their attention? How can you be unique, creative and thoughtful in your presentation? How can you create something that your audience will want to keep? Display on their desk? Put up on their wall?

Self-promotional pieces can take many forms such as postcards in a box, poster series, small artist books, CDs/DVDs, pieces that relate specifically to the employer's business (bookmarks for a book publisher), interesting/unique package designs, folders with sample printouts of work, business cards and/or CD, sample (reduced) portfolio of works or e-mail newsletters.

In his article on www.creativelatitude.com, "Self-Promotion—Finding Your Theme," designer Kevin Potts notes that "Your own promotional material is completely self-generated. There is no creative brief to get the project rolling, and all timelines or budget constraints are self-imposed. You are essentially creating something from nothing, and 100 percent responsible for the final product. A cold engine is harder to start than a warm one, and getting the creative pistons firing at full speed requires time and focus. It may require altering your schedule. Set aside paid assignments. Don't mow the lawn. Work late a few evenings. Without taking the time to sit down and simply work through ideas, the canvas will remain forever blank.

"When you do start sketching out ideas, it is important to remember that unabashed honesty is a critical ingredient in creating designs that successfully represent you as an artist. If it deceives the audience, it is self-defeating. If you willingly project a false identity through your own design, how useful are you to clients?

"Sometimes, you have to dig a little deeper and find unique inspirations—your own theme. It is imperative to avoid shallow self-design built for the whiz-bang wow factor. These hollow attempts at promotion are almost too easy to find—they are too flashy or too corporate or too high concept. They have no passion. No soul. … Finding our own unique theme for self-design requires coming to terms with ourselves, and not just as creative lifers but also as people. Like many forms of art, it can often seem like public self-examination."

APPLICATION: PLANNING AN EFFECTIVE SELF-PROMO

- Research your targets and be relevant to their needs. Get to know them and tailor your self-promo to connect with their needs and interests. Make some notes.

- Work within your branding. The best self-promos complement your résumé package, web site, portfolio, etc. All these pieces should have a certain look and feel—a consistent application of color, fonts, textures, etc.

- While being consistent, you can still express yourself. The self-promotional piece is a great place to express your creativity, have fun and show your energy.

- Always pay attention to details. Proofread everything, make sure you have all the names and titles correct, watch your craft, etc.

- Connect with the right people. Make sure you do your research on who should specifically receive your materials. If you send your self-promo to a generic "Creative Director" or "To Whom it May Concern," it will end up in the trash.

- Consider sending a series of self-promos. Send a "teaser" that gives only a portion of the information, then send more pieces that culminate in a "reveal."

- Make sure to follow up a week or two after your mailing. The point is to maintain a dialogue between you and your prospective employer.

- Keep detailed records regarding your correspondence and follow up.

RECORD OF CONTACT: SELF-PROMOTION
Date Sent:
Date/Time of Follow-up:
Conversation:
Action Items:

CHAPTER 6
INTERVIEWING SKILLS AND ETIQUETTE

Effective interviewing comes naturally to very few people. Most of us have to work on developing the skills necessary to communicate our knowledge, energy and capabilities. This is truly something for which you need to take responsibility. Courses, seminars and workshops on effective interviewing can be helpful in giving you an overview and specific tips, but the things you hear there generally won't make sense until the rubber meets the road—until you actually start having interviews.

Meta Newhouse, Creative Director at GroupBaronet describes two scenarios, "Scenario A: Potential employee shows up a little late. There is a typo on his resume. His boards are cut in different sizes. He is argumentative. His overall attitude is, 'What's in this job for me?' Scenario B: When potential employee calls ahead to make appointment, he asks what the employer is looking for and tailors his book. He researches the website and comes to the meeting (early) with several questions for the interviewer. The presentation is spotless, consistent and understandable. His overall attitude is, 'What can I do to help make your company even more successful?'"

As the examples above point out, it is very helpful to look at the interviewing and job search process from the perspective of the employer.

Which of the two people described would you hire? In a recent www. howdesign.com article entitled "Finding Entry-Level Job Candidates," written by The Creative Group to employers, they note six important pieces of interviewing advice: look for real-world experience such as internships, client-based projects in class and extracurricular work, or volunteer work; take note of professional behavior, etiquette and communication skills; look for good chemistry and "fit" with your company culture; look at the educational credentials, but don't get "hung up" on them; take note of an enthusiastic attitude and a positive approach; and check the references. Notice that the portfolio is barely mentioned, as your design skills are only a part of who you are as an employee. All of the points above focus on personal and professional skills, and all of these characteristics will or will not be communicated during the course of your interview. It's up to you.

INTERVIEW BASICS

There is no set recipe for a successful interview. It's very important to realize that every company and situation will be different. You need to be prepared and flexible. It's important to "go with the flow," but you should also have some consistent goals for any interview:

- Expand upon the information that's available on your résumé and fill in the gaps.

- Express your personality and professionalism.

- Communicate your qualifications and credentials for the job and your fit with the company.

- Show your interest and enthusiasm for the position and your knowledge of the company.

- Gain additional information about the company so you can better assess possible employment opportunities.

Types of Interviews

There are several different types of interviews that you will encounter. Each employer approaches interviewing differently, and they may use one or all of these approaches:

• **Phone:** You may be interviewed by phone, especially for a first/screening interview or if the employer is farther than driving distance. If you are going to be interviewed by several people over a speaker phone, it's good to get some prior experience with this situation, if at all possible, as it can be quite disorienting and confusing. Be well prepared for a phone interview. If it doesn't go well, you won't get the in-person interview. Make sure you have a quiet spot to talk.

• **E-mail:** You may be asked to fill out a questionnaire by e-mail or web, possibly including some quick assignments to test you out. I've found that this approach is a bit frustrating for the applicant, because they don't really get to "show their stuff" in a web questionnaire—the questions and information being gathered are rather controlled. Companies use these forms because they are efficient ways to collect the key facts they need to then move on (or not) to the next level.

• **In-person:** Depending on the company and their interview procedures, an in-person interview can be a shorter screening interview that will be followed up by a longer selection interview, or it can be your one chance to speak face-to-face. The number of interviews can vary greatly from company to company. You might visit the office only once or many times. You might interview with only one person, with several people together or with a series of people individually. Treat each interview like it's your one and only chance to make a great impression and to communicate your qualifications. You can ask for details regarding the interview so you might better prepare, such as how many people will be interviewing you, but don't be surprised if this changes at the last minute.

- **Informational interview and portfolio review:** So far, we've talked about interviews for specific job openings, but how can you connect with the company you are interested in that has no job openings? Jeff Fisher of Jeff Fisher LogoMotives suggests, "Research companies that are of interest to you. Then contact the principal, creative director or art director for an informational interview. Many will be happy to take the time to talk with you about what their firm does, the local market or their own careers. My initial informational interviews led to referrals to other firms, contract design work, job interviews with other companies and relationships with individuals in the advertising and design industries that are now approaching three decades."

Interview Preparation

Preparation for interviewing is paramount. Of course, you know yourself and your work, but do you know how to talk about it in a concise and positive manner? What do you know about the organization you are interviewing with? Have you looked at their web site? Have you studied their work and their client list? As Mark Hamilton, Associate Director of Marketing and Creative Services at the College of Saint Rose, suggests, "Don't consider yourself some hot shot rock star designer. You might be great, but so are a whole lot of others. And if you really are great, humility goes a long way in making you even greater. Do tell me about yourself and what makes you tick. What inspires you, the book you want to write someday and most importantly, tell me about those "crummy" jobs you may have worked. Admitting that you once pumped gas or worked in a grocery store says more about your work ethic (that you weren't afraid to work), in comparison to those who did nothing over the summer and lived out of their parent's pockets. Do your homework. Know about the company for whom you are interviewing, whether it is a design or ad agency or a corporation."

Clearly define your career goals prior to the interview and consider how you are a match for the company and their needs. A recent design graduate, Nikki Glibert, Designer, Branding Brand, elaborates, "A voice from one of my college professors sang in my head, 'When you go to a job interview, you are interviewing the company as much as they are interviewing you.' Not only was that idea extremely comforting at the time, I realized later how true it actually was. I decided that whatever happened would be for the best. I went into the interview excited to show my work and completely confident in my skills and personality, thinking that if the company didn't like me for me, then we wouldn't work well together anyway. The best advice I can give when it comes to interviewing for that first design job is to be yourself, to know your work and to show your passion for design. The rest will take care of itself."

APPLICATION: MATCHMAKING

It's important to consider how you and your prospective employer(s) match up. This will help you effectively interview and ensure that you are interviewing with the appropriate companies. How can you demonstrate a good "fit?" Here's an example:

YOUR CAREER GOALS	PROSPECTIVE COMPANY 1	PROSPECTIVE COMPANY 2
SAMPLE		
Upward mobility into Management	✓ Large Corporation	Small Design Firm
Work with Multidisciplinary Team	✓ Team-based Organization	Some Team Projects
Challenging Environment	✓ Large Projects	✓ Variety of Clients

YOUR CAREER GOALS	PROSPECTIVE COMPANY 1	PROSPECTIVE COMPANY 2

Making a Great Impression

Making a great first impression is more important than you realize. I've interviewed a lot of people, and I can tell you from personal experience that I make a good many mental notes about a person in just the first few minutes of the interview. And, as an interviewee, if you get a bad start, you have to work extra hard during the remainder of the interview to improve the impression. It seems to go without saying that you should dress professionally, but I've seen some pretty inappropriate outfits. Don't overdo it and be dramatic or distracting to your own work. It's OK to show a bit of personality, but you want the interviewers to be staring at your work, not you. Be punctual and arrive five to ten minutes early so you aren't rushed. Be courteous and kind to everyone you meet. Smile, give a firm handshake and direct eye contact. Bring extra copies of your résumé and reference sheet because you never know how many people will be interviewing you. It's also a good idea to bring some paper and a pen to take notes during the interview. This will show that you are prepared, interested and engaged.

During the interview, do not refer to notes. You need to be able to speak about your work in a natural way that doesn't sound canned or memorized. If you forget something, or if you are asked a question, it's OK to pause for a minute to gather your thoughts. There's nothing worse than listening to someone who is trying to fill time with disconnected comments and *umms*. It's very important to show confidence, enthusiasm and passion, without coming across as arrogant. The STAR method will help you keep your thoughts organized and your comments efficient: When discussing your work, focus briefly on the *S*=situation, *T*=tasks involved, *A*=actions taken and *R*=results.

STAR METHOD EXAMPLE

• **Situation:** This poster is part of an identity campaign I created for a nonprofit organization's annual fine arts festival. I worked with the event committee to develop the theme.

• **Tasks involved:** I created a cohesive branding package for the festival consisting of the logo, event poster, program and various advertisements and promotional items. I also worked with the committee to develop a marketing and implementation strategy.

• **Actions taken:** I met with the event chair and committee on a weekly basis to give them updates and to receive feedback on my design work. I supervised the work of freelance photographers and art directed a photo shoot. I also worked with the printer through all aspects of the production phase for each piece that was produced.

• **Results:** The attendance for the fine arts festival increased by 25 percent, partially due to these increased effectiveness of this promotional campaign.

Interview Questions

There are several different types of questions that an interviewer might ask you.

• **Direct questions** are focused and elicit specific information from you, such as "What's your name?"

• **Open-ended questions** allow you to bring more information into your answers and elaborate on topics you want to discuss, but make sure that all the points you bring up are relevant—you have limited time; don't wonder off and waste your time on a tangent. An example of an open-ended question would be "Tell me about this project." The STAR method will help you focus and concisely describe the project and solution.

• **Behavioral questions** are designed to determine how you react in certain situations, such as "Give me an example of a time you handled a particularly stressful situation." Behavioral questions are probably the trickiest type and they are becoming more commonly used. It's very important to stay positive and engaged when answering these types of questions. The interviewer might be "fishing" to see if you will negatively complain about former colleagues and work situations. Your interview will go badly if you start down a negative path.

• **Questions about weaknesses** are one of the biggest difficulties for most people is answering—and these can really come in any of the forms above. Be honest, talk about what you specifically have learned from particular situations and certainly don't lie. Some people say to turn weaknesses into strengths, but be careful that this doesn't sound evasive, manipulative or canned.

SAMPLE INTERVIEW QUESTIONS

Write out your responses and practice verbally answering the questions.

Tell me about yourself.

Which piece from your portfolio is your favorite? Why?

Which is your weakest piece? What would you do differently if you created this piece again.

What do you do well?

What don't you do well?

What was your most important experience(s) in college?

What things outside of design influence your work?

Tell me about a specific situation in which you effectively handled stress.

How do you handle multiple tasks?

Where do you see yourself in five years?

What is the biggest contribution you made to your classmates' education?

What was your favorite thing about a job you had in the past?

What do you think would be the ideal job?

Under what conditions do you work best?

When faced with conflict, how do you handle it?

Describe how you work as part of a team?

What personal qualities distinguish you from other applicants?

Why did you choose to be a graphic designer?

What factors do you consider most important in evaluating yourself and your success?

Why should I hire you?

It's also important for you to have questions for the interviewer. One reason to have that pen and paper for notes is to jot down questions as they occur to you during the course of the interview. Normally toward the end, you will have time to address these. It's important to be prepared with intelligent and insightful questions that show your interest in the position and your knowledge of the company. Try not to ask obvious questions about information that's readily available—on their web site or printed materials—this shows you didn't do your homework. For instance, don't ask "Who are your clients?" since that's information you should have discovered in your research. Ask instead, "I noted on your web site that Company X is one of your clients. I think it would be very interesting to work with them. Are you currently working on a project together?"

If the interviewer appears to be pressed for time, don't be pushy about your questions; you can ask them at another time or through e-mail. It's fine to ask when you will hear more about the status of the position.

REAL WORLD ADVICE: INTERVIEWING

COLE JOHNSTON, JUNIOR DESIGNER, LANDOR ASSOCIATES, RECENT DESIGN GRAD:

- Be humbled you were asked to interview but confident there is a reason.
- Interviewers want to see passion, seeing good work is icing on the cake.
- Explaining your process and articulating your ideas succinctly is key.
- Know more about a company than what their web site can tell you. If there is a book, read it.
- Learn the lingo that the company you are interviewing for uses and use it in your interview.
- Be kind to everyone, including the receptionists, they can sometimes give you insight as to what kind of day the company is having.
- Always follow up and write genuine thoughts.
- If you can get your interviewer to remember why he loves his job, you have gotten the job.
- Listen whenever you can. Ask your interviewer questions.
- Never speak poorly about anyone, anything or any place. Negativism doesn't get you the job.
- Smile!
- Be open to criticism. This goes back to being humble.

- Compliment the people who helped you get to where you are.
- You will be rejected; don't let that distract you from your goals.
- You are a brand; decide what message you want that brand to make before you walk in the door.
- Don't show work you are not 110 percent sure about.
- You get better at interviewing the more you interview.
- Interview for an internship; it can turn into a job offer.
- Have conversations with your interviewer, not lectures.
- Don't be stressed; there is always another job out there.

FOLLOWING THE INTERVIEW

Your job search doesn't end with the interview. In fact, in many ways it has just begun. Your behavior following the interview can make or break your chances of getting the job. This is the time to really differentiate yourself from the crowd by showing your attention to detail, courtesy and professionalism.

Effective Follow-Up

Don't just sit there and wait for the phone to ring. Employers value initiative and enthusiasm and this is a great opportunity to express those qualities. Don't wait too long to send a thank you note as a follow-up (see Chapter 4: Persuasive Résumés and Business Correspondence). You might also correspond by e-mail or phone to stay connected and answer questions. Keep all of your communication brief and to the point. Jeff Fisher of Jeff Fisher LogoMotives mentions a good example, "Be persistent and patient. Hiring someone for the position that interests you may not be the number one priority of the company at the time. A designer friend was just interviewed and hired for a position almost two months after submitting a résumé and hearing nothing during that period. Still, every couple weeks he would place a phone call to leave a message or drop a postcard in the mail."

Evaluating Yourself

Immediately following the interview, whether it was by phone or in-person, spend some time evaluating your performance and listing your areas of strength and your areas for improvement. Look at each interview experience as a learning opportunity. You can and should get better with each interview, but you'll only do this if you reflect and make notes. Be confident in yourself and don't give up. Even bad interviews can be great learning tools.

Evaluating the Offer

If there's a match, the employer will extend a job offer. This offer is normally made by phone or e-mail, and then a more formal letter outlining the details may follow. At this point, a time frame is usually set for your decision. A normal time frame is a few weeks. If you feel the company isn't giving you enough time to make a decision, it's acceptable to negotiate and ask for additional time. Understand that they also have to look out for their best interest. If you don't accept the position, then they need to move on to their second or third choice. If you take too long, that person may no longer be available.

If you receive multiple offers, you need to examine each very carefully. As part of your job search process, it's best to develop a list of criteria to judge offers against. Prioritize the items that are most important to you: the scope of work, the company's client list, the location, the salary, etc. This criteria list is absolutely necessary when judging offers, especially when comparing multiple offers against one another. Develop a pro/con list for each offer. This will allow you to come to a thoughtful decision.

In evaluating offers, it's important to be deliberate, but you need to balance out the analytical with the emotional; trust your instincts. Your criteria list will only give you so much information. In the long run, you will probably have to just leap and trust that gut feeling. Pay attention to the feelings you have about the company during all your interactions with them—phone calls, the interview and e-mail exchanges. Does it feel like a match to your personality and skills? Try to base this decision on interactions with not just one, but multiple people. Additionally, try to gather other opinions—how do people outside of the company think and feel? Talk to people you trust about your job offers and get their reactions and opinions, but remember that the final decision is yours.

Salary Discussions

Generally speaking, you don't talk about the specific salary until an actual job offer is made. If an employer pushes you for a salary range early in the process, be prepared with a broad range, so you don't get pigeonholed. When discussing salary, it's important that you have a specific idea about how much you want and need to make, but don't offer up this information to the employer right away. Be positive and considerate during the salary negotiations to demonstrate your willingness to be a flexible employee.

In addition to the salary, you must also consider the benefits package (such as health insurance, vacation and sick pay, tuition reimbursement and retirement plans) that the employer is offering. It is my experience that many young designers don't realize the importance of this package, as it is a more long-term perk. It can be extremely important, especially in circumstances where an individual has health issues of one kind or another. It's also important to think about retirement benefits early in your career, even in your early twenties. The value or quality of a benefits package is somewhat subjective as it can be dependent on your personal situation.

Once you've agreed to a salary and benefits package, the employer will put everything in writing. You may even be asked to sign a copy for your permanent job records. If the employer doesn't offer this up, you should ask. It's important to have these details in writing so there are no misunderstandings later in your employment. This letter should include the starting date, salary, benefits, job title and any other important details for your particular situation.

PART THREE

PRACTICING CRITICAL SKILLS

Design is all about people and all about communication—not just visual communication. Today, more than ever, designers are called upon to have strong communication skills.

As designers, we are interacting in the business world and our work is influencing business decisions on a daily basis. Your key business and communication skills can make or break your career in design, no matter how talented you are or how beautiful your work is. If you cannot communicate in an effective manner with business people and clients, you will not be a successful designer in today's marketplace.

Additionally, the market is quickly evolving. Even designers who have been in the professional setting for some time must be flexible and fluid in their approach. You must stay up-to-date on developments and directions. Evolution is key to design within a business context.

The following section highlights critical skills for a young professional to possess. From communication to time management, it's important to be intentional in the application of these skills. They will serve you well throughout you career as a designer, and in many cases, even in your personal life.

CHAPTER 7
BASICS OF EFFECTIVE TIME MANAGEMENT

I don't claim to be an expert on time management. I credit my parents for any natural organizational skills I possess; they are both incredibly organized—more than I will ever be, or maybe even want to be. But I have found that having a good grasp of time management skills can make you a happier, more balanced and certainly more successful person. Most importantly, these skills can reduce work and personal stress—something we all need. As a design professional, you will have stressful times, but good time management skills will assist you in functioning more effectively even during high-pressure situations.

Here's the secret: You must be proactive in the application of the principles shared in this section. They will not happen on their own; you must actively apply them. You have the choice. We can blame a lot on our ancestors, our upbringing and our environment (and these things are certainly factors in how we all behave), but ultimately, we can overcome and take a different and better path. We have the power of imagination and great potential. I know it sounds cliché, but it's really true. Your perception is your reality, and you have the choice to alter your perception and your actions.

Focus on enjoying something in each task, even the most mundane. Count your time as extremely valuable, because it is. If you remember that your time as a design professional is worth 50, 100 or 150 dollars per hour, you will think twice about wasting a moment, especially if you imagine billing yourself for those lost and unsatisfying hours.

PRIORITIZE

Our priorities manifest themselves as tasks and actions. For example, if my children are important to me, then I demonstrate that priority by doing things with and for them. And I need to balance those personal priorities with my professional ones. It's important to know what tasks are important and to perform those first before lower value activities. As C. Ray Johnson, business planning coach and author, notes, "Prioritizing is the answer to time management problems—not computer efficiency experts or matrix scheduling. You do not need to do work faster or to eliminate gaps in productivity to make better use of your time. You need to spend more time on the right thing."

The 80/20 Rule states that, generally, 20 percent of the causes affect 80 percent of the outcomes. For instance, in business, 80 percent of the sales would come from 20 percent of the clients. In time management, if you prioritize and spend 20 percent of your time on the most important tasks, you won't get just 20 percent value, you'll get 80 percent value. That's why you get so much done a few days or hours before something is due— because you are forced to concentrate on the most important tasks. If you could always focus on those most important tasks, then procrastination would not be an issue.

Prioritizing is all about making choices. One of the key tricks to making prioritization work for you is learning to identify "important" versus "urgent" tasks. Important, or high priority, tasks are those that help you achieve your long-term goals or have meaningful or significant long-term effects or consequences for others or you. At first glance, many day-to-day tasks seem equally urgent and important. Yet, if you take a moment to look more closely, you will hopefully see that many of our urgent activities throughout the day are not really important in the long run and do not have a significant long-term impact on your life or the lives of others. At the same time, the parts of your life that are most important to you, like improving your skills, and yourself, or spending time with family, would often not be classified as urgent.

Urgent items should always be held to a high standard in order to truly be classified as such: They are the tasks that would get us into a crisis or trouble if they didn't get completed on time. They are not the tasks that keep you busy so you can avoid important work or decisions; they are not the problems that are really the responsibility of others (it's certainly nice to help people, but don't enable another procrastinator!); and they are not the constant interruptions by e-mail and phone.

How do you know what is important in the long term? You know by understanding yourself and your personal goals in your various roles and parts of your life: health, family, financial, intellectual, social, professional and spiritual. You probably already have many of these goals figured out, but they may be vague and unclear. Writing them down can help to clarify and organize these goals.

APPLICATION: MAKING A PLAN

Planning is preparing and organizing a series of action steps to achieve a goal. If a plan is thoughtful and applied effectively, it can significantly reduce the amount of time it takes to achieve a goal.

A thorough plan consists of:

1. writing a goals statement(s)
2. listing tasks or actions to achieve the goals
3. prioritizing the list according to importance/preference
4. developing the tasks into an action plan (in the form of a calendar or timetable)
5. monitoring the implementation of the plan (keeping a checklist)

6. adjusting the plan based on self-evaluation (You always need to be flexible, as things may take longer than you expect, or you may have new, unanticipated assignments that need attention.)

SAMPLE GOALS STATEMENTS AND TASKS/ACTIONS:

First Goal: Decide on an area of interest

- Research fields of interest in the library and on the web.
- Talk to professors and/or colleagues and show them my portfolio.
- Job shadow interest areas.
- Talk to professionals about first jobs and get their advice.

Second Goal: Design a portfolio with interest area in mind (print design).

- Evaluate existing work and determine strengths and weaknesses.
- Expand upon annual report design layouts.
- Design a Gallery Guide using my fine art work (drawings and paintings).
- Finish poster series focusing on typography skills.
- Have professional photographs taken of three-dimensional work.

Third Goal: Research job market and determine list of "targets."

- Determine career goals.
- Research companies that fit my career goals and interests.
- Research average starting pay and benefits packages.
- Apply to companies.
- Keep good records of company interactions.

Once you have your tasks/actions, put them into a calendar/timetable form that becomes your action plan. It can be difficult to determine how long particular tasks can take, but with experience, this becomes easier and easier; you can also ask a more knowledgeable and experienced person for help.

DELEGATE WHEN APPROPRIATE

One of the ways we can be more efficient in our work and get more of the tasks completed is through delegation. More hands on the job should get it done faster. Especially with a large project, it's very important to assess the entire project to know when and if to delegate a task to someone else. For instance, you obviously need to design all your own pieces in your portfolio, but you don't necessarily need to make your portfolio case. For some people, this might be a priority, and they might schedule the time to accomplish the task. But for many people, this would take too much time away from more important revision and improvement of previous projects. This is where delegation comes in. You can purchase your portfolio case from a company, or, if you want something unique, find another person with the skills to create it for you.

Delegation is a form of project management, and for it to work well, you have to monitor the process of the task execution to ensure that it is satisfactorily completed. If you are in charge of the project, you are still ultimately responsible for the work. So that you aren't caught in a very difficult situation, it's extremely important to assess skills, strengths and weaknesses of those to whom you want to delegate the work. For instance, say you're a junior designer and you're working with interns on the implementation of a project. You might informally interview those individuals to make sure they have the skills and the interest to complete specific tasks. If you are confident in those you have delegated to, you will not have to worry about getting the job done. It's poor time management to delegate but continually check up on, and ultimately do, the work of others. This will make more work for you, so make sure you pick the right people for the job.

CHOOSE TO AVOID PROCRASTINATION

Procrastination is often caused by a lack of clear goals, improper prioritization, feeling overwhelmed, waiting for the right time or mood to do the job, underestimating the difficulty of tasks, unclear standards for the task outcomes, feeling as if the tasks are imposed on you from outside, tasks that are too ambiguous, underdeveloped organization or decision making skills, fear of failure or success, and perfectionism.

Most people procrastinate to some degree. Even highly effective time managers may procrastinate about specific tasks that are burdensome. Most procrastinators are not slackers, but work diligently, often in an apparent frenzy of sorts. Most of the time, the issue is focus. They are doing many things, often in a hurried manner, so they aren't working efficiently. We've all experienced situations where the time just seems to disappear and we've gotten nothing done. Examine your habits and search for new ways to change or eliminate those moments of procrastination and distraction.

First and foremost it's key to learn to recognize when you are procrastinating. Many people don't even recognize these actions, especially if the avoidance behaviors are in themselves positive or appear to be urgent. Be aware of the following:

- focusing on less important jobs, like doing the laundry, instead of tackling that big, important job that's been haunting you (It's important to have clean laundry, but you can probably do it another day.)

- reading your e-mail or texting instead of starting your high priority tasks

- continuously going for coffee or taking breaks to talk with coworkers

- having an item on your to-do list for a very long time without addressing it

- saying "yes" when others ask you for assistance in order to avoid your important work

Here are some strategies to help solve procrastination problems:

- Examine your own habits and become more aware of your own work behaviors and patterns.

- Force yourself to at least begin the task. Even if you don't get very far, when you go back to it later, it will be easier to take up where you left off.

- Use peer pressure if you have to. Let your colleagues keep you accountable for your responsibilities.

- Focus on an unpleasant consequence. For me, my most powerful motivator is the thought of the stress that will result from my procrastination.

- Use positive reinforcement. Give yourself a reward for your hard work and effective scheduling.

- Break a big project into smaller pieces that are manageable and not so psychologically overwhelming. This is an extremely effective strategy for me. I tend to get involved in very large and complex tasks (like writing books!), and I find the beginning of the project to be particularly difficult. Once I organize and subdivide the job, it's less cumbersome.

- Start with smaller, quicker portions of a big job, so that you feel you are making some key progress. Once you get rolling, the momentum will help your motivation.

- Use your dead time wisely. Every minute can be used—your time in the car, walking, waiting, etc. Even if you only have ten minutes while you are sitting in a doctor's office, how can you use that time?

- Find a place to work that is free from distractions.

- Schedule regular reviews of your progress.

- Block out specific time for tasks. Just as with meetings, block out your calendar so that certain times are protected for big tasks.

- Most importantly, you need to know yourself. What are the things that help you work at your best?

KEEP TO-DO LISTS

Part of your planning process can be spending five to ten minutes each day in organizing your tasks into to-do lists, whether using one of the many digital tools now available, or just the simple, old-fashioned way. Writing down your tasks is very important, unless you only have a few things to do each day. (I don't know any designers with that sort of life.) The process of writing the to-do list will help you clarify the urgency of the tasks as well as assess the time allotment for each one. Review your to-do list and decide on the priority of each task. Give the highest priority to the tasks that get you closer to your goals, using something like the ABC method. Mark the tasks on your to do list with As if they are directly related to your goals or are assessed as being "urgent" and should be done that day. *B*s are less important tasks that can wait until you are done with *A*s. *C*s are the ones that can be safely moved to a later day.

Remember, a to-do list is not an endless, overwhelming list with no sense of priority. By organizing the list, you will decrease stress. Even if it takes a bit more time to prioritize, your time will be much more effectively utilized in the long run. If you don't prioritize the list, it will only add to your stress by making you feel that you are drowning in work.

One other caution: I have known people who spend time writing to-do lists each day as an avoidance behavior, and I've done this myself from time to time. They don't use the list to help them organize their work, they just spend time creating it as busy work, as a means of keeping them from doing bigger and more important tasks. The to-do list is not an end in and of itself. It is merely a tool to help you get to work.

TIPS AND TOOLS FOR TIME MANAGEMENT

- Don't trust your memory; write and organize your list.
- Prioritize your tasks; focus on your important goals.

- Plan your time; don't let life just "happen" to you.
- Learn to say "no"; assess requests against your priorities (things that are important to you) and sweet spots (things that you are good at and enjoy).
- Start fresh; don't kick yourself for mistakes in the past.
- Use an activity log; evaluate how you are spending your time.
- Learn about yourself; know what works for you and identify bad habits.
- Have high standards, but don't be a perfectionist; it's not possible for everything to be perfectly done.
- Watch out for filler tasks; don't keep yourself busy to avoid important work.

DISCOVER YOUR "SWEET SPOTS"

You've heard about the "sweet spot" in tennis, baseball and golf. It's the part of the racquet, bat or club that allows you to get the most impact for the least effort. When you hit the sweet spot, the ball goes in the right direction and for a long distance, and it makes the game fun and enjoyable. In the same way, people have certain interests, talents and skills and when they live in this zone, life is more enjoyable and less stressful.

That's not to say that you can only live there. We all have to do the laundry and tackle projects that might not be our strength. A variety of activities stretches us and expands our horizons, but if we know our sweet spots and work them in effectively, we can use our time more wisely to meet our goals and interests a majority of the time. For example, my career-oriented sweet spots include teaching and curriculum development, design and branding, organization and big-picture problem solving, and project management.

Sweet spots give you a good measuring stick for making decisions and setting priorities about how to use your time. If someone asks you to do something, you can measure the request against your sweet spots. Does the activity distract you from working and living within your strengths and priorities? If so, maybe the activity is still worthwhile for a short time—perhaps you're helping someone with their sweet spot—but don't let it deter you from your priorities and distract you for the long term. We'll talk more about finding and using sweet spots in Part Five: Working With Others (page 161).

TIME MANAGEMENT ONLINE RESOURCES

- Online to-do list and task management tool: www.rememberthemilk.com
- Sharable calendar service from Google: www.google.com/calendar
- Organizational tool and online sharable calendar: www.30boxes.com
- Web-based task manager: www.vitalist.com
- Easy to use to-do list and task manager: www.todolist.com
- Daily weblog on "getting things done" tools: http://lifehacker.com

CHAPTER 8
GENERAL COMMUNICATION SKILLS

To communicate effectively you must understand the content of your message, the audience you are connecting with and how the message will be perceived. You must also consider the circumstances and environment surrounding your communication messages, such as cultural or situational context. Additionally, since communication is two-way, you need to consider how you receive and respond to the messages of others.

An article on www.mindtools.com, "Communication Skills–Start Here," states that, "In a recent survey of recruiters from companies with more than fifty thousand employees, communication skills were cited as the single most important decisive factor in choosing managers. The survey, conducted by the University of Pittsburgh's Katz School of Business, points out that communication skills, including written and oral presentations, as well as an ability to work with others, are the main factor contributing to job success."

NONVERBAL COMMUNICATION

Various examples of nonverbal communication include eye contact, facial expressions, body posture and gestures, clothing and jewelry, and how you relate to the space and people around you. It's extremely important to think about your own nonverbal cues, as well as the cues you pick up from of those around you. An understanding of what is actually being said can be highly colored by different gestures and looks. Also, be mindful of cultural differences. (This is an interesting and large topic. There are many online resources and books on cultural and personality differences.)

Although what you say is verbal, the way you say it is nonverbal. Your tone of voice is extremely important. Watch the tone, volume and pitch of your voice, as your tone communicates your feelings about the subject and person you are speaking with. Be mindful of listening to your own tone and be conscious of how you are speaking. Train yourself to notice the volume of your voice. This takes self-control, but it can be done. The Institute for Management Excellence reports that research by Dr. Albert Mehrabian, psychology professor and communication expert, explains that words alone are only 7 percent effective in completely communicating your message, tone of voice is 38 percent effective, and nonverbal cues are 55 percent effective.

E-mail correspondence can also have a tone of voice. When people read, they sense a tone or voice to the writing, and e-mails, because of their informal and quick nature, can communicate a short and sometimes rude tone. Be especially cautious of miscommunication of your intent through e-mail or instant message. (See page 110 for more information about e-etiquette.)

Reading body language will help you read between the lines of a message. For instance, a client may tell you they are satisfied with your logo design, but they may have their arms crossed and have a furrowed brow and a frown. If that's the case, you should dig deeper. Ask them specific questions about things they like and dislike. If they are truly unsatisfied, even if they are telling you something different, you will ultimately pay the price. They may eventually come back to you to redo work, and at that point, it will probably be more difficult to change and refine.

Also, be conscious of your own body language. Think about how others may be reading your behavior. What are you communicating to your clients and coworkers? Do you express an openness and confidence with your calm demeanor? Or do you pace around the office, tap your feet under the desk during meetings, play with your pencil instead of looking at the person you're speaking with or work on your laptop instead of listening to the presentation that's being made? Your body language can and will communicate your true intent. You can say you're interested in what someone has to say, but if you aren't giving that person your full attention, your behavior will communicate the opposite.

ACTIVE LISTENING

Listening attentively, or actively, is key to performing your job, meeting client expectations and connecting with work colleagues. Active listening means understanding the perspective of the other person—getting into their head to grasp their point of view. It is listening that is engaged, not passive and distracted. It is noted in various research that people speak at 100–175 words per minute, but can listen and think at a much faster rate—that's why it's easy to get distracted when listening to someone. Remember, that what someone says and how you interpret what he or she is saying can be quite different—and vice versa. Personal beliefs, cultural contexts, judgments and assumptions can all color how people receive and perceive messages. It's best to make sure you understand and have clearly heard the other individual by echoing back what you hear in your own words. Generally speaking, we listen to gain understanding and context, to gather information, to solve problems and to connect on personal and professional levels. Make sure you are sensitive to your goals in listening to others and be responsive to the needs of others in the conversation.

In addition to active listening, it's important to ask the right questions. Think about what you need to know, organize your thoughts and ask open-ended questions to get at these important issues and information. Consider carefully how you can best gather the information from the people around you. Given the particular situation: Who should you ask? How should you ask? What should you ask? Don't just indiscriminately fire off questions to anyone who happens to be standing in front of you.

It's important to listen carefully to the answers of others, but what about listening to their questions? You cannot effectively answer someone unless you have carefully listened to and understood his or her question. When someone is asking you a question, concentrate on her, don't be distracted, and if you have any questions about what she is asking, echo back the question to her. Make sure you understand before you respond, otherwise miscommunication is likely to occur. Sometimes, people will even formulate a response before they've heard the question; you may have known and been irritated by someone like this.

TEN STEPS TO EFFECTIVE LISTENING

**FROM DIANNE SCHILLING'S "BE AN EFFECTIVE LISTENER!"
(HTTP://WWW.WOMENSMEDIA.COM/NEW/LISTENING.SHTML)**

- Face the speaker and maintain eye contact.
- Be attentive, yet relaxed.
- Keep an open mind.
- Listen to the words and try to picture what the speaker is saying.
- Don't interrupt and don't impose your "solutions."
- Wait for the speaker to pause to ask clarifying questions.
- Ask relevant questions—don't disrupt the speaker's train of thought.
- Try to feel what the speaker is feeling.
- Give the speaker regular feedback—summarize or simply say "uh huh."
- Pay attention to what isn't said—to nonverbal cues.

COMMUNICATION WITHIN THE CORPORATE CULTURE

In a new position, it's very important to understand and become a part of the corporate culture. This term refers to any size firm, not just large corporations. As a new employee, it's your task to figure out that culture, be sensitive to the needs and interests of those around you and work to connect on multiple levels. Grace Ring, Managing Designer for HOW Books and Writer's Digest Books notes, "When you're a designer working in a corporate environment like ours, it becomes all too easy to be isolated in your own work. I've found that the best way to fit into the office culture is to be social. Ask questions. Speak up in meetings. Share your crazy ideas. Be interested in other designers' projects. Your coworkers aren't going to seek you out unless you make yourself known."

Much of this comes down to effective communication. Get to know and understand the communication preferences of your coworkers and managers. There are e-mail people, people who prefer to talk in person, IM people and people who leave notes on your desk. Work to connect with people using their preference. If you know that someone doesn't respond well to e-mails, but will answer your questions quickly if you leave a brief note on their desk, you'll be less frustrated and more productive if you're the one who bends and uses their preferred form of communication. If you are stubborn and narrow, you will have difficulty fitting in. Employers love flexible, adaptable employees; work to be one.

That being said, there are situations in any corporate culture that warrant a particular style of communication. For instance, if you have something controversial or confrontational to discuss, you need to address this in person. Whether professional or personal business, you should handle sensitive issues firsthand. Telling someone off via e-mail is immature and inappropriate, especially if it's your supervisor. It's very important to resolve these types of issues in person. It can be difficult, and perhaps you just want to avoid it, but your supervisor will need to speak with you anyway, so you might as well be the one to make the first gesture of reconciliation. Whether with your boss or a coworker, try to approach a confrontational situation with a nonconfrontational approach—something like, "From my perspective, it appears that we aren't seeing eye-to-eye. I'd like to discuss this with you so that we can better understand one another's viewpoints."

REAL WORLD ADVICE: COMMUNICATION ACROSS CULTURES

JENNY LANICCA, DESIGNER, DELICIOUS DESIGN

Communication carries exponentially more importance when you don't share a common background and culture. While I was with CNN.com, I worked with individuals from almost ten different countries. My creative director was Icelandic, my design director was Japanese and my art director was Norwegian. The bureau's editorial staff were of English, American, Australian, South African and European descents. The way design can transcend those boundaries is powerful and inspiring, but you have to work much harder to both understand and be understood. If you rely on your own culture's shorthand way of communicating something (idioms, slang, accents), you can cause confusion. In the role I was in, it was very important to get the facts exactly right.

COMMUNICATION WITH CLIENTS

Most young designers have little to no experience with client communication (see Chapter 14: Partnering Effectively With Clients). It's easy to assume, after years in the classroom with group and class critiques, that client presentations will have much the same flavor. This isn't the case, and it's important to understand the communication dynamics that go into client communications and presentations. Preparation is key. You will be asked various questions that you will answer either orally or in writing. Many points of clarification and planning will be presented in the project proposal. (See Chapter 19: Pricing, Proposal and Contract Basics.) Clients will want to know the answers to questions like:

• How much will it cost? It's fine to say "I'll prepare a proposal for you." or "Do you have a budget in mind?"

- How long will it take? Again, this can be part of the proposal; make sure you have enough information to give an accurate answer.

- What are your qualifications? Be truthful and describe any related experiences you have, whether or not you were paid for them.

- Can I add work to the project? Be clear that the proposal covers a specific project scope. If they add work, then you will do a new estimate.

Don't answer questions too quickly, think carefully and take your time. A successful approach to client interaction, whether you are working freelance or in a large studio, is to think of your client as your partner. Don't set up an adversarial relationship. Your client is the content expert so it's smart to take advantage of that knowledge.

If you are going to effectively communicate with your clients and truly understand and solve their problems, then you need to research their business and get to know their industry vocabulary as much as possible. Learn their acronyms, lingo and technical terms. And at the same time, see your interactions as an opportunity to educate your client about the language and value of design!

REAL WORLD ADVICE: A WRITING PRIMER FOR DESIGNERS

JULIET D'AMBROSIO, EDITORIAL DIRECTOR, ICONOLOGIC

It's a strange paradox: So many designers whose work speaks so fluently in images flee in terror when called upon to communicate with the written word. After all, designers are nothing if not communicators, and communication is most fully realized when image and word unite.

It's time to conquer that fear. One look through any recent annual's credits will confirm that, in this era of shrinking budgets, designers are more frequently called upon to serve double duty—writing everything from taglines to full-blown annual reports. For those who tackle the challenge, it can be highly rewarding, enriching the creative experience and extending the boundaries of expression.

And all it takes is practice. Here a few tried-and-true verbal brainstorming techniques designed to help you find the right words for your next project.

- **Begin with the words.** While it may feel more natural to begin the process by sketching images, starting with the words will help you quickly zero in on the concept and inspire images in line with the language.

- **Get to know the territory.** Pore over the annuals—they're rich with examples of excellent writing. Read and absorb the winning entries. Take note of the techniques used by those you admire and get a feel for how the format you're working in—ad, brochure, web site, whatever—sounds and feels.

- **Find the key(s).** Creative briefs abound with keywords that serve as guide-posts to the brainstorming process. Identify and compile a list of those words that evoke an emotion, that seem particularly important to the client or that speak to you.

- **Create a mind map.** Take every word on your list and free-associate. What other words does that one bring to mind? What images does it inspire? Are there connections between them? It's also a good idea to get comfortable with a dictionary and thesaurus. Many words have nuances in meaning or unexpected synonyms that can provide fertile ground for ideas.

- **Get it all out.** When it's time to actually sit down and write, it's often best to just let yourself go creatively. Allow yourself to write thoughts as they come, without stopping to second-guess or edit. Don't even use full sentences. It's surprising what can come from these stream-of-consciousness ramblings.

- **Organize and edit.** This is the hard part: sifting through what your subconscious produced in the previous step and whipping it into shape. For long copy, identify one main point or theme and make every sentence support it, ensuring that every thought logically leads your reader to the next. For short copy, like headlines, select your top five and refine. Request feedback from someone you trust, and keep an open mind.

- **Simplify.** Be merciless with your red pen. The fewer words, the better.

E-ETIQUETTE 101

Over the last decade, e-mail has changed the way people communicate. Beyond just becoming a new medium for written communication, it has transformed the way we do business and the way we connect on a daily basis, both professionally and personally. Because we are not trained to use e-mail in the same way, we are taught more formal methods of written communication and many people use e-mail ineffectively and improperly.

The following advice will help you avoid some embarrassing mistakes and perform your job more efficiently:

- Be concise and to the point—avoid long sentences and long e-mails, but don't be overly blunt. An e-mail of a few paragraphs is fine—if your e-mail looks more like a letter, then it's too long.

- Use proper grammar and punctuation, and check your spelling; it's important to proofread. Don't use texting abbreviations in professional e-mails.

- Answer any and all of the questions asked in the e-mail sent to you—and preempt further questions as much as possible. There's nothing more frustrating than asking someone a series of questions in an e-mail and having them answer only one or two.

- Answer as promptly as possible. This doesn't mean that you have to answer e-mails the minute they come in; it's best to set aside two or three times per day to respond to e-mail.

- Do not attach unnecessary or unusually large files to your e-mails.

- Do not overuse the high priority option. People will just ignore it after awhile.

- Do not write in all capital letters. It's very difficult to read, especially on screen, and it implies that you are yelling.

- Don't leave out the message thread—people need context for the information they are reading and trying to understand. Always write at the top of the thread/string.

- Be careful about using "Reply to All." Only reply to the people that need to see the message.

- Don't forward chain e-mail; it's unprofessional and time-consuming.

- Don't copy a message or attachment without permission to do so.

- Do not use e-mail to discuss confidential or highly personal information. An e-mail trail is easy to retrieve. Additionally, any message you send can be so easily forwarded, either by accident or with intent; you should always assume that others can and will see your correspondence.

- Use a meaningful subject line so you and your contact can easily search for the e-mail at a later date.

- Generally copy (CC:) anyone mentioned in the e-mail and make sure to copy everyone that needs to know the information in the e-mail.

- Your signature line should not be overly long or personal—keep it professional.

- Avoid using picture attachments as backgrounds.

- Keep your e-mail address professional.

- Don't use e-mail to attempt to resolve a conflict of any kind. In e-mail you aren't getting any nonverbals. All sensitive issues should be handled in person.

- To ensure that people aren't put off by the brevity of an e-mail sent from a smart phone, put some indication in the signature line that it was written on a phone.

EFFECTIVE PRESENTATION SKILLS

In many settings, both professional and personal, you'll find that you need to have solid presentation skills. This doesn't mean that you have to be the most eloquent public speaker. It means you need to know the fundamentals of creating a clear and cohesive presentation of your thoughts and ideas—one that engages your audience so they're involved and learning. An effective presentation requires:

1. Preparation and practice: Start preparing early as you will need the time to write, format and practice. This takes more time than you think. Also, it's important to let the presentation sit a while. When you come back to it, you'll notice portions that need improvement or revision. Run through your presentation several times, practicing it just as you will be doing the final. If you have presentation slides, then practice with them so you can get a sense of timing and click through the slide animations. It's also good to practice in front of an audience, however small, especially if you have any stage fright. They can offer up suggestions for improvement and encouragement.

2. Knowing your audience: While writing the presentation, make sure you are keeping your audience in mind. Who are they and why are they coming to your presentation? What do they want to get out of it? What interests do they have and how are they engaged with the topic? Are they novices or experts? This is an investment of their time, so you want to make sure that it's worthwhile for you and them.

3. Knowing your purpose: Are you educating your audience about a particular topic or are you trying to persuade them to understand and embrace a specific viewpoint? Start with an agenda for the presentation that outlines what you are going to share with the audience, then go through your points and end with a summary and conclusion. What do you want them to take away from the presentation? What do you want them to comprehend following the presentation?

4. Starting with a strong introduction: Your first impression is very important, and it's essential that you catch the audience's attention and interest. If the beginning of your presentation is confusing or vague, then you will lose your audience, and it will be very difficult to regain their attention later in the presentation. If the audience is unfamiliar with you, it's important to introduce yourself and establish a certain amount of credibility. In your introduction, you also need to orient the audience by giving them a presentation agenda. This doesn't have to be a literal agenda slide, although many times that is appropriate. Tell them what you will be covering and what the important points are. Set the tone of the presentation.

5. Having strong organization: Most strong presentations have a clear and simple organization that's easy to follow. Only the most experienced speakers can talk spontaneously without a clear outline to their presentation. Outline your points to create a clear and logical argument. Prioritize the points and spend the greatest amount of time on the most important ones. Don't overwhelm the audience with many smaller points. Organize three to seven main points with supporting statements. It also helps convey information more effectively if you develop a pattern that can be easily followed, such as talking about each point as "cause and effect" or "problem/solution."

6. Bringing your presentation to life: Use examples, quotes, stories and statistics to give your presentation relevance to the audience. Your main points might be rather abstract without application points or anecdotes that relate to everyday life. If you are making points that are difficult to believe or understand, then it's especially important to present statistical or other evidence to back up your statements. Quoting well-known experts is another good way to lend credibility to your arguments.

7. Thinking about all the senses: What types of media might you use in your presentation to engage more than hearing? How about visuals? Video? Audio? Even touch and smell? Depending on the topic, almost all of the senses can be engaged. People learn and understand in a variety of ways, and if you can speak to visual, verbal, auditory and kinesthetic learners, for instance, you will be more engaging and inclusive of the entire audience. In addition, your presentation will be more interesting and memorable to everyone because of the variety of the approach.

8. Pulling the ideas together: At the end of the presentation, it's important to summarize key points and repeat the main takeaway lesson for the audience. What is the main thing you want them to remember and learn from your presentation? There needs to be strong and clear closure in a presentation, just like a paper or book. What are the conclusions you want to share?

9. Practicing your presentation style: Don't read your presentation, even if you're nervous. Talk through the bullet points you've outlined and speak in a conversational tone. Speak from your experience and knowledge. You're giving this presentation because you're the expert; speak with confidence. Use your body language to reinforce that confidence. Don't speak and stand in a rigid fashion but try to use relaxed gestures and motions. Even move about the room if it's appropriate. If the audience is small, it's especially important to look directly at them and engage them with your eyes and manner. Try to avoid repetitive gestures, like pacing or fidgeting with a pen.

10. Checking out the room: It will help if you are familiar with the setup of the room before your presentation. What size is the room? As the speaker, what's the relationship between your placement and the audience? Are there any distractions you need to be aware of, like a loud air conditioning system? What is the AV setup? Do you need to bring any extra equipment or adapters for your laptop? Will you use your own laptop or theirs? If you are using their laptop, can you preload your presentation and make sure that everything looks OK, such as the fonts. Working through these sorts of details can give you a greater sense of preparation and confidence. There's nothing worse than working diligently on a great presentation and then having the whole thing unravel because of some unforeseen issue with the room or equipment.

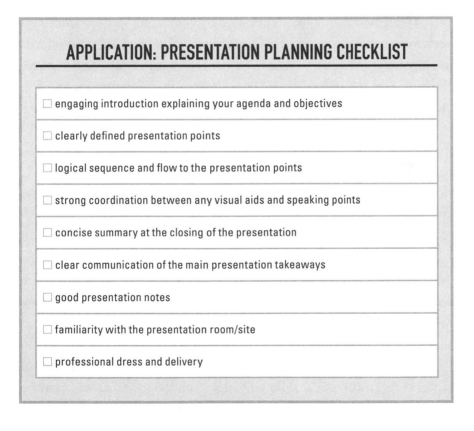

APPLICATION: PRESENTATION PLANNING CHECKLIST

☐ engaging introduction explaining your agenda and objectives

☐ clearly defined presentation points

☐ logical sequence and flow to the presentation points

☐ strong coordination between any visual aids and speaking points

☐ concise summary at the closing of the presentation

☐ clear communication of the main presentation takeaways

☐ good presentation notes

☐ familiarity with the presentation room/site

☐ professional dress and delivery

CHAPTER 9
KEY ETHICAL GUIDELINES

Ethics is an important topic in any discipline, and most professional organizations speak to some type of ethical code of conduct. These standards are key to establishing a consistent level of expectations for designers, their vendors and their clients. There are specific competencies and policies that should be met by any designer. AIGA, the professional association for design, has outlined these standards of professional practice in a series of brochures that are available for download at www.aiga.org/content.cfm/design-business-and-ethics. Much of the information below is a synthesis and summary of these brochures, since they set the standard in our discipline.

I can't emphasize enough how important this information is, even for student designers. It's essential, especially early in your career, to understand these ethical practices and to get in the habit of living them out. If you are an ethical person in your personal life, you probably think ethical behavior in your professional life will come naturally and without thought. This is not the case, and you should not delude yourself into believing so. Many of these policies may be unexpected to you. Especially in our current culture of "just download it from the Internet," you may be surprised to find out that certain things are unethical practices. Much of ethics is about understanding issues from multiple sides and looking out for the welfare of others. Sometimes seeing things from another's shoes doesn't come all that naturally. Read the standards with care and thought and use them to guide your professional behaviors.

AIGA STANDARDS OF PROFESSIONAL PRACTICE

"A professional designer adheres to principles of integrity that demonstrate respect for the profession, for colleagues, for clients, for audiences or consumers and for society as a whole. These standards define the expectations of a professional designer and represent the distinction of an AIGA member in the practice of design."

—"STANDARDS OF PROFESSIONAL PRACTICE"
WWW.AIGA.ORG/CONTENT.CFM/STANDARDS-
PROFESSIONAL-PRACTICE

Designers have various responsibilities to their clients, such as:

- Knowing the client's business and act in their best interest.

- Never work on projects simultaneously that create a conflict of interest without client agreement.

- Never divulge client information without their consent.

- Don't accept instructions from a client or employer that violate this code of conduct.

- Provide an estimate for projects, and get advance client approval for any changes to that estimate. Provide all scheduling and terms.

The designer has certain responsibilities to other designers, such as:

- Support fair and open competition based on merit.

- Don't take over a client project until there's a clear termination with another designer/firm.

- Don't compete with another designer by means of unethical inducements, like bribery and blackmail.

- Be fair in criticism and never denigrate the work of a fellow designer.

- Don't accept instructions from a client that involve infringement of another person's property rights without permission.

- When working in another country, become acquainted with and follow the code of conduct of that country.

The profession has guidelines regarding the charging and collection of design fees, such as:

- Don't undertake work for a client without compensation, except in cases of gift, charity or nonprofit work.

- Reasonable handling or administrative charges can be added, with the knowledge of the client, to reimbursable items.

- Don't accept kickback, hidden discounts, etc., from contractors or suppliers and inform clients of any financial interests in suppliers.

- Don't base recommendations of other designers on receipt of payments.

There are guidelines regarding the authorship and publicity of design work, such as:

- Don't claim sole credit for a design in which you collaborated with other designers.

- Identify your specific role on collaboratively created work.

- Self-promotion, advertising or publicity must not deliberately mislead regarding your level of experience or competence.

- A designer may allow a client to use his/her name for promotion of work designed.

The designer has the following responsibility to the public:

- Avoid projects that will result in any public harm.

- Communicate in truth and make no false claims or knowingly mislead.

- Respect the dignity of all audiences and value individual differences. Avoid the stereotyping of people or groups.

The designer also has responsibility to society and the environment:

- Don't do anything while engaged in the practice of design that knowingly constitutes a deliberate disregard for public health and safety.

- Don't accept instructions from a client or employer that involve infringement on a person's or group's property or human rights.

- Never discriminate on the basis of race, sex, age, religion, national origin, sexual orientation or disability.

- Support and act upon the principles of free speech, freedom of assembly and access to an "open marketplace of ideas."

Lastly, don't undertake speculative projects, either alone or in competition with others, for which compensation will only be received if a design is accepted or used. (AIGA has more information and specific guidelines about spec work on their web site in "Position on Spec Work" at www.aiga.org/content.cfm/position-spec-work.)

AIGA STANDARDS FOR THE USE OF FONTS

"Fonts are creative, intellectual property, similar to designers' creative work or a proprietary business product. Since type seems so ubiquitous, and fonts are so easy to share among computer users, the legal and moral issues of the simple process of using a font are often overlooked."

—"USE OF FONTS" WWW.AIGA.ORG/CONTENT.CFM/
DESIGN-BUSINESS-AND-ETHICS

Here are five rules that guide ethical practice for font licensing:

- Make sure you have a license to use a font, which means you own the font.

- If you want to install a font on your computer, make sure you or your employer have a license to install the font.

- If you have any questions about your font license, contact the foundry or supplier of the font.

- Don't lend or give a font to others to use.

When sending a job to a professional printer, they may request the font(s) you used in the design. It is best practice to embed the font into a PDF file, so you don't have to provide the font separately. If the printer wants the original file format (such as an Illustrator file), then create outlines/paths of the fonts, so they become art and don't have to be provided.

With all the fonts available for free download online, some people might consider these rules to be antiquated. It's important to view this issue from the perspective of the font designer and foundry. If you've even attempted to design a typeface, you know how challenging and time-consuming it can be. It requires the utmost attention to detail and design sensitivity. Type designers deserve to be properly compensated for their work.

AIGA STANDARDS FOR THE USE OF ILLUSTRATIONS

"AIGA is interested in encouraging the use of original illustration in design solutions. Illustration can provide a unique sensibility to certain projects."
—"USE OF ILLUSTRATIONS" WWW.AIGA.ORG/
CONTENT.CFM/DESIGN-BUSINESS-AND-ETHICS

Each illustrator brings a different perspective and a unique style to a project. Using original illustration for a project can be quite powerful and compelling and can enrich a design solution.

To choose an illustrator, designers normally look at a portfolio in person or online. Speculative work within the illustration community is also considered unethical so don't request an illustrator to do work without proper compensation, whether through competition or contest. There are archives of preexisting illustrations readily available on numerous web sites. These can be stock images where you pay for each use of the image or royalty-free where you pay for the image and can use it as much as you like. There are also groups of illustrations that can be purchased as a collection. Stock or royalty-free imagery is generally less expensive than custom work, but you have to live with a precreated image that may or may not be perfectly matched to what you need. Price is directly related to the use and location of the illustration.

All agreements with an illustrator should be made in writing, and just as with your own design work, excessive refinements or changes required of the illustrator will probably result in further charges.

One of the most misunderstood parts of this whole process is that you are not purchasing the original artwork. The artwork belongs to the artist. You or the client (depending on who pays) are purchasing the right to use the work for specific purposes and only those purposes. Additionally, the original artwork should not be altered.

One of the most important things to consider when working with an illustrator or photographer is that you are hiring a collaborator—someone to partner with you to make your design a stronger and more holistic piece of communication. Bring the illustrator in early to help you conceptualize the project; she is a creative, experienced individual who will bring much to the table. Use her skills and knowledge throughout the process. Respect her abilities just as you expect to be respected by your client.

AIGA STANDARDS FOR THE USE OF SOFTWARE

"Just as design is a designer's creative property, computer software is intellectual property that is owned by the people who created it. Without the express permission of the manufacturer or publisher, it is illegal to use software no mater how you got it. That permission almost always takes the form of a license from the publisher, which accompanies authorized copies of software. When you buy software, what you're really doing, in almost every case, is purchasing a license to use it. Rather than owning the software, you acquire limited rights to use, reproduce and distribute the program according to the terms spelled out in the license."

—"USE OF SOFTWARE" WWW.AIGA.ORG/CONTENT. CFM/DESIGN-BUSINESS-AND-ETHICS

Installing software that you haven't licensed or using a single license on multiple machines is unethical. There are usually provisions allowing you to back up a copy for archive in case you lose your hard drive. Uploading, downloading or transmitting unauthorized copies of software can result in civil or criminal action. It's very important to keep your original install disks in case you need to reinstall your software or you need access to your licensing numbers. Different software packages have different license policies; look at the original license for specifics. For instance, there are cases where you can load one license on both a desktop and a laptop computer.

Not only are you respecting the software developers and companies by following these guidelines, you are also protecting your computer and your work. A legitimate copy ensures you're getting the quality product you expect and one that won't have issues. Be careful when buying software online. If the price is too good to be true or if the software is without documentation or manuals, it is probably pirated. You could get a piece of software that causes compatibility issues, is corrupted or doesn't work properly. The same is true of pirated fonts. Ultimately, this will waste your time and money and could damage your machine.

AIGA STANDARDS OF THE USE OF PHOTOGRAPHY

"Use of photography in design work involves choice and responsibilities. With the growth of digital libraries of images, stock photography has become far more accessible to every designer, although there are also strong reasons to commission photography specifically for a project."

—"USE OF PHOTOGRAPHY" WWW.AIGA.ORG/
CONTENT.CFM/DESIGN-BUSINESS-AND-ETHICS

Designers should be careful when contracting with a photographer. If you, the designer, are responsible to pay for the photography services, then you must be sure the client will reimburse your expenses. It may be easier and less risky to have the client contract the photographer directly. Additionally, if the client wishes to own the rights to the imagery, it's best for them to pay directly.

Detail all specifications, fees and requirements for the project in writing, just as you would with any other vendor, such as an illustrator. Be clear about art direction requirements and be concise about what form the final product will take. Be explicit about your schedule and how the photographer will work within it. It's very important to allow enough time for photo shoots and for reshoots because they may be necessary. Additionally, authorship credit should be established and approved in writing.

Just as with illustration, the right for the use of imagery must be clearly specified and there are various options. "Work for hire" should be avoided, as it gives the copyright to the client, giving the photographer (or designer) no protection. For legal purposes, the photographer should get a release from any models/people in photos to protect the photographer, designer and client and to ensure that these individuals have given their consent to be photographed and their permission to have their image published. If you are using stock photography, it's important to understand the license agreement and to not exceed it. These work in much the same way as the illustration stock and royalty-free license agreements already discussed.

DESIGNERS' RESPONSIBILITIES TO AUDIENCE AND USERS

In his article on the AIGA web site, "In Search of Ethics in Graphic Design," Paul Nini, AIGA member and design educator, proposed an addition to the current ethical guidelines outlined by AIGA. These included responsibilities specifically related to the audiences and users that design work engages. He outlines these important points:

- Designers must recognize the need to include audience members and users whenever possible in the process of developing effective communications and to act as an advocate for their concerns to the client.

- The designer's main concern must be to create communications that are helpful to audiences and users and that meet their needs with dignity and respect.

- Designers must not knowingly use information obtained from audience members or users in an unethical manner so as to produce communications that are unduly manipulative or harmful in their effect.

- Designers must advocate and thoughtfully consider the needs of all potential audiences and users, particularly those with limited abilities, such as the elderly and physically challenged.

- Designers must recognize that their work contributes to the well-being of the general public, particularly in regard to health and safety, and must not consciously act in a manner contradictory to this well-being.

- Designers uphold the credibility and dignity of their profession by practicing honest, candid and timely communication and by fostering the free flow of essential information in accord with the public interest.

APPLICATION: BEING ETHICAL

Think about a difficult ethical dilemma you've experienced or could imagine experiencing. Perhaps you're approaching a big deadline and you need imagery or a new font for your project. How will you get it? Or maybe the client of your current employer has approached you and he would like you to do freelance work on the side? Write a reflection about what you would do given the information you learned in this chapter.

PART FOUR

STAYING FRESH

Even young designers find that it's difficult to stay up-to-date in this fast-paced discipline. It's not just technology that's changing, but the very fabric that makes up graphic design is constantly evolving as well, demonstrated by the growing integration of design principles and practices into strategic business decisions. We are a curious, demanding, unsettled bunch who don't like to rest and hate boredom. We yearn for challenge and love to learn. We understand that it's important to stay fresh if we are going to remain a competitive and contributing member of the team.

But everyone gets stuck in a rut at some point in her career. The creative lull can last for a couple of hours, days or even months. There are many, many ways to continue growing—to reinvigorate and reinvent. You simply need to take ownership of your own growth and development. One of the many wonderful things about the design community is the countless points of inspiration that can be found—you just have to look for them and connect. That inspiration might be found in a person, a place, a workshop or an organization. This section highlights some great ways for you to move past the creative lull that may be caused by a lack of intellectual and creative stimulation.

CHAPTER 10
CONTINUING EDUCATION AND PROFESSIONAL DEVELOPMENT

You have to continually renew and reinvent yourself, seek educational opportunities and strive for professional development over the course of your entire career. Whether you like it or not, and I hope you at least accept it, this is a field that is constantly evolving. There are daily changes in graphic design, and if you are going to have a successful career over more than a few years, you have to continually learn and develop with the discipline. This can seem overwhelming at times, especially when it comes to the technological side of things, but it's critical to have a positive attitude and be curious. When it comes to continuing education, there are a wide variety of choices at various levels of involvement and commitment.

GRADUATE SCHOOL

If you have an undergraduate degree and you're interested in pursuing further education in a formal and focused environment, then graduate school may be the best option for you. There are a variety of programs that offer master of arts or master of fine arts (or equivalent) degrees, and it's very important to carefully research and analyze the different offerings to see what works best with your particular situation.

Begin with Research

Gather as many catalogues as you can. It only costs you a phone call, and a great way to assess a school is through the materials they send you. Additionally, you will find a wealth of information on the web. Study the school web sites carefully and compare them to one other. Carefully look through all the promotional materials and rank your choices. Some will obviously not be what you are looking for, some will fit into a gray area and some will be at the top of your list.

Not all of your questions will be answered by the catalogues or web sites, so develop a list of questions, make some phone calls and send some e-mails to the graduate directors of the schools you are interested in. This will help you to determine if the schools in the gray area should really be at the top of your list. After you have gathered as much information as you can, try to plan a visit to the schools at the top of your list. Many schools are very different when you visit them in person. Talk to the faculty, but more importantly, talk to the students and get their opinions.

There are various criteria that you might use to assess your choices:

- **Subjects available to study:** What diversity of coursework is available?

- **The school's philosophy:** How do the school's key ideas match with your goals and needs?

- **Studio, facilities and technology:** How up-to-date are the facilities and technology? What's available?

- **University or art school:** Do you want to have access to liberal arts coursework? Or be more focused on an art/design curriculum?

- **Faculty experience and continuity:** Will the mentor you want to work with be available and not on sabbatical?

- **Diversity and interdisciplinary connections:** Do the graduate students work with any other majors? Are there students from around the country and world?

- **Quality of life, opportunities with business/community:** Are there opportunities to interact with the community?

- **Location:** Is the school located in a thriving community? Are there stimulating events/activities available?

- **Library and museums:** What cultural institutions are available for your research and enrichment?

- **Employment potential following graduation:** What have graduates done following graduation?

- **Size of class:** How large/small is the class and how many students will you be interacting with?

Additionally, it's important to understand the difference between a master of arts (MA) and a master of fine arts (MFA). These are two very different degrees, although they sound similar. A master of arts is not a terminal degree, meaning the final degree available in a particular discipline. For most academic disciplines, there is a PhD available and this is the terminal degree. For most practice-oriented degrees (design, fine arts, music performance, etc.) there is no PhD. (Although there are now a few PhD programs available in graphic design, the MFA is still considered terminal.) MA degrees are usually half the number of hours of MFA degrees (thirty versus sixty, for instance). All good colleges and universities require their faculty to have the terminal degree to teach in a full-time, tenure track position.

The Application Process

Graduate school is an important investment in time and money, and you want to put a lot of thought into the decision. Apply to your top schools. Most applications are due at the beginning of the calendar year, similar to undergraduate schools. Use the official forms and get written references. There will also be an application fee. Be certain that you make a good impression by watching your spelling and grammar. Also, your presentation of digital materials should be neat and well considered.

Be especially careful in your writing of the statement of intention. You should offer insightful comments about why you want to go to this specific graduate program. This letter is often very important because it communicates to the school what sets you apart from other applicants. Why should they accept you, specifically, and how do your interests match with this particular school? You should tailor this letter tightly to the school, and it should not feel like a form letter.

Once your materials are submitted, you will need to wait. Most graduate schools narrow their pool to a small number to interview. They don't pay for this, so be prepared for the cost. If you get to the interview stage, you will be asked to show a portfolio, and you will probably talk to faculty and students. As with any interview, present yourself professionally. Following the interview, you will again wait. You will get a letter of acceptance or rejection in the mail. If you are rejected from the school you are dying to go to, apply again the next year. Schools keep track of applicants from year to year. Persistence has been known to win out! These are generalizations. You will find that each school has different admission guidelines.

REAL WORLD ADVICE: ONLINE GRAD SCHOOL PROGRAMS

SAMANTHA PERKINS, MFA STUDENT IN GRAPHIC DESIGN

I received a BS in architecture where the primary focus was centered around the field of design and theory. To start my graduate school selection, I ran a number of online searches, spoke to colleagues and did a series of 'blind' approaches, researching schools I'd heard of previously. It took awhile. My current location provides many options in terms of a graduate education within architecture. However, since my focus of design media had shifted towards graphic design, the traditional brick-and-mortar university system became rather limiting. In addition, I needed to attend a program that would allow me to continue my teaching, provide time for my family and give me time to seriously focus on my projects. Ultimately, I chose an online program due to the option of accessing course materials whenever I had the time, the reputation of the graphic design program offered and the caliber of work coming out of the program.

About a week prior to the start of the term, the school sends out a set of content disks for each course. These disks are to supplement the scheduled lectures, which are provided on the school's web site, as well as provide specific paths for project investigations where necessary. Instructors/professors hold "office hours" via scheduled online chat hours, and answer e-mail or blog questions rather quickly. To take courses, students log onto the course site, "attend" the lectures, check instructor messages, review comments. Any assignments are uploaded to the instructor using the site, commented upon by the instructor and reloaded for student review. If we're working on sketches, or something else manipulated by hand, we scan it to the computer and upload that instead. Twice within the program course, the student is required to actually meet with the faculty—once after the first year of studies to present a graduate thesis topic and again at the end of the thesis process to present findings for critical review.

PROFESSIONAL DEVELOPMENT

Graduate school isn't feasible for everyone because of limitations of time, location, family and money. Additionally, many people aren't looking for such a long-term experience. You might be interested in learning about something very specific, such as sustainability, or perhaps you just want to pick up a new skill or learn some software tricks. There are many opportunities for this level of continuing education. These opportunities pair well with real world experience in the workplace.

Some universities and community colleges offer night and weekend classes with focused topics or training (software, for instance). Some large professional printing or paper companies offer workshops for design professionals. I once took a wonderful course in paper manufacturing and specification that was offered by the local distributor of a national paper company. If you are looking for something specific, it's best to do a search on the web.

Bryan Gaffin, Senior Vice President and Group Creative Director at Rapp Collins Worldwide, talks about his experience. "The best thing to do is to seek out continuing ed classes. When I first came to New York, I had a very polished design book that had no edge to it at all. It was well designed, but didn't pop and wasn't memorable. These classes gave me a great book, which I used to get my first New York job. Not only are these classes taught by real working creative directors, but you'll make connections with other people starting out in the industry, and they can help you hone your book and give you emotional support."

And you can take courses away from home as well. Many conferences offer courses before, during or after the conference program. I was recently at an AIGA design educators conference and there was a Processing workshop for a couple of hours one morning. Many people took advantage of this opportunity to learn a new programming language and to understand applications for use in design education. This format has many benefits: You are already taking time away from your job, you are with colleagues interested in the same topic and there are often opportunities outside of the workshop to network and establish new relationships and contacts.

There are also many resources available online for training and education. Lynda.com is a vast and cost-effective resource for online courses. You can check out their offerings by going to the web site. Additionally, there is training through the Adobe web site; you can select online courses for their various software applications for a reasonable fee. Virtual

Training Company (VTC) also offers a wide variety of video tutorials, as do many other companies. As a benefit to the employee, some companies pay for these types of training opportunities.

NATIONAL DESIGN CONFERENCES

- The AIGA Design Conference is a biennial gathering to celebrate the design community and to discuss the state of the design profession. (www.aiga.org)

- The AIGA Regional Educators Conference enables the AIGA Design Education community an opportunity to gather, present current design research and share information on new teaching methodologies. (www.aiga.org)

- The DUX (Designing for User Experience) conference gathers together researchers and practitioners of various design disciplines and related fields to discuss the needs and goals of both users and businesses. (www.aiga.org)

- The AIGA Business and Design Conference (Gain) is a biennial conference focusing on design's impact on business success. (www.aiga.org)

- Image, Space, Object (A Rocky Mountain/High Ground Workshop in partnership with AIGA) brings small teams of participants and studio mentors together to create multidimensional environments, human interactions and brand strategies. (www.aiga.org)

- The HOW Design Conference provides an annual forum for design, and business advice for new and seasoned professionals. (www.howconference.com)

- HOW and Marketing Mentor's Creative Freelancer Conference focuses on business and creative information for freelance designers, illustrators, photographers and copywriters. (www.creativefreelancerconference.com)

- The Flash Forward Conference is an annual forum for the best minds in the Flash design and development community. (www.flashforwardconference.com)

- The Type Camp has a limited number of participants to provide an intimate experience between the campers, instructors and their love for typography. (www.typecamp.org)

- The WebbyConnect Summit focuses on sharing ideas and evaluating new trends in interactive media, entertainment and advertising. (www.webbyawards.com/webbyconnect)

- The Design Dump has an updated list of conferences and resources for graphic designers (www.designdump.com).

CHAPTER 11
COMMUNITY INVOLVEMENT

Getting involved in your community is your opportunity to focus on issues that reflect your personal passions and concerns. As Jennifer Morla, Morla Design, notes, "Design that moves others comes from issues that move you." I hope you agree that a paycheck isn't the only reason to design. Many designers believe that they have a social obligation to actually make a difference by contributing to a cause in which they strongly believe. Through your design work, you can help others communicate that cause effectively and efficiently, hopefully making a difference for them and those they serve.

DESIGN FOR A CAUSE

One of the great benefits of our profession is that we can use time and talents to give back to the community—locally or globally. There are several different ways you can work with groups and organizations to reach their communication goals.

Many designers donate their skills by doing pro bono projects or projects "for the public good." It is design work that is donated free of charge to an organization, institution or cause. Many designers do pro bono work for nonprofits or independent causes that may not have the formal organizational structure of an official nonprofit. For instance, perhaps there's a small group of individuals who are interested in environmental concerns in your local area. They need to promote themselves to create momentum and draw people to meetings. They may call on your services as a designer to create a logo, flyer and web site. Perhaps you are even a founding member of this group, and you volunteer your services knowing that this is the best way to spread the word and develop an awareness of these issues. Many designers and firms work this way on promotional materials for social causes and social responsibility at local, regional, national and international levels.

It is important to create some personal guidelines about donated time. You need to decide for yourself what matters to you personally and how you will commit your time (see Chapter 7: Basics of Effective Time Management). Most designers are donating their efforts to these projects at the same time they are doing many for-profit jobs. You need to limit your pro bono projects so you don't overextend yourself and have difficulty finishing work for your paying clients. Work it into your overall budget so you know exactly how much time/money you are investing in this type of work. Don't just go about it blindly; make donated time and work part of your business plan. Keep in mind that you cannot deduct your time or services from your taxes, but you can deduct any expenses. Keep your receipts!

Designers can donate their time for free or at a discount, and many design firms and ad agencies do a percentage of pro bono work. Doing pro bono or nonprofit work can be part of a company's business plan and can increase visibility for the firm and its favorite causes. Paul Ghiz, Founding Partner of Global Cloud, explains, "We have a dedicated division that serves the nonprofit sector, which makes up 50 percent of our client base. Everyone shares a passion of giving back to society and helps in many ways. It is important to us to stay connected and assist nonprofit organizations with their missions." You can create a strong network of business allies through community involvement projects. This can be especially beneficial for one-person firms because it gives them a way to connect with others who have similar interests and concerns, while increasing visibility for their work.

SOCIAL CHANGE AND IMPACT RESOURCES

Organization that calls attention to social issues using their creativity and activism: Design for Social Impact: www.dfsi.org

A nonprofit design resource: PureVisual: www.purevisual.com

International advertising giant's award for world-changing ideas: Saatchi & Saatchi: www.saatchi.com/worldwide/innovation_award.asp

Design online resource and company directory: Core 77 Design Directory: www.designdirectory.com

---

Beyond increased connections and the great feeling of giving back, there are several other benefits to doing work with nonprofits. In many cases, you can ask for increased credit or creative freedom in exchange for free work. Many institutions will be happy to grant you this added flexibility. Additionally, because the topic is one you are passionate about, the work is usually extremely enjoyable and interesting. Lastly, this is a great opportunity to teach someone about the power of design. Many nonprofits start off with bare-bones communication pieces. With your expertise, they can see the dramatic increase in their visibility and impact. Even if the work is discounted or free, it's important to give them an estimate for how much it would cost in the real world. This will ensure that the work isn't taken for granted and that they understand its true value.

REAL WORLD ADVICE: NONPROFIT WORK

MIKE ZENDER, DESIGNER AND DESIGN EDUCATOR

I've been doing nonprofit work my entire career, since 1973. I started with a project for my church promoting a conference on small groups. After graduate school, I did a consistent stream of projects, pro bono and paid, for arts and cultural organizations. My favorite clients, because they serve my favorite people, are nonprofits. Faith and philosophy agree that we are the stewards of a long chain of work by others passing our work on to those who follow us. This means that we are stewards, not owners. Therefore, as stewards, we have a responsibility to share our time and talent with others for the greater good, not just for our own good. I believe there was something said about this when I received my master's degree at Yale, that we are responsible for using our training for the good of all. Work for paying clients is work for the good of all, but all includes those who can't pay too, or those nonprofits who can't pay much.

Design matters: It is intended to make the world a better place and people better, happier, more honest, more grateful, more faithful in it.

OTHER WAYS TO GIVE BACK

Beyond donating design work, there are many ways for you to impact society. Throughout your career, it's important to donate your time to organizations and causes you believe in:

- Become a board member for your local AIGA chapter or be a mentor to a college design student.

- Create a blog or contribute to one that promotes the causes that are important to you.

- Get involved with raising funds for a needy cause.

- Create a contest to promote your cause and get people involved and excited to participate.

- Use your design and art talents to connect with kids or older adults. Give a community-based art course or workshop.

REAL WORLD ADVICE: VOICES ON NONPROFIT DESIGN

JENI MOORE, CREATIVE DIRECTOR, PLUM DESIGN

I do work for United Cerebral Palsy of Chicago and I have worked for Chicago Chamber Musicians and Merit School of Music. Though, this year, I donated my time to the Avon Breast Cancer Campaign. It's important to give back, pitch in and make a difference, no matter what you do. It makes you feel good, it gives your job purpose and it helps.

HOLLIS OBERLIES, PRESIDENT, PURPLE ZANTE, INC.

Remember, nonprofit doesn't have to be no profit for you. Many of the nonprofits have money to spend on their good causes. Good budget or not, it's a complete joy to work for organizations and schools with a mission to better the place we live in some way. I've always enjoyed local nonprofit work since that work is so greatly appreciated and impacts/enriches the lives of many in the community. Often times, there's a bit more creativity allowed too.

JEFF FISHER, ENGINEER OF CREATIVE IDENTITY, JEFF FISHER LOGOMOTIVES

I've been doing work with nonprofits since I first started working as a designer over thirty years ago, and actually, I was donating my time and energy to nonprofit causes as early as my grade school years. My parents were both very socially conscious and were involved in many causes themselves. ... I have set boundaries for myself of limiting pro bono efforts to children's/education causes, grassroots arts organizations, HIV/AIDS groups and an occasional event or group that piques me interest. It's important to set limits for yourself—and your firm—so as not to be overwhelmed with such work and so you are able to say no to some requests without guilt. It's also very important for me to treat such projects as I do my real projects. Project agreements (contracts) are used to define the project for both parties involved.

CHAPTER 12
CREATIVITY AND INNOVATION

There are many ways to expand your thinking and build your creativity on a day-to-day basis, or in a more focused way, for the particular problem you are trying to solve. Below are ideas and approaches. Take these and build upon them.

COLLECTING CREATIVE "BITS"

There are plenty of opportunities to get inspiration and creative ideas from the world around us. Unfortunately, most people, even visual people like designers, just don't pay attention to all the visual and verbal "bits" that present themselves throughout the day—bits of ideas, bits of influence and bits of solutions. It might be the leftover plane or movie ticket that you found laying on the ground. It might be that cool brochure that you picked up on your last trip. The trick is taking these bits and connecting them with what is relevant to your creative problems and the problems of your clients.

There are many ways to find and record imagery, ideas and influences. Many people keep sketchbooks and scrapbooks of visual inspiration during their college lives, but often this good habit doesn't translate into their professional lives. I recently visited the Cincinnati office of Interbrand, one of the largest branding firms in the world. I met with five individuals from various roles in the company. We sat around a large high-top table in a brainstorming room, and each person had his or her own sketchbook to write thoughts and ideas in during the session. Interbrand has made this practice part of their corporate culture because they understand the value of recording ideas and gathering inspiration. Employees are even encouraged to collect things that are seemingly unrelated to their current projects, such as images from magazines or pieces of packaging, because they know this inspiration will come in handy at a later date. They share these sketchbooks with one another so individuals can be influenced by their colleagues' views of the world.

EXPANDING YOUR THINKING

There are many ways to expand your thinking to new levels. Many designers get comfortable with where they are, and they stop really pushing their design aesthetics and solutions.

Think in extremes and try to push your ideas all the way to the ends of the continuum. You can always come back to something that's more practical, but you may never come up with the truly creative idea unless you allow yourself to move to the extremes. Sometimes, this works most effectively in group brainstorming because unique perspectives can push ideas to places where you would never go on your own.

Learn the rules of the profession and respect them, but don't allow them to become a straightjacket. If there are good reasons to break certain rules, then do so, especially when it means your solution is more innovative and effective in solving the problem at hand. It can be especially important to break the rules when it means more effective communication. Perhaps there are certain typographic or compositional rules that you would normally follow, but your problem really calls for breaking those rules in order to exaggerate the communication point being made. For instance, maybe it's more appropriate for the poster to be aesthetically "ugly" to communicate the message.

Expanding your thinking can relate to visual brainstorming, but it can also be verbal. Create a word list that extends your verbal ideas. Start with one or several words that describe your problem or idea and try to expand them as far as possible. Use a thesaurus to expand your word list and extend this thinking as far as you can.

Another method of verbal brainstorming involves creating a mind map or word web by putting your key word in the center and build out from it. The central word radiates a ring of different word associations. From each association radiates secondary associations, generating an outer ring. The rings will contain words that directly or indirectly relate to the central word.

NINE WAYS TO KEEP GROWING

BENNETT HOLZWORTH, ART DIRECTOR, NEBRASKA BOOK COMPANY

1. Volunteer your services. For example, if you want to design identities for a living, you have to have some samples in your portfolio. Seek out projects for nonprofits that you would like to help. Since the project is pro bono, push for more creative freedom.

2. Attend local AIGA events. This should be a no-brainer. Hang out with like-minded people and learn from some of the best in the industry.

3. Do something you don't think you are capable of. Find something you are interested in and tackle it. Whether that is expanding your capabilities in writing, video editing or book design, find something that will force you to keep learning.

4. Self-initiate projects. Produce your own T-shirts, print a line of greeting cards, develop new web ideas, create a graphic novel, etc.

5. Create a blog. Do this for yourself and others will see the honesty in your writing. Even if you never get Digg or Design Observer to link to you, you are still thinking and solidifying ideas.

6. Read books. It doesn't matter what kind. Just read.

7. Socialize outside of design. When I moved to a small town, I knew I would miss my regular involvement with my AIGA buddies. I did, but I was also forced to find people outside of design to learn from. Look to local college professors, musicians and fine artists. They will expand your horizons and maybe even turn into some great creative freelance work.

8. Enter competitions. The fact that you are entering competitions will hopefully make you approach each project to make it the best it can be. But don't design projects with the sole goal of winnings awards.

9. Get a hobby or pursue your crazy ideas. Letterpress, glass blowing, camera collecting, fencing—anything but watching primetime television.

LET OTHERS INFLUENCE YOU

Designers can't isolate themselves. It's very important to develop a community to push your thinking and learning as a designer.

• Work in a multidisciplinary manner. Fresh ideas can come from people who aren't experts in your field. Experts in each profession are trained to think in a certain way, with a particular point of view. Someone from another discipline will approach the problem differently and may come up with a more innovative approach. Depending on how your workplace is structured, this may be difficult or easy. Try to seek people out, even if it's just to have lunch, to discuss ideas and share perspectives. Go to conferences of related disciplines (an architecture conference may give

entire business models. Creativity and innovation are big business and are the key to differentiation in this new economy.

Even back in 2005, *BusinessWeek* was focusing on the importance of design and innovation, starting their online portal www.businessweek.com/innovate. An August 1, 2005 *BusinessWeek* special report "Get Creative!" explained, "You're thinking 'this is all hype,' aren't you? Just another 'newest and biggest' fad, right? Wrong. Ask the 940 senior executives from around the world who said in a recent Boston Consulting Group Inc. survey that increasing top-line revenues through innovation has become essential to success in their industry." Out-of-the-box consumer experiences require a shift in process toward creativity and design strategy. (See Chapter 13: Design Thinking and Strategic Synergies.) All of this points to the growing importance of creative problem solvers in today's marketplace, and selling yourself as such is vital to your success.

REAL WORLD ADVICE: STAYING FRESH

GRACE RING, MANAGING DESIGNER, HOW BOOKS AND WRITER'S DIGEST BOOKS

In our office there's little to no interaction between the design teams. In order to keep everyone feeling energized and creative, we schedule regular lunch forums and off-site brainstorms for everyone to get together. This gives us a chance to share information and ideas, see what everyone else is working on and promote social interaction across teams.

JEFF FISHER, ENGINEER OF CREATIVE IDENTITY, JEFF FISHER LOGOMOTIVES

Push yourself away from your computer and get out into the world! I travel the world. I read all the time—books and magazines on a wide variety of topics, including design and business. I am physically unable to walk by a bookstore without going in to peruse, smell and touch books. I am surrounded by friends who own a variety of businesses and are a wealth of information (vacations together tend to become business incubators). I'm constantly visiting galleries, museums, new retail establishments, the latest new restaurant and more to soak up the design all around me. A great source of inspiration is the local farmer's market or a neighborhood art fair.

PAUL GHIZ, FOUNDING PARTNER, GLOBAL CLOUD

We conduct ongoing internal knowledge-sharing seminars where each employee is responsible for leading a presentation on a relevant topic. Global Cloud has an open door policy where ideas for making the environment and culture better are embraced.

MARK HAMILTON, ASSOCIATE DIRECTOR OF MARKETING & CREATIVE SERVICES, THE COLLEGE OF SAINT ROSE

Design books and magazines are great sources for inspiration, but they shouldn't be your only source for inspiration—it becomes too easy of a source to copy from. Creative inspiration can be found in a myriad of places. You may find it walking down the street and just by looking at patterns and colors of a neighborhood, or you may find inspiration at your local library. Children's books offer an immense wealth of ideas.

JENI MOORE, CREATIVE DIRECTOR, PLUM DESIGN

I go to conferences or open houses or shows. I travel a lot, take breaks when I need to and keep in touch with colleagues from other jobs/school. I especially like to travel; its refreshing to change your environment, experience something/someplace else, do things a little differently for a few days.

TRENDING

It's critical to realize that trending, an understanding and analysis of current perspectives on design, shouldn't be approached as superficial and ungrounded. In fact, it should be very grounded in research and an understanding of social context. For instance, during the aftermath of the 9/11 tragedy, the use of the red, white and blue palate became very common—it reinforced our unity as a nation and our sense of patriotism. And during times of economic or social chaos and complexity, people are often drawn to design solutions that provide simplicity and clarity in their lives.

Callison, one of the world's largest design and architecture firms, uses trending to inform their design solutions. Joan Insel, Associate Principal, details their process: "Tracking and identifying consumer trends is a crucial way to understand what consumers are doing now and next. When we track trends, we gain a better insight into the motivations, needs and desires of the user, and more importantly, we learn about the values of the customers for whom we design.

"Understanding the user is key to creating spaces and places where people want to be. To better understand our users, we read what they're reading, we watch what they're watching and listen to the music to which they're listening. The Internet, social networking sites (e.g., YouTube, Flickr, MySpace and Facebook) and Google's Zeitgeist have provided an over-abundance of information to track general trends and, more specifically, fads and fashions. We supplement this secondary research with primary research as well as gleaning insights from our colleagues and clients.

"Callison designs projects all over the world, so it is imperative for us to understand the user specific to a region or culture; just as Seattle is very different from New York, Beijing is very different from Shanghai.

"In the end, understanding trends helps us to plan ahead and anticipate the needs of users, spark creativity for our design teams and ignite new thinking with our clients. People trends is one thing we track."

CHAPTER 13
DESIGN THINKING AND STRATEGIC SYNERGIES

Today, more than ever, with heavy competition both in national and international markets, business owners must think about how their company or product will stand out in a sea of visual clutter and consumer overload. Many companies understand that little "d" design is important—they know that an effective logo or brochure can help them communicate their company's goals or connect emotionally with consumers, but few truly understand and use design as a strategic asset. Design is often thought of as a creative and finite endeavor: Identify a project; execute the art; put it into the marketplace. Big "D" design is defined by connection, the design disciplines (graphic, interior, industrial, architectural) working together and influencing one another. "D" design is about this synergy and developing a holistic approach to design; it connects design with fields like business, engineering and psychology by strategies based on thoughtful analysis and planning.

Traditional definitions of design focus on the process of design. They lack the connection with business processes or strategy development that are integral to today's design. The evolution to a broader definition of design is the recognition of the wide-ranging impact that has transformed traditional design disciplines, moving design (with a small d) to Design.

BIG "D" DESIGN

Developing a design strategy isn't about a one-time "event" or about an end product or solution. Design thinking and design strategy are becoming a part of business process. This involves a more comprehensive look—analysis of competitors, measurements for success, analysis of user/consumer needs, etc.—and touches every aspect of the company. Thinking like a designer and understanding design strategy have become powerful business tools. Business professionals are looking to designers for an innovative approach to solving problems and understanding audiences/users. Designers help consumers actually experience and visualize the business strategy through consumer interaction and touch points.

NEW THINKING FOR DESIGN

This emerging design thinking incorporates a new philosophical approach to managing and creating across disciplines. In a recent *BusinessWeek* article by Harry West, "The Cross-Discipline Design Imperative," "The word 'design' has different meanings in different schools, and as these meanings intersect, design becomes bigger, something that sits well above vocational skills and techniques. Design is a set of principles and ways of thinking that help us to manage and create in the material world. It values creativity as much as analysis. It is a way of seeing and painting a new, bigger picture." On the website of the Stanford d.school, (dschool. stanford.edu) a well-known design-thinking educator adds, "Having designers in the mix is key to success in multidisciplinary collaboration and critical to uncovering unexplored areas of innovation." Design methodology, focusing on iterative process (repetition of a process resulting in greater and greater refinement), creates a more fluid environment that allows designers and other professionals to learn from experimentation.

Multidisciplinary, iterative problem solving is essential since today's problems, such as large environmental or sustainability issues, are often too complex and ambiguous to be solved from one disciplinary perspective. Multiple points-of-view are needed to innovate. Additionally, it is no longer enough to merely design products, buildings, web sites or interiors. The overall user/audience experience must be considered in a holistic fashion that engages all senses. Communication isn't just about the visual or verbal, the heart or head. It requires connecting with the whole person.

Design Thinking

Victor Lombardi discusses the central characteristics of design thinking in "What is Design Thinking?" on the blog Noise Between Stations (http://noisebetweenstations.com). These key points are adapted from his article.

- **Collaborative:** working with others who have complementary experience to generate work that encompasses different perspectives
- **Innovative:** inventing ways to create new and better solutions
- **Iterative:** prototyping and testing and then repeating the process to discover what works most effectively
- **Personal:** considering the unique problem context and understanding the needs of the people involved yielding human-centered design
- **Integrative:** perceiving an entire system and its linkages
- **Interpretive:** framing the problem and judging the possible solutions

---

DESIGN THINKING: BOOKS AND ARTICLES QUOTED ON VICTOR LOMBARDI'S BLOG, NOISE BETWEEN STATIONS

EDWARD DE BONO, *WHY SO STUPID? HOW THE HUMAN RACE HAS NEVER REALLY LEARNED TO THINK*

What now matters is the design and delivery of value. That needs design thinking. That needs creative thinking. Judgment thinking alone is not going to be enough. Most people, in business and elsewhere, have done very well on judg-

---

ment thinking. Such people are rarely aware of the need for 'design thinking.' They find it difficult to conceive that there is a whole other aspect of thinking that is different from judgment thinking. It is not that such people are complacent. It is simply that they do not know that there is another aspect to thinking.

BILL BREEN, "MASTERS OF DESIGN"

Design's power runs far deeper than aesthetics. ... If you are mapping out a sales strategy or streamlining a manufacturing operation or crafting a new system for innovating, you are engaged in the practice of design.

ROGER MARTIN, "THE DESIGN OF BUSINESS"

In the end, design is about shaping a context, rather than taking it as it is. When it comes to design, success arises not by emulating others, but by using organizational assets and integrative thinking to identify, build on and leverage asymmetries, evolving unique models, products and experiences—in short, creative business solutions.

JEANNE LIEDTKA, "STRATEGY AS DESIGN"

The most fundamental difference between [design and science] is that design thinking deals primarily with what does not yet exist; while scientists deal with explaining what is. That scientists discover the laws that govern today's reality, while designers invent a different future is a common theme. Thus, while both methods of thinking are hypothesis-driven, the design hypothesis differs from the scientific hypothesis.

BRUCE NUSSBAUM, "REDESIGNING AMERICAN BUSINESS"

Designers are teaching CEOs and managers how to innovate. ... They pitch themselves to businesses as a resource to help with a broad array of issues that affect strategy and organization—creating new brands, defining customer experiences, understanding user needs, changing business practices.

TIM BROWN'S SPEECH AT THE ROTMAN BUSINESS DESIGN CONFERENCE IN 2005

Really, what we're doing as designers is, ultimately and inevitably, designing the business of the companies that we're working for. Whether you like it or not, the more innovative you try to be, the more you are going to affect the business and the business model.

The Development of the "T-shaped" Person

The "T-shaped" individual has a strong disciplinary specialty (their vertical/depth) balanced with the ability to extend that specialty to related areas and the vocabulary and understanding to connect with other disciplines (their horizontal reach/breadth). As the world and its problems become more complex, "T-shaped" people are highly sought after for their skills and knowledge, as well as their abilities to communicate and connect with others. You need to become a "T-shaped" individual to be a leader in tomorrow's economy. Try to develop this attitude in college, if possible, by taking courses in other fields. Be a sponge and learn wherever you are and whenever you can. If you've already graduated, then do some research online or interact with other disciplines through environments such as blogs or conferences.

The Increased Importance of Technology

Technology is much more than just a tool. It is a media, a way of integrating the process of thinking, knowing and learning. Designers need to develop a shared community vision of the evolving capacity of technology to assist with problem solving and exploration. The rapid evolution and transformation of technology demands that those who engage in it continually learn and relearn this language and retool themselves and their skills. This requires extreme flexibility of approach and an evolving understanding of what will be expected in tomorrow's evolving environment. Commit yourself to being open and curious about technology. Set some time aside each day, or each week, to experiment with new software and to research new developments.

The Client-Based, Problem Solving Approach

Traditional art disciplines generate much of their content and inspiration from within the individual artist. The essence of design is that the problem to be solved, and the strategy to be developed, originates from the client—from the outside. There is a fundamental difference between problems that originate from the outside, as opposed to from the inside. Limitations are also a distinct characteristic of design. Learning to work creatively and innovatively within limitations imposed from the outside is one of the most important things a young designer must learn. The solution must function within its appropriate human-centered problem context, budget and time constraints.

Aesthetics is obviously an extremely important part of design, but it is not the only part. The disciplines of design have broadened in the last decade to interact with and embrace the disciplines of psychology, communications, business, marketing, English, journalism, film, engineering and computer science, among others. The links to these disciplines have become as strong, and sometimes stronger, than the original links to the traditional art disciplines from which design grew.

FIRM PROFILE: IDEO'S MODEL FOR INNOVATION

IDEO is a global design consultancy whose slogan is "We create impact through design." They believe the following ingredients are essential to discovering breakthrough solutions:

GATHER NEW/CLEAR INSIGHTS ABOUT USERS THROUGH DIRECT AND CAREFUL OBSERVATION:

- The number of people/situations observed is not as important as the depth of the observation.

- Observe situations that are both directly and indirectly tied to your problem. Gathering inspiration from related, but not the same, situations can yield fresh insights.

WORK WITH "T-SHAPED" PEOPLE:

- Work with people who display disciplinary expertise (forming a strong vertical stroke), but who balance that depth with the ability to branch out and view the world from various perspectives (the horizontal stroke).

- Strive to be open, positive, flexible and empathetic.

- Collaborate with various disciplines to brainstorm, develop a depth of ideas and collectively problem solve.

PROTOTYPING IS ESSENTIAL:

- Prototyping is the process of enlightened trial and error. It's important to test your ideas by building and testing them in the world, and to keep refining those ideas until they are ready to bring to market.

- Prototyping allows you to uncover problems and successes in your design, and gives you a story to tell about the problem solution.

DESIGN IS ALL ABOUT EVOLUTION:

- An idea is always evolving and even once it's in the marketplace, the most successful products are continually being further developed and refined.

- Since the market is always changing, so must the strategy. A flexible and evolving strategy is key to remaining relevant. A brand identity, for instance, must be able to adapt and evolve over time and with consumer interests/needs.

APPLICATION: THINKING DESIGN

Craft a pitch to executives in your corner of the business community convincing them of the importance of the design process and strategy. List the key points and elements of your pitch here. Make sure to keep you potential clients first in your mind as you brainstorm.

PART FIVE

WORKING WITH OTHERS

Design has always been a business of partnerships. We can't do the job completely by ourselves. There are always collaborators—photographers, illustrators, printers, paper vendors, other designers, marketers, writers, etc. Today, partnerships have become increasingly important as the problems to be solved have become more complex and integrated. Working with others comes more naturally to some of us than to others, but it's an area where we can all continue to learn and grow.

Nancy Owyang, Creative Director and Owner of Eye 2 Eye Graphics, has some great advice: "As for interactions with vendors, clients or anyone for that matter, be up-front, honest and build a relationship with them. Do business with integrity, honesty and respect. Don't be afraid to ask questions! We are always learning, so if there is something that comes up that you aren't sure how to handle, go to your network of design mentors and ask to see if anyone has been in a similar situation."

This section gives specific advice on partnering effectively with those we create work for: our clients and those who help us create the product, our design colleagues and other creative professionals.

CHAPTER 14
PARTNERING EFFECTIVELY WITH CLIENTS

WHAT ARE CLIENTS REALLY LOOKING FOR?

As a design professional, whether working on your own or in a large international firm, it's critical to be a proactive partner with your client. Below are some key characteristics you need continually to develop over the course of your career. Many of these qualities will become second nature over time.

Creativity

Clients are coming to you because they need your expertise—your design knowledge and skills. They want your creativity and your unique approach to problem solving because that's not something they have within their organization. As a "creative person" interfacing with "noncreative" professionals, it's important to understand and appreciate different approaches and languages. Approach the client with respect, but don't be afraid to be creative and use design-thinking methodologies with your clients.

Communicate your creative vision in a language and form the client can connect with and understand, whether that means a written proposal or PowerPoint presentation. The design process can help clients solve their problems in innovative ways by revealing unique and diverse perspectives. In addition, most of the time, "the problem" involves communication with an audience. How can you use your creativity and analytical skills to solve that communication problem and allow the clients to connect with their audience? You create that link.

Understanding

Clients really do appreciate it when you judge their level of understanding of design and then meet them where they are. Nine times out of ten, your client will have no training in design and little understanding of visual literacy. Unlike verbal communication, visual communication isn't part of our secondary schooling process; this isn't the client's fault, so don't get frustrated with them when they don't understand the importance of white space. It's part of our job as designers to educate the client about design in general, the specific process and expectations for the project and the critical place of design within business. Especially with a new client, this type of education process is important. Sometimes, it's difficult to be sure that your points are getting through. Your client may nod, smile and give every indication that they understand, but then when it comes to developing a project schedule, for instance, they may want to give you only two days to do a complex project that really requires two weeks. It's important for you, in this case, to be flexible, and use this situation as an opportunity to discuss the complexity of the design process and be clear about why it takes time.

Always approach the client with respect and a nonpretentious attitude. It's important to be confident in your own disciplinary expertise and at the same time, be humbled by the client's disciplinary expertise. You are both experts and deserve to be treated as such. You need to be open to the client educating you about their business; they are extremely knowledgeable when it comes to the topics and issues you will be visually communicating in the design work. Make sure to use that expertise to your benefit.

Ask the client these questions to get to know their business:

- When you speak to your audience/consumers, how do you describe your products/services?

- When you speak to your business peers, how do you describe your products/services?

- Do you have business literature I can look through in order to educate myself about your business?

- What web sites or books would you recommend I read in order to better educate myself?

- I've studied your web site. Is the information current? Is there content you would add or change? What? Why?

Communication

Mark Hamilton, Associate Director for Marketing and Creative Services at the College of St. Rose, describes the importance of effective communication with clients, "Success and failure of your work lies in words. Speaking and talking are very important. But also be a good listener. Ask questions and listen to answers; involve the client with a vested interest. Clients do live and breathe their work; recognize that. At the same time, do not be afraid to approach other people on the client side if necessary—advocates are helpful, sometimes necessary. Always stress process. When presenting, begin with words before showing any visuals. Make sure you have done your homework; know who's in charge and who's in the meeting. State your goals for meeting and what decisions you expect to make, repeat goals and objectives of a project that were discussed in previous meetings and state your concept clearly before you show any visuals. Also learn to be articulate and take the time to pick up the lingo of your client."

Confidence

You're the design expert—make sure you act like it. That doesn't mean you shouldn't ask questions, and it doesn't mean you are a know-it-all. But it does mean that you are there to confidently guide the client through the process, thoroughly answer any questions they have, find the answers if you don't know them, show your knowledge of your field and your professionalism, and learn as much as you can about the client's business. Humble confidence that expresses itself in actions, instead of showmanship and words, will give your client the important sense of comfort that the job is being done correctly.

Trust

Your client relationships should be strategic partnerships. Build trust by being dependable and keeping your deadlines and promises to the client. Building trust is one of your most important tasks. People will not work with someone they cannot depend on. A good partner never promises something they can't deliver. It's better to tell the client "maybe" or "I'll try my best" than to promise and not follow through. You can also suggest a compromise depending on the situation specifics.

You will, of course, make mistakes—everyone does. But don't let your mistakes damage the trust of your clients. You need to immediately take responsibility for any mistakes you make and quickly plan a course of action to remedy any adverse effects. If your words and actions express an honest and responsive solution, this can actually build trust with your client instead of damaging it.

Flexibility

You need to be the flexible one in this relationship. If the client strongly prefers to be billed monthly and you usually bill quarterly, then change your practice. If they would like to meet at their office instead of yours, be accommodating. How can you learn to set aside your own preferences and routines? Start with one client and see the difference it makes. When you see the results, you'll also be able to identify the benefits to you and your business. If you are easy to work with and you are careful to consider the clients' needs before your own, you will win a lot of future work for you and your company. There's nothing better than having a client call your boss and request to work with you specifically because you provide such good customer service. It's probably the best way to get a raise.

There are times when you can be too flexible. If you feel that you, your skills or your time aren't being respected and that the clients requests have crossed a line of some sort (asking you to be available 24/7, for instance), it's your responsibility to stand up for yourself and work out a compromise that doesn't damage your self-respect and your ability to do your job effectively.

Excellence

Shoot high and plan to exceed the client's expectations on every occasion. Excellence includes consistently high marks in communication, confidence, trust and flexibility, while anticipating the future needs of the client. This foresight is another great way to get projects and business. If you can get to know the client's business so well that you can see their needs before they do, and sell them on those needs, then you will always be busy. You are approaching their business from an outside perspective. This can be a real advantage in "seeing the forest"—the larger context—while the client is busy "looking at the trees" and putting out forest fires, absorbed in the smaller details. Approaching the client with a new idea can be very exciting for both you and them. Proactive excellence is one of the most critical characteristics to success and a true differentiating factor between strong designing businesspeople and strong designers.

DEVELOPING YOUR CLIENT RELATIONSHIPS

It's critical to continually work at developing your client relationships. There are a number of ways you can effectively nurture those partnerships, but the key is that you read your client to see what will work for them; your approach needs to be personalized and individualized.

REAL WORLD ADVICE: CLIENT MANAGEMENT

BRIAN SOOY, WWW.BUSINESSOFDESIGNONLINE.COM

There are two mantras you should recite every morning before starting your day:

1. I will manage my client's expectations.
2. I will lead my clients.

Managing a client's expectations starts with a great relationship, where they value your input and respect your recommendations. Understanding the relationship informs how you will lead. These are mantras that declare your intent to focus on their needs and expectations in a proactive manner and make the experience of working with your firm easy.

I WILL MANAGE MY CLIENT'S EXPECTATIONS

Too often, we can't lead our clients because we haven't:

- understood how the client wants to work with us
- defined our expectations (to the client) of the collaborative relationship

To manage your client's expectations, you need to make clear your policies and procedures. Do you expect timely approvals? Put it in your contract and make it clear to them. Do you provide weekly status reports? If so, are they aware that you do? Should they call you for every little edit? If not, whom do they call? If a client doesn't understand how your firm works, then you will constantly be responding to their requests, instead of proactively anticipating their needs.

It's two-sided: The client has needs and expectations; the design firm has (or should have) workflow procedures. Your procedures will have anticipated their expectations, and the client will make it clear if those will work for them.

Of course, it's not a one-size-fits-all approach, but it all starts with the relationship that your firm has built with the client.

I WILL LEAD MY CLIENTS

Do you wait for the client to call or send copy, or is your firm proactive in monitoring the project schedule? It's easier to wait for the "trigger," the e-mail from the client that indicates you need to drop what you're doing and fight that fire. Do you wait for input from your client, or do you take the lead role in the collaborative relationship?

Anticipating deadlines, respecting timelines and awareness of your client's needs will allow you to manage your time and lead your clients. This thinking can be applied to everything from business development to project management. It allows you to control the relationship and the workflow, rather than letting it control you. It allows you to lead your clients and guide them—not let them pull you along.

My recommendation: Develop your leadership skills. Your clients will notice. The rest will follow.

In her www.howdesign.com article, "Connect With Your Clients," Ilise Benun notes that using multiple approaches is key: "On the phone: Make sure that a human being, preferably a caring, professional receptionist, answers the phone. If you cannot hire a receptionist, make your voice mail system easy for callers to navigate and assign a real person to respond when a caller presses zero.

"In the mail: Don't overlook the power of the personal note. When you open your mailbox to find a letter that's been hand-addressed to you, don't you think, 'This must be from someone I know?' and don't you spend more time reading or looking at that piece of mail? It takes time, yet it makes a stronger impact than any flashy direct-mail piece ever could.

"In person: Look for ways to interact with you potential client base face-to-face. Speak at trade conferences. Offer to meet with your prospect rather than shipping off your portfolio. Get involved in pro bono projects that offer you a chance to connect with leaders in your community."

As noted in Chapter 8: General Communication Skills, it's critical to read the client, or any person for that matter, to find what type of communication method works best for them. Your client might respond well to e-mail or might love to chat on the phone. Perhaps having a hard-copy version of your proposal is important for their file-keeping or maybe they prefer to keep solely electronic files. You should make it your mission to discover these preferences and tailor your actions to their needs. This is part of being a flexible, dependable working consultant. It will also save you a lot of headaches and time in the long run. Say you constantly e-mail your client, because that's your favorite form of communication, but your client checks e-mail irregularly, you'll be frustrated and unable to move the project forward. If you know that you can get the information you need quickly by phoning her, then do so. If you are stubborn and inflexible, it will be your undoing in the long run, and communication stalls will constantly hold you up.

In the www.entrepreneur.com article, "Building Client Relationships," Tom Hopkins mentions "People like to do business with people who are like them, who demonstrate that they care about them beyond making the sale. That type of treatment makes them feel important. It's in your best interest to offer that type of treatment and cultivate relationships that customers can count on." By being the flexible one in the relationship and meeting the clients needs, including bending to their communication style, you will show your concern for their best interest.

WHEN SOMETHING GOES WRONG

So what happens when something goes wrong—there's a mistake that's been made or a communication breakdown of some sort? Your client is unhappy and worried about the project. What's your best course of action?

• Call the client, or better yet, go talk to them in person if you can. Personal contact is key when you have an unhappy client. You need to see their nonverbal communication and hear the tone of their voice. They may say everything is okay, but their tone and posture might tell you something different. It's important to talk through the problem until you are sure they are comfortable with the action plan to move forward. Never e-mail when there is a confrontation; it will communicate that you don't have the guts to solve the problem head on.

• If a mistake of some type has occurred, then consider possible solutions to the problem before you make the call. Have a solid plan of attack, present it confidently and ask your client for their honest feedback. This will give your client the sense of reassurance that they need: You're on the job to fix the problem.

• If it's a miscommunication that's occurred and an apology is appropriate, then offer one as promptly as possible. Don't wait around a day or two. Call right away and smooth things out.

• For the remainder of the project, try to add extra value and go over-and-above what you would normally do. This will help to reinstate trust and confidence in you and your business. In addition, it might be appropriate to keep in closer touch with the client, especially if the error involved communication. Give them more frequent and more detailed updates on your progress to assure them that it's moving ahead without problems.

In the vast majority of cases the client will accept your apology and will allow you to move on with your work, but if the client is unwilling to accept your best efforts you may need to end the relationship. It's key to do this in the most professional and respectful manner, while leaving as little wake as possible.

Mistakes and miscommunication will occur. Even the most careful people will encounter problems at some point in time. The key is to own up to the mistake and work confidently and diligently to make it right for yourself and the client. Never try to hide a mistake or blame someone else. This is immature behavior, and it will hurt you in the long run.

SETTING REASONABLE BOUNDARIES IS IMPORTANT

Being flexible and accommodating of your clients is very important, but there are situations where you need to set some boundaries. You do have a life, and you don't work 24/7. Respect is a two-way street, and you should not allow yourself to be used and abused. Once you start down that slippery slope with a client, it's very difficult to make it back up the hill to a place where you have a relationship of mutual respect and equal partnership. The client won't respect you or your time if it's clear you don't respect yourself.

Your client should have your business hours and should know that you are available for calls during those hours. Other than emergencies of some sort (a midnight press check gone wrong, for instance), all phone communication outside of business hours should be kept to a minimum. If your client learns that you always answer the phone, no matter the time, then you may set up a situation where you get calls at all hours of the day and night. This isn't healthy for you or the relationship.

If a client demonstrates behaviors that make your life difficult and don't follow the standards you set up in your letter of agreement or proposal, then it's time to have a conversation. Don't continue to do the job if your client is months behind on payment, for instance. Or if you aren't getting the feedback you need and your questions aren't being answered, then let the client know the project schedule is being compromised. Send a revised schedule that indicates how the due date is slipping. Or if the project scope keeps growing and every time you hear from the client they want more for the same price, it's your job to manage that scope by setting clear expectations for yourself and your client; make sure you don't experience "scope creep."

APPLICATION: PLANNING DIFFICULT CONVERSATIONS

What do I want to get out of this conversation? What are the specific points I want to make?

How can I present my points without sounding overly critical, difficult or pretentious?

What does the problem look like from the client's perspective?

What might I be doing wrong in the situation or what could I do better?

What is my body language communicating when I speak with my client?

How can I avoid/control my anger during the conversation?

If you are working on your own, remember that you have the option to decline working with a client. This is one of the advantages of working independently. Unless you are desperate for the money, continuing to work with an extremely difficult client is probably not the best thing for you or the development of your business. Choose to work with people who partner effectively with you. This will decrease your personal and work stress and increase your time and happiness. Thankfully, these types of issues never arise with most clients. The vast majority of clients are respectful and responsive.

REAL WORLD ADVICE: WHAT ARE CLIENTS LOOKING FOR?

KIM CORNWALL MALSEED, INDEPENDENT B2B B2G MARKETING COMMUNICATIONS & PR CONSULTANT, COPYWRITER

Clients want: a solution to their particular problem(s) and to know what's in it for them and their organization if they use your services, so clearly explain this in your marketing efforts; experience in their particular industry (not a requirement but helps greatly); proof your work quality is what you say it is (portfolio of samples or similar); fee rates consistent with your level of experience/quality of work; and flexibility, responsiveness, and overall, being easy and enjoyable to work with.

THOMAS H. GILMORE, DIRECTOR OF BRAND STRATEGY, RGI DESIGN

While the goals of each client and project engagement can be considerably different for a design professional, overall objectives are often the same. Clients are looking for creativity and a varied perspective from designers. As experts in their particular businesses, clients are in need of designers that can provide innovative methods of creativity, communication and collaboration, as well as project management. Often, the innovation needed for a project to succeed must come from someone removed from the immediate management of the client's business. Designers may offer valuable leadership, helping to gain consensus and build upon cross-functional ideas, as well as raise aesthetic awareness.

ERIK BORRESON, SENIOR GRAPHIC DESIGNER, MARSHFIELD CLINIC

Remember to value the client's input, but don't act like a production person. You are there to make the product better. If all you are there for is putting their idea in an InDesign file, you really aren't designing. With that being said, get as much information about them and the project as you can. Find out what the budget is, how many printed pieces they need, and who their target audience is. Be honest and command respect. Be sure they know what to expect. Communication is key—and makes the job easier on both sides.

CHAPTER 15
COLLABORATING WITH OTHER CREATIVE DISCIPLINES

There are many design projects in which you will be partnering with other creative disciplines in order to achieve the best possible product for your client and their audience. Whether you are working with photographers, illustrators, writers or programmers, you will need to address how to most effectively and efficiently work together. You speak similar languages, but there will be specific nuances that may catch you off guard. It's important to be aware of those similarities and differences so the job will go smoothly.

MAKING THE RIGHT CHOICES

In Chapter 9: Key Ethical Guidelines, we discussed the use of illustration and photography, especially as it relates to existing and stock images. If you have the budget to work with an illustrator or photographer to create new and unique imagery for your project, how do you go about making the right choices to ensure that the working relationship ends with the best possible results? What are the best strategies for researching the skills you need, whether it's writing, photography or illustration?

Stock or Not?

First of all, you'll have to decide whether or not to use stock photography/illustration or to work with a professional to achieve something truly unique. When is it appropriate to hire a photographer or illustrator? It's especially important if you are trying to communicate something with the imagery that you can't find in stock, or perhaps you want your graphic or typographic ideas to work into the imagery. Tailoring the imagery to the concept of the piece works more effectively than tailoring the piece to stock imagery. Collaborating with a photographer or illustrator may be the only way to truly achieve your vision for the project and most effectively meet the communication needs of the client.

With this approach, you and your client are also sure that the images won't show up elsewhere, perhaps in a competitor's promotional materials. This is an important way to differentiate your design work and the image of the client's brand. A certain style of photography or illustration may become part of the brand identity, just like the color palette and type family choices. This strengthens the voice of the company, allowing them to more clearly communicate and differentiate their message from the sea of competitors.

Portfolio Reviews

Keep a running file of the promotional cards that illustrators and photographers send out. Look through them and the sourcebooks and annuals you have on your shelf. Talk to other designers and get recommendations. But the most effective and up-to-date tool for finding the right creative partner is the Internet. Photographers and illustrators publish their work on their own web sites as well as group portfolio sites. Do a search and look for the style you are interested in using. In his www. howdesign.com article, "How to Commission Photography," Alan Klehr explains key points to consider when inspecting portfolios (these ideas can be adapted to illustrators as well):

- Make sure the photographer can duplicate the style you require/desire for your job. Does their photographic style match what you need for your job?

- Are the portfolio pieces for real clients or personal work?

- Does the photographer's experience (as represented in the portfolio) match what you need for your job?

- Can you assess how manipulated or "doctored" the photographs in their portfolio are? A lot of Photoshop work may result in a more expensive job, and you need to be prepared for that, or avoid it all together.

CONSIDER YOUR BUDGET

Make sure you get an estimate for the job before you begin. Photography, illustration, writing and programming charges can vary quite a bit, so never assume that because your last job cost a certain amount that the next one will be about the same. Ask that the estimate be specific and cover all costs of the job. Also discuss the schedule of the job and agree to the timing. If the estimate is too high for your budget, you can always go back and attempt to negotiate the costs. There may be ways to bring the price down by adjusting certain aspects of the job, such as shoot location or timing.

You may also want to get estimates from various creative professionals so you have several choices and a way of comparing costs. If you do this, it is referred to as "bidding" the job. Ethically, it's important to be clear from the outset that this is a competitive situation and that others are bidding on the same job. This may impact whether or not the individual wants to participate in the process.

The usage and rights to creative work, such as photography, will probably affect the price. Look to Chapter 9: Key Ethical Guidelines and Chapter 20: Intellectual Property Basics for Designers for more information about copyright and usage. In most situations, you should only pay for what your client needs at the time, but for some specific images, for instance, the client may want more extensive rights—perhaps it's an image that will become closely associated with the brand and may be used in many different contexts. You or your client need to negotiate these rights with the photographer.

DIFFERENT WAYS OF CHARGING FOR CREATIVE WORK

- **Day Rate:** Refers to the cost of showing up for approximately a one-day period.

- **Usage Fee:** Fee based on how a creative image or text will be used (where, when, how many times and how long).

- **Project Rate:** Includes the scope of the work and may also include the copyright/usage (but always check).

- **Expenses:** Studio fees, supplies, travel, talent and props may be added to the job separately.

- **Hourly Rate:** Cost based on the specific length of time it takes to do the job. Creative work and production work may have two different rates.

- **Money Up-Front:** Some individuals/companies will request a certain percentage of the fees up-front.

DEVELOP A RELATIONSHIP

It's very important to develop a strong relationship with your creative partners, whether they are photographers, illustrators, programmers or writers. When you are assessing those portfolios, also look at the individual and what they bring to the table in terms of personality, people skills and communication style. Try to meet with them in person to see if there's good chemistry between you. This will be a close working relationship, perhaps only for a few days, but it's still very important to ensure things will go smoothly. This individual may eventually meet with your client (perhaps it's a photographer who needs to do a photo shoot with the CEO of the company). Your choice of that photographer will reflect on you and your decision-making skills. If that individual comes off as crass and rude, then it will reflect poorly on you.

Ideally, this relationship will last more than just a few days. Many designers and their creative partners develop mutually beneficial relationships that last for many years. Strive for this goal. It's wonderful for a designer, especially one that works on his own, to have a stable and trusted group of collaborators that are resources for talent and inspiration.

One way to establish strong relationships is to bring people into the process as early as possible. These partners are important to helping you more clearly define your concept. They will offer new perspectives and ideas on the project—ways of solving the problem from a different viewpoint. Listen to them. Use this expertise to your advantage. Whether it's the programmer who can offer you new ideas on motion graphics or the writer who has a different take on how the words and imagery might work together, these individuals have a lot to offer. Make sure to be open to their ideas, ask for their input and give them the time they need to do their work.

REAL WORLD ADVICE: WORKING WITH OTHER CREATIVE DISCIPLINES

MARK HAMILTON, ASSOCIATE DIRECTOR OF MARKETING & CREATIVE SERVICES, THE COLLEGE OF SAINT ROSE

Simply, work with [the person] you can trust as a creative partner and learn to be a partner yourself, and if you have to, leave your ego behind. Often, photographers and illustrators can make your ideas even a hundred times better than you originally conceived, and writers can be just as visually inclined as yourself. Be the director and let the photographer or illustrator take care of all the technical needs. This even applies when working with programmers and interactive designers.

JEFF FISHER, ENGINEER OF CREATIVE IDENTITY, JEFF FISHER LOGOMOTIVES

Put the "creative type" egos aside and work with, rather than against, writers, photographers and illustrators. These people are your allies on a project and, most often, are the only other players in a project effort that speak the same language as a designer. Establish the boundaries and "rules" of a project early in the effort so the creatives are not walking all over each other in the process of meeting the client's needs. Always give credit where credit is due—writers, photographers and illustrators need their strokes just as much as a designer does.

BRYAN GAFFIN, SENIOR VICE PRESIDENT, GROUP CREATIVE DIRECTOR, RAPP COLLINS WORLDWIDE

Learn the interactive channel. In this day and age, the digital channel is as important as anything, and those creatives who try to keep themselves siloed as 'just print,' will find their opportunities narrow as time goes on. This doesn't mean becoming an expert overnight, but it does mean taking the time to learn the basics of digital. Take a class if possible or teach yourself (lynda.com and Visual QuickStart being my favorite self-help tools). Get magazines like *Wired* and *Fast Company* and follow the trends. Learn the capabilities of Adobe Flash Player and Autodesk Maya; you don't have to learn how to use them, just understand what they can and can't do. The best way is to be a regular web surfer and see what people are doing. When you've done that, you can work well with developers or interactive designers because you'll speak and understand the same language.

ERIK BORRESON, SENIOR GRAPHIC DESIGNER, MARSHFIELD CLINIC

When working with writers, photographers and illustrators, value their input. These professions can make your work a lot better and your job a lot easier.

I think the most difficult part about working with writers, photographers and illustrators is that there are so many different types of personalities and styles. It is the graphic designer's job to make these elements work together in a successful layout.

For that to happen, I believe a designer must, before anything else, have a vision of what they want the completed piece to look like. Know the styles that you want to use in the piece. Talk with them a lot in the front end; have an open door policy with them if they have any questions; have examples of styles (if possible) for illustrations, photography, writing that you like. Be sure the writer, photographer or illustrator is capable of doing that type of work too.

THOMAS H. GILMORE, DIRECTOR OF BRAND STRATEGY, RGI DESIGN

When sourcing contributions from photographers and illustrators, a designer must remember to communicate specific project objectives, clear artistic direction, timelines and success criteria. While great emphasis is placed upon initial meetings and communication, a post-project follow-up should be given equal importance. This enables refinement to project process, communication, timing and quality. Once an ongoing relationship has been built with outside services, additional efficiencies may be realized.

ELLEN PETTY, CREATIVE DIRECTOR/ PRINCIPAL, IDENTITY KITCHEN

I find it very easy to work with writers, illustrators and photographers; their business models are almost identical to those of designers. Just treat them like we would like to be treated by our clients and colleagues. Respect their work, give clear direction and compensate them as best you can. If the scope or direction of the project changes because of wavering from your client, try and get a good handle on the new direction before giving new instruction. Also, try and give a little bit of room for them to interpret the project. If you have hired a writer, illustrator or photographer whose work you admire, they might give you something you did not think of, and sometimes, these are the perfect solutions.

I read a bit of advice once that said, know how to do every job in your company. When hiring a programmer or interactive designer try and understand what it is you are asking them to accomplish. If you don't understand, ask them to explain how they are going to accomplish the goals you have set in layman's terms.

CHAPTER 16
WORKING WITH OTHER DESIGNERS

We talked about working with clients and other creative disciplines, but what about working with other designers? Whether you are working on projects alone or as part of a team, you will be interacting and interfacing with designers almost every day. And sometimes, it is most difficult to work with people of like minds because there is more sense of competition. So what makes for successful relationship between designers?

COOPERATION NOT CONFRONTATION

Try to develop a spirit of collaboration with your fellow designers. It doesn't help anyone, especially yourself, to have a confrontational or negatively competitive personality. You will find that you are rewarded for being a team player. Work to develop a reputation for cooperation—be someone that is easy to work with. This doesn't mean being a pushover. People will only respect you if you have standards of excellence, but don't be difficult and stubborn. It's a balancing act.

Be as helpful as possible. Seek out opportunities to assist with a big project or help out a colleague that's overwhelmed. Even though this means more work for you in the short term, it will lead to rewards and opportunities in the long term. As the concept of business has moved away from hierarchical structures to one that is flatter and more team-driven, these types of skills have become increasingly important for success. Helpfulness and cooperation make for a less stressful work environment and happier employees.

It's critical to learn to function smoothly in a crisis situation when there's a lot of pressure on you or your team. Graphic design is a stressful business and there will be plenty of times when you need to keep a cool head. When there's a setback, calmly analyze the situation, gather any facts you need, make a plan (perhaps with the team) and develop specific action steps—then get started.

STAY CONNECTED

Because jobs aren't as segmented and subdivided as in the past, it's even more important to develop a good network of contacts, especially if you work at a larger company or corporation. You need to keep up with developments that are occurring both with the company as a whole and with individual people, especially key players. Don't mistake this for gossip by the watercooler. These connections should be positive and constructive, not negative and destructive. This means keeping current with the organization and developing a clear understanding of how you fit within that context, as well as how you can fit in the future. This network should include the designers you work with at the office, as well as designers in your city or region.

FIND A MENTOR

In her www.howdesign.com article, "How to Find—or Be—a Mentor," Laurel Harper tells this story, "In Homer's literary epic *The Odyssey*, when Odysseus departed to fight the Trojans, he left behind a trusted friend—a wise old seaman named Mentor—to guide his son Telemachus. Mentor taught Telemachus not just the physical skills but he also cultivated the boy's mental prowess [and] his father's morality. Through the years, the word 'mentor' has come to mean 'trusted friend' and 'counselor.' But in today's social climate, where so much attention is focused on climbing the career ladder, mentor has taken on a new connotation—'career guide' or 'executive nurturer.'"

In my own experience, mentors have been instrumental to my success and happiness on the job. A good mentor can guide you away from poor decisions, make you more politically aware of sensitive situations, give you a broader perspective, lend you her wisdom and support, teach you a great deal and become a dear and trusted friend. If you aren't formally assigned a mentor by your employer, then seek one out on your own. Pay close attention in formal meetings and informal interactions and connect with people who are compatible with your personality, people who are smart and savvy and who you can look up to for advice and guidance. Developing a relationship with these people will be rewarding and beneficial.

Two Can Be Better Than One

Sometimes, it's difficult for one individual to completely fit the bill. You may have needs and questions that should be addressed by two, or even several, mentors. Seek out experts in the various areas with which you need assistance. One person might not have all the knowledge and skills you need. You can always build a primary relationship with one very trusted individual, while also seeking advice from other people who have greater experience in particular focused areas. For instance, perhaps the colleague who's been around the block for many years has great organizational/company knowledge, but he may not have the technical savvy for guidance with software conundrums.

Learn as Much as You Can

Mentors have a great deal to share with you—skills, experience and knowledge. Seek out mentors who will challenge you and get you out of your comfort zone. Sometimes students fail to realize that learning doesn't end with college. The most successful people learn and challenge themselves throughout their careers. Your mentors can be great guides along that path.

Deidre Evans, Mentoring Co-Director for AIGA Cincinnati, describes the mentoring experience, "It's nothing too difficult. Just being there is enough. You might be asked to review a portfolio, critique a résumé or hammer through a thesis. It's very possible to just meet for lunch and pick each other's brains. Mentoring can be ten minutes of your time or you might end up with a mentee for life. I know one thing, mentees aren't looking for all the right answers. They are just looking for direction and insight. And no matter how short or long you have been in the profession, you have that. Otherwise, I have found to expect little, and I gain a lot. And just the fact that you are taking time out of your day to be a mentor means you'll be perfect."

Don't Mimic Your Mentor: Be Yourself

It's important for both the mentor and mentee to realize that mentorship isn't about teaching one person to act like the other. Each person has their own gifts, strengths and "sweet spots," and it's essential that the mentor discover and nurture those characteristics. The mentor should not try to remake the mentee in her image. This will result in a strained and unhealthy relationship and may make the mentee less confident in his own abilities. As the mentee, it's important to be aware that this can happen and to be sensitive to these issues. If you feel your mentor is being overbearing, have an open discussion about your relationship.

Developing a Strong Relationship

It's very important that the mentor and mentee approach the relationship in the proper manner:

- Both should be open to listening and learning. The mentee won't get any benefit unless he respects the experience and wisdom that the mentor offers. At the same time, this isn't a one-way street. The mentor should also be open to learning some things from the mentee, especially as he grows. If the mentor is doing her job well, then the mentee will be able to offer up a developing experience and knowledge level to the relationship. Allow the relationship to develop and evolve. Over time you may move from the mentor/mentee relationship to one of valued friends/colleagues.

• Value critique and feedback; don't be threatened by it.

• The mentor must be willing to openly share her knowledge, experience, skills and savvy. The mentor should share her secrets for success without fear of competition with her mentee.

• There needs to be a measure of chemistry between the mentor and mentee. This doesn't mean that they should be alike. Sometime opposites attract. Putting two quiet people together might result in nothing by silence. Putting two chatty people together might result in nothing but frustration because neither can get in a word.

• If you are assigned a mentor and the relationship just isn't working out, you should still work with that individual, as they will always have something to offer. But you should feel free to seek out other individuals who might actually be a better match for you.

• Don't restrict your mentors to people that are obviously older or more experienced than you. A great mentor can be someone who allows you to see a different perspective or challenges you with her own strength in creativity or intellect, even if she is younger or a peer.

Give Back, Be a Mentor

Once you've had some experience, try the mentor role yourself. If you've had an effective mentor, then you will have a wonderful role model to fashion your mentoring style after. You can even start to mentor very early in your career. Perhaps there's an internship/co-op program at your company. Even as a first or second-year employee, you can train and mentor college students so that they have a more positive, enriching experience at your company. The best way to assess your mentee's needs is to have an open discussion about what he wants to get out of the relationship.

BE A LEADER AND A FOLLOWER

Leadership skills are important to nurture, especially in a team environment. Someone has to lead the group, and it isn't always the person with the title. You can show leadership abilities at any level, even if you are a junior designer.

• One aspect of being a good leader is to be clear about expectations for yourself and other members of your group. If everyone is clear about their responsibilities, then the job is much more likely to be completed well and on time.

• Be consistent so that people know where you're coming from and can depend on you. If you communicate mixed messages, or if you are on one minute and off the next, you will confuse your coworkers and make them uncomfortable. Effective leaders have a consistent style that breeds confidence and cooperation among the group. I'm sure you can look back in your own experience to fellow designers/students who were highly productive for one project and could care less for another, or perhaps they were moody in their relationships with colleagues. It's difficult to deal with people if you don't know how they are going to respond to you or the project at hand.

• Work well under pressure. As I said previously, this is especially important for a leader. People will look to you for your calming spirit. Don't escalate the situation by asking frantic questions and acting panicky. Try to consciously quiet the commotion with your confidence and problem-solving abilities. Be the one that stops for a moment, takes a breath and thinks through the situation. Don't send verbal or nonverbal messages that "we are doomed," but instill the confidence in your team that "we can do it!"

• Set a good example for your coworkers. Don't participate in office behaviors that you know aren't appropriate, such as gossip or undercutting your peers. Demonstrate integrity and honesty in your work and personal practices. Build strong working relationships with your coworkers by being kind and helpful.

Sometimes it's just as important to be an effective follower by being supportive and dependable. If the group already has a leader or leaders who are directing and guiding the work, then listen and learn from them. Don't try to fight them for the leadership position. If you disagree with them for one reason or another, then give respectful suggestions and try to see things from their perspective. Especially if you are a new employee, it's important to develop relationships before you can be trusted with official or unofficial leadership responsibilities.

WORKING TOGETHER AT THE DESIGN FIRM LPK

In LPK's *Tips for Success: An Active Guide to Understanding Company Culture for Employees*, the company identifies and outlines six critical skills necessary for success within their corporate culture:

LEADERSHIP

• understands our company's Statement of Purpose, embraces and applies our values, principles and processes
• recognizes opportunities and champions ideas and people to get breakthrough results internally and externally
• demonstrates uncompromising integrity and respect for the individual

- demonstrates "employee owner" approach to work, actively taking on responsibilities
- possesses ability to earn respect while instilling in others the inspiration to identify, set and achieve challenging goals

CREATIVITY AND INNOVATION

- uses logic, data, insight and intuition from a variety of sources to define problems and develop a solid plan of action
- learns from successes and mistakes to solve problems better
- recognizes developing problems and involves the appropriate people, managing the issue in a timely manner

FUNCTIONAL MASTERY

- consistently provides a product or service that meets or exceeds client expectations
- achieves technical mastery and help develop it in others
- consistently demonstrates fiscal responsibility using resources (time, space, materials, equipment, people)
- understands and adheres to policies and procedures
- exhibits working knowledge of commitment to product and process excellence

PRIORITY SETTING

- recognizes the most important issues, makes effective plans, gets resources in place to achieve key objectives, takes appropriate risks
- handles multiple priorities well

WORKING EFFECTIVELY WITH OTHERS

- works effectively across the organization

- recognizes and respects diversity of culture, viewpoint and approach
- adheres to team covenants and honors commitments to others
- exhibits an excellent "customer service" approach both internally and externally, providing distinguished service

COMMUNICATION

- seeks first to understand, then to be understood
- consistently provides accurate and timely information
- organizes and expresses thoughts clearly in both written and oral form

PART SIX

DOING YOUR OWN THING

If you're considering venturing out on your own, whether it be as a free-lancer right out of college or a more experienced designer who wants to start your own small firm, understanding what it takes is critical. Do you know what does it take to be successful? You were trained as a designer, but are you prepared run the business side? How do you know if doing your own thing is right for you?

In this section, we will investigate the ins and outs of working independently, figuring your pricing, writing contracts and proposals, understanding your intellectual property rights and setting yourself up for success. You'll hear from experienced designers who struck out on their own fairly recently or some time ago and get some legal advice from experts on intellectual property.

Careful, confident planning is the best way to ensure success in your own business. Follow William A. Ward's four steps to achievement: "Plan purposefully. Prepare prayerfully. Proceed positively. Pursue persistently," to build your own business on a successful foundation.

CHAPTER 17
FREELANCING AND RUNNING YOUR OWN FIRM

Most graphic designers find themselves freelancing at some point in their career, whether it's while they are still in school, on-the-side while working full-time at a firm, as a part-time situation while looking for permanent employment or in a full-time capacity. Many firms and agencies hire freelancers on a regular basis to help them complete projects when they are too busy for their own staff to handle everything. Additionally, many companies and organizations will hire freelancers to do smaller jobs when they don't need the assistance of a larger firm.

Petrula Vrontikis, in her HOW Conference presentation, defined a freelancer as "a solo-practitioner who primarily works on a particular part or phase of a project." He or she might also create a one-time end product, like a logo design. The U.S. Department of Labor Bureau of Statistics reports that, of graphic designers, "about 25 percent are self-employed; many do freelance work in addition to holding a salaried job in design or in another occupation." Often, people think of freelancing as a way to keep the money flowing while unemployed, but many freelancers aren't between jobs. They choose to take advantage of the lifestyle of freedom and flexibility that this type of situation offers. Freelancers often work at any time of the day or night, arrange their own schedules and decide on what clients they work with or not. Some people really enjoy this lack of externally imposed structure.

The line between being a freelancer and running your own full-time firm can be confusing and fuzzy. Normally, a practitioner in a firm works directly with clients; often a freelancer works temporarily for a firm whose representatives (designers or account executives) meet with the clients. A one-person firm requires the development of longer-term client relationships and requires more business management. (A one-person firm may hire its own freelancers during busy times, for instance.) Also, firms normally handle larger, long-term projects from start to finish.

Vrontikis groups freelancers into five main categories:

- those with specialized skills: typography, illustration, lettering
- those who are moonlighting while working full-time elsewhere (for money or creative motivations)
- those transitioning from one job to another or to running a one-person studio
- those being "tested" by prospective employers
- and those who choose freelancing as their main career choice

THE MAIN REASONS TO HIRE FREELANCERS

- They provide a specialized skill for a particular job.

- They can provide fresh ideas/approach, especially when the current staff is low on ideas or tired of a particular project.

- They can help with overflow work during especially busy times and be available on an "as needed" basis with no need for a long-term commitment.

- They can be less expensive for the short-term than a salaried employee.

- They are a great way to "try out" a potential future employee.

ARE YOU READY TO FLY SOLO?

So, are you ready to venture out on your own? There are a variety of important characteristics and attitudes that you need to possess or acquire in order to be successful as a freelancer or as a solo firm:

• **You need to be an organized person.** This includes carefully tracking your expenses and hours, keeping your paper and digital files neat and billing your clients.

• **You need to be a self-starter.** You need to find jobs and clients, supervise your own work performance and interact with a variety of different people and companies on a daily/weekly basis.

• **You must have good business sense.** Whether it's marketing your skills or figuring your finances, you will need to have a handle on this important aspect of the job.

• **You have to be willing to learn.** If you don't have experience, get advice. Some people start out freelancing in college and can do fairly well. You just want to make sure that you have more experienced people around you that can answer questions and give advice. You will need it. The more experience you gain, the easier it will be, and then you can help the "newbies."

• **You need to be flexible and resourceful.** Things will happen, with your clients, with your paper company and printer, and with your day-to-day life. When you're on your own, you don't have a lot of people around you to help solve problems and pick up the pieces when things go wrong. You need to be able to "roll with the punches," keep a positive attitude and figure out Plan B quickly, without panicking.

• **You must be productive and able to work fast.** Your time is money, and if you're on your own, your hours are the only ones you can bill for. Wasted time means no pay.

- **You have to be committed to building a positive reputation.** If you are a good listener, an eager partner with your clients and reliably deliver a quality product on time, you will keep your client base happy and grow it over time. People will want to work with you, and will even seek you out, if you have a reputation as a high quality team player that they can trust to do a great job and make ethical decisions. Many, if not most, design jobs are found by word-of-mouth, so it's critical that people say good things about you and your work ethic.

- **Finally, you need to be visibly passionate.** Being passionate about your work is essential to keeping up the high energy and motivation needed to work alone. And by showing off your passionate attitude, clients will be attracted to what you have to offer them.

APPLICATION: YOUR STRENGTHS AND WEAKNESSES

Look over the following list and carefully assess whether or not each characteristic/skill is a personal/professional strength or weakness. If it's a weakness, do you have the energy and interest to improve in that area? If not, is it something you can hire out, like accounting services? How can you improve on your weaknesses and maximize your strengths?

CHARAC-TERISTICS/ SKILLS	STRENGTH	WEAKNESS	DESIRE TO IMPROVE	WAYS TO IMPROVE
Organized				
Thorough				
Budgets/ Finances				

CHARAC- TERISTICS/ SKILLS	STRENGTH	WEAKNESS	DESIRE TO IMPROVE	WAYS TO IMPROVE
Marketing/ Promotions				
Self- Motivated				
Legal Issues				
Professional Experience				
Flexible/ Resourceful				
Productive/ Efficient				
Ethical				
Dependable				
Sensitivity/ Listening Skills				
Drive for Excellence				
Political Savvy				
Overall Passion				

Once you have completed the chart, assess your findings. There's no magic percentage of strengths versus weaknesses that will tell you whether or not working on your own is right for you.

REAL WORLD ADVICE: FIVE DESIGNERS ON THEIR OWN

KATIE RUNDELL, OWNER, GINKGO CREATIVE, CHICAGO, ILLINOIS

Q: How do you describe your firm and its particular direction/focus/mission?

A: Our firm is a small graphic design firm specializing in printed materials for small to large businesses. Our philosophy: Don't make anything too hard. Be thoughtful, decisive and direct. Embrace and revere color and educate. Be educated. Hear, look for and recognize other's needs and honor their suggestions. Work should be as fun as you can make it, and you should surround yourself with people you not only really like, but are in awe of.

Q: What motivated you to start your own business?

A: I was motivated to start my own business because I was lucky enough to work with my business partner at a previous job, and we knew we had a great working chemistry. We really wanted to work together. We enjoy what we do and have fun.

Q: What are the joys and pitfalls of owning your own business?

A: The joys of owning my own business are the flexibility and [ability to do] what I love to do. The pitfalls include the months when work is slow, therefore the paycheck is slow to come. It's also difficult to take a day off when you're responsible for everything. Even when I'm sick or on vacation, I need to take some time out to e-mail or make a few phone calls to make sure things are running smoothly. But, when you love what you do, it doesn't seem like such a chore.

Q: What advice would you have for someone considering starting her own design business?
A: I would say be prepared to work a lot in the beginning to establish a client base. Go on as many portfolio showings as you can to meet as many people as you can. You can't be shy: Ask existing clients, family and friends for referrals. Be prepared for slow months and be prepared to get help for the busy times. Meet other designers, both senior and right out of school.

HOLLIS OBERLIES, OWNER, PURPLE ZANTE, INC., CHAPEL HILL, NORTH CAROLINA

Q: How do you describe your firm and its particular direction/focus/mission?
A: Founded in 2001, Purple Zante takes a creative and results-oriented approach to working with clients, who are considered partners in the design process. We pride ourselves on building long-standing relationships through teamwork, trust and open communication, which are key to any successful partnership. We take the time to listen to our clients and ask the right questions, which enables us to understand each client's unique needs and challenges. Our goal is simple: to achieve results for you and your organization. We know our continued success is dependent on yours.

Q: What motivated you to start your own business?
A: I eased into it by opening a satellite office for my last employer. I knew I could do it, and finally realized it's what I wanted/needed.

Q: What are the joys and pitfalls of owning your own business?
A: These are both joys and pitfalls: As owner, one constantly thinks about the business side and where the next project is coming from. And, as owner initially, you are the wearer of many hats; designer, creative director, client liaison, boss

man. When employing others, one spends quite a bit of time mentoring and working closely with the staff. This takes away from creative time on projects and puts the owner in more of a role of management, however, at the same time, that can also be a joy.

Q: What advice would you have for someone considering starting their own design business?

A: Go for it. You know when it feels right. You'll also know when it's the right time to add employees. Being a business owner is so satisfying. It is a freeing feeling to set up and run a business the way you want it run. It helps to have experience working at multiple other firms and know aspects, philosophies, systems that you like and don't like before running your own business.

JENI MOORE, OWNER, PLUM DESIGN, CHICAGO, ILLINOIS

Q: How do you describe your firm and its particular direction/focus/mission?

A: Our business offers creative design services, primarily for the real estate/ architecture market, focusing mainly on print work.

Q: What motivated you to start your own business?

A: I didn't like managing people, but I was motivated to start my own business because I wanted to have a family. My job is easier to do from home than my husband's. I'd reached a position in my previous job that was as far as I could go, and it was furthest from what I was really good at/loved to do.

Q: What are the joys and pitfalls of owning your own business?

A: A lot of freedom. I'm able to see my kids all day long, teach art classes at their school and go on their field trips. Plus, I work in my pajamas and don't need a lot of space to do what I do. The only real pitfall, so far, is managing cash flow. I wasn't a business major, so as far as I've gotten with this has all been on gut instinct, and that really isn't enough.

Q: What advice would you have for someone considering starting her own design business?

A: If you are determined, it will happen. Be confident, and humble. Be aggressive, but gracious. Have patience. It's a lot of fun.

LISA KUHN, OWNER, CURIO PRESS, CINCINNATI, OHIO

Q: How do you describe your firm and its particular direction/focus/mission?

A: Curio Press is devoted to high quality book design and packaging. We pride ourselves in weaving the content and design for each book seamlessly to provide a package that communicates cohesively in both visuals and in written word.

Q: What motivated you to start your own business?

A: I started in the field as the art director of HOW Books and Writer's Digest Books, and I began to get requested by outside publishers to do covers and interiors on a freelance basis. I realized that there was a big need for what I do and that I didn't need to work as a designer for just one company to be profitable. I also desired to have a more flexible schedule as well as more diverse projects.

Q: What are the joys and pitfalls of owning your own business?

A: One of the best things about owning my own business is the flexibility. I work when I can and need to, and the hours are based on getting the job done, not a forty-hour work week. That can be the pitfall as well because there can be dry times when there's nothing available and then the next month there could be more than I can handle.

Q: What advice would you have for someone considering starting her own design business?

A: I would advise them to make sure they have the right skill set to be a business owner. It takes a lot of organization and a certain type of personality to make it work well. I would also make sure that that person has a safety net in place when making the jump to starting her own business, both financially and relationally. I've found that I've needed a lot of advice and help from others along the way.

ADVANTAGES AND DISADVANTAGES OF WORKING ON YOUR OWN

There are many advantages to working on your own. At the top of the list for most freelancers is the flexibility and the control over one's schedule. Depending on when you work your best, you can wake up at 3:00 A.M. or work until 3:00 A.M. Sometimes, this sense of control is more in perception than reality. Freelancers do have to work with other people and that means working with their schedules and trying to be flexible enough to meet the needs of collaborators and clients. But for many people even the feeling of control is enough of a reward. Perception is reality after all.

There are also some financial advantages to freelance work. There are some income tax advantages and write-offs so you can keep more of the money you make (this can vary depending on economic and political leaders and their decisions). In addition, freelancers generally make more money per hour than salaried employees if they are working for/within a company, because employers don't have to pay benefits and deal with as much overhead. Of course, freelancers don't have the benefits that a salaried employee has, so there may be expenses like health insurance that come out of the hourly rate. Designers today can set up a studio with very low overhead. With a desk, a souped-up laptop and a nice color printer, you can be up and running, so the cost of actually setting up an office can be very minimal.

Working on your own can also give you a feeling of greater control over your job satisfaction. You are the boss, and you can focus your work in the direction that best suits your philosophy, attitude, interests and passions. Additionally, you can work closely with various firms. You may find that one suits you quite well, and by working with them on a temporary basis, discover that you want to transition to full-time work with them. Trying out an employer in this way can set you up for greater success because you know more about the firm and how they match your own work style and needs.

But there are some disadvantages to the freelance life. Top of the list for most people is the irregular income stream. Some weeks you will be busy, and other times it can be quite dry. Being ready, financially and emotionally, for the dry times is extremely important.

- It's critical to be prepared with a plan of action for times when you don't have enough income.

- You need to have a detailed budget so you know how much money it takes to do the job, as well as your financial priorities.

- Follow your budget so you know if it's realistic or not. Revise as needed to make your budget as accurate as possible.

- Make hay while the sun shines. While times are good, try to keep as busy as possible.

- And save for the rainy day. Make sure you have a healthy savings account just in case you need it.

Being the only employee can have its problems as well. It can be lonely, and it's important to seek out other designers and collaborators for feedback and interaction. Connecting with other creative people through organizations such as AIGA is a great way to network. You will have to generate your own motivation and thirst for challenge, since there's no one there to push you to get up in the morning. Identifying the benefits of your work is one of the best motivators; try to always be aware of these benefits and never take them granted. In addition, there can be a lot of pressure to wear too many hats. Jeff Fisher lends some good advice, "When it comes to the actual business aspects of operating a firm—one-person or otherwise—a business owner also needs to determine what they like, want, dislike and won't do, or there will be major problems. I love the marketing and promotion aspects of a business. I detest the bookkeeping, taxes, paperwork, etc. That's why people exist to do those specific jobs. I always recommend that a business owner surround himself with a team made up of a bookkeeper, tax professional, banker and attorney. That allows me to do what I need to accomplish and what I enjoy most. I want to be having fun with my work." You can't be good at everything. Especially as your business develops, it's important to realize that getting help in certain areas, such as financial planning and accounting, will actually benefit you, even at a certain financial cost.

WEBSITES AND BLOGS FOR FREELANCERS

• Active community, articles, resources and advice for freelancers: www.freelanceswitch.com

• AIGA professional organization advice for freelancers: www.aiga.org/content. cfm/design-and-business

• Business of Design Online blog about starting your own business: www.businessofdesignonline.com

• Graphic Artists Guild web site with information about the *Handbook of Pricing & Ethical Guidelines*: www.gag.org

Another drawback is working on projects with a limited scope. As a freelancer, you may be coming into a firm to work on a fairly narrow portion of a project. It could be that your specialized skills are only needed for one part, or maybe someone is going on maternity/paternity leave and you have to pick up a job that's already three quarters of the way completed. These situations can be frustrating for people that want more control over the whole job. As a freelancer, you need to have an attitude of helping out where and when you're needed. Ego needs to be put aside.

AVOIDING COMMON PROBLEMS WITH FREELANCING

Communication problems can be quite common between freelancers and the companies or clients who hire them. When you are working on your own, it's extremely important to have clear procedures for correspondence, the writing of estimates and contracts (see Chapter 19: Pricing, Proposal and Contract Basics), work process and follow-up. There can also be a lack of clarity about usage and rights regarding your work, especially when you are collaborating with others. It must be clear from the beginning of the relationship who owns the work: the freelancer, the firm or the client. (See Chapter 20: Intellectual Property Basics for Designers.)

If you were a freelancer for Design Firm A doing work for Client B, it's very important to be clear about that on your résumé, web site and promotional materials. You cannot and should not say only that you worked for Client B without mentioning your relationship to Design Firm A. They were your collaborators on the project, they hired you, and they may own the rights to the work depending on the situation, so it's very important to give them their due credit. Also, be clear about your specific role and the amount of the project you were responsible for. Ask the person who hired you what you can and cannot use in your portfolio and, specifically, how you should describe the relationship. The main point here is that everyone deserves credit for their role on the project and their part in the relationship.

Freelancers should also be especially careful to act in an ethical and responsible fashion. You will be working in various environments for different periods of time. You'll meet and interact with a lot of people with very different personalities and working styles. It's your responsibility to keep sensitive information to yourself. Don't talk about one company to another. Don't bad mouth one design director to another. This type of behavior will haunt you faster than you can ever imagine and can even ruin your career as a freelancer. No one hires people they can't trust or who spread dirt. The design world is very small, especially within certain communities.

In addition, as a freelancer, your relationship to clients needs to be carefully managed. Freelancers should never directly court the clients of the companies that hire them. Also, if you are working on-site with a company, it's inappropriate to work on the projects of your other clients, including speaking to them by phone or corresponding by e-mail.

Once you finish your specific assignment, it's very important to leave clean, organized and complete files for the company's records. You may not be around when the client comes back with a question in six months. The company needs to be able to quickly and easily track down anything you worked on. It also important to clarify if you are permitted to take any digital files with you and how you are allowed to use them. This is especially important when a confidentiality agreement is signed. (See Chapter 20: Intellectual Property Basics for Designers.)

Freelancers need to be dependable, timely and committed. At the same time, the company needs to be provide access to the right project mentors and decision makers and to provide adequate project orientation or supervision to the freelancer. Some companies have worked with freelancers for many years and, through experience, have set up a good system and communication strategy for effective and efficient workflow. Unfortunately, others do not have such a system. If you feel that the communication and workflow between you and the company isn't going well, it's up to you to go to the right person and suggest clear ideas for how to improve the situation.

CHAPTER 18
SETTING UP A SUCCESSFUL WORK ENVIRONMENT AND BUSINESS STRUCTURE

Setting up a successful work life has many dimensions. You need to be inspired by the environment you've set up for yourself (whether it be a corner in your apartment or a rented space). You need to feel comfortable in the relationships you've built related to your business (accountants, printers, illustrators, other designers). You need to develop boundaries with a positive work/life balance. You need to feel confident about both the business and design aspects of the field. And you need to create a network beyond your day-to-day work environment that supports and grows your career.

First, take a minute to dream: What is your dream work life? What type of visual environment inspires you? Do you need wonderful imagery on the walls? Color? Simplicity? Visual activity? What type of audio environment inspires you? Do you need quiet? Music? White noise? What activities make you most creative? Do you need toys around you? What type of schedule do you like to keep? How do you stay current with what's happening in the design world? Friends? Blogs? Books?

BUILD AN INSPIRATIONAL ENVIRONMENT

You must feel comfortable and inspired by the place you choose to do your work, whether that be in the coffee shop down the street or your own corner office. Today, there are many choices with good quality office furniture at reasonable prices. Just look on the web and you'll find many options. At minimum, you'll need a desk, a good ergonomic chair, good lighting, a computer loaded with software and memory, and dependable peripherals like a printer and scanner. I've found that a color multifunction printer/scanner/copier/fax is an excellent and cost-effective option, plus a space saver. You'll also need room for paper storage, various supplies and books.

Fill your space with things that inspire you. Design work that you aspire to, like beautiful images of places you dream about visiting, snapshots of your family and friends, quotes about design and innovation, playful and humorous items—things that make you smile and lighten up.

One of the great advantages with today's technology is that you can do much of your work almost anywhere. With a laptop and the Internet, you can stay connected to your clients and vendors with great ease while traveling abroad or just around town. I have a friend that does work for clients while sitting in her minivan waiting in line to pick up the kids from school—now that's making a good use of your time.

PUSH TO STAY CURRENT

All designers need to have an environment of learning and growing. This is particularly difficult for designers working on their own. For designers to stay effective, confident and successful, they need to stay current with the field and its developments. Going to continuing education events is particularly helpful, including design organization meetings, software workshops and university programs. (See Chapter 10: Continuing Education and Professional Development.) Subscribe to design magazines and keep up with the changing pages of their web sites. For instance www.howdesign.com and www.commarts.com are wonderful sources of inspiration and information. Always be looking for ways to improve yourself and what you have to offer to your clients. Continually challenge yourself with new methods and approaches and don't be afraid to learn a new piece of software or a new technique.

Make it a habit to look at design blogs on a regular basis to see what's new and to catch the buzz of the design community. There are blogs of all sorts and specialties. If you love typography, there are blogs for you. If you want information about sustainability, there are blogs for you. You can just read and take it all in, or get involved in the conversation by posting your own thoughts and ideas. Here are a few blogs to start with:

- Writings on design and culture: www.designobserver.com

- Design magazine and resources: www.core77.com

- Inspiration for graphic design and typography: www.aisleone.net

- *Creative Review* magazine: www.creativereview.co.uk/crblog

- Design portal with the latest design news: www.dexigner.com

- NYTimes.com design editor, Khoi Vinh: www.subtraction.com

- For web designers and developers: www.smashingmagazine.com

- Resources for green design: www.inhabitat.com

CONNECT AND NETWORK

One very effective way to stay current, as well as build your business, is to make sure you're connected to other designers both in graphic design and in related fields. Join your regional AIGA chapter or the local design or advertising club. Go to their events and get involved in the organization. Work towards being part of the leadership group. You have the potential to make great professional and personal connections that may last your entire career. If you are working on your own, or in a small office with just a few people, it's especially important to meet others and have a wider sphere of inspiration and influence.

Work with a team of designers on a project that will impact your community. Working together on a goal for the greater good is a wonderful way to bond with new design friends and a great way to give back. Perhaps you know of a nonprofit that needs design assistance to get the word out about their important cause. Maybe they also need a marketing and promotional plan. Pull a team of marketing and design professionals together to make it happen.

Especially if you are a younger designer, it's key to find a mentor (see page 183 in Chapter 16: Working With Other Designers)—one or two people that you look up to and whose opinions and advice you trust. Whether you are working on your own or within a large corporation, this is equally important. You need someone with whom you can share thoughts and get feedback. It's critical to feel that you can really push your ideas and challenge your assumptions in a safe environment where you can get nonjudgmental reactions.

MARKET YOUR BUSINESS

It would be great if all you had to do was focus on doing great design work and, somehow, the word magically spread about your design expertise. This does happen on occasion—if you have a really vocal and well-connected client who loves you. But for the most part you will have to promote yourself in various ways. (See Chapter 5: Effective Portfolio and Self-Promotion Strategies.) There are many methods to market yourself and encourage referrals. In their www.howdesign.com article "Freelancing Finesse," The Creative Group offers the following ideas:

- Send regular e-mails to former and current clients to keep you top of mind.

- Send your clients promotional packets so they can refer you to their networks.

- Create a distinctive business card that will capture attention.

- Follow up and always thank those who recommended you for a job.

- E-mail a periodic newsletter about the exciting things happening with your business, such as new awards you've received.

- Send out press releases focusing on current client projects and your accomplishments. (Make sure to get approval from the client.)

- Create a well-organized web site with useful and persuasive information.

- Do even more than you promised. Deliver a project early or provide something over and above what's written in your letter of agreement.

CREATE THE APPROPRIATE BUSINESS STRUCTURE

Whether you are a freelancer or setting up your own firm, it's important to consider creating the appropriate business structure to meet your needs. You could set up a sole proprietorship, a partnership or a corporation. You need to know your business and how each of these options works to find out what's best for you. This is an essential part of setting up a successful and profitable business environment.

Even if you are working temporarily as a freelancer, you need to be aware that if you earn four hundred dollars or more per year in your profession, you will need to pay taxes on that income (the amount could change with tax reforms, so check to make sure). You should be classified as self-employed and set up a business structure that identifies you as an employee of the business.

In her www.howdesign.com article "Choose a Business Structure," Poppy Evans describes the considerations and issues related to setting up the appropriate business structure to meet your needs. There are three different structures, for tax purposes, that Poppy addresses: a sole proprietorship, a partnership or a corporation.

Sole Proprietorship

"As a sole proprietor, you are responsible for any debts, legal obligations and liabilities, and you reap all of the profits from your business. No legal forms need to be drawn up. You simply file a Schedule C 'Profit or Loss from Business' at tax time along with your Form 1040." This structure is the one that most creatives use when they first set up their businesses because it's easy and simple.

Partnership

"A partnership involves two or more people in a situation where all profits, losses, legal obligations and other business liabilities are shared by the partners. Each partner's share is determined by a percentage of his interest in the business." This percentage can be based on the amount of financial investment by the partners, or the reputation and expertise of one partner versus the other.

Corporation

A key difference between corporations and sole proprietorships and partnerships is that "a corporation (which can be made up of one individual) is considered separate from the individual who owns it. Forming a corporation will safeguard you from personal liability, meaning your personal assets won't be affected if your corporation goes bankrupt."

Many professionals begin as sole proprietors and grow into corporations. It's important to realize that you can be flexible and change your status as your business grows and develops.

APPLICATION: DECIDING WHAT'S BEST FOR YOU

BUSINESS STRUCTURE	ADVANTAGES	DISADVANTAGES	FIT FOR MY NEEDS
Sole Proprietorship (Your business is you)	• You reap all the profits • No legal forms, just file the proper paperwork at tax time • Simplest structure • Good for starting out	• You are responsible for any debts, legal obligations, liabilities	
Partnership (2 or more people)	• Each partner's share is based on their contribution to the firm and the percentage of their interest in the business	• You and your partner(s) share any debts, legal obligations, liabilities	
Corporation (general)	• Considered separate from the individual • Protects you from personal liability	• Can be expensive	
C Corporation (step 1)	• First step in the process	• Pay corporate taxes on all profits • Profits distributed to you are also subject to personal income taxes	
S Corporation (step 2)	• Avoid double taxation because the business profits are taxed once as income	• Second step in the process	

CHAPTER 19
PRICING, PROPOSAL AND CONTRACT BASICS

There are entire books, websites and blogs devoted to the topics of pricing, and proposal and contract creation. (A great reference is *The Designer's Guide to Marketing and Pricing* by Ilise Benun and Peleg Top, another book in the Designer's Guide series.) This chapter is meant to be an introduction to some of the basic issues related to these written agreements. Even though most designers would prefer to avoid such topics (including myself), I'd also like to emphasize the importance of understanding and implementing these practices, at least at a fundamental level. Having a clear, well thought-out plan from the beginning will prevent problems later.

Many designers are uncomfortable forming written agreements with their clients. Sometimes people believe putting an agreement on paper will result in tensions or alter the relationship with the client. Actually, the opposite is true. Failure to work out important details in writing can result in misunderstandings and miscommunication and even end in legal troubles. In addition, there are several other reasons for putting things in writing: It helps ensure appropriate compensation because you have to consider all aspects of the job up front; it provides a good record of the project so you can go back and reference the decisions and details of each job; and it provides some protection in case any issues arise.

There may be some cases when a written agreement isn't needed. For instance, for some long-standing relationships, where parties understand one another, a handshake may be enough. Or perhaps you've been asked to do a very quick turnaround job and there may not be time for formal paperwork. Unless you are certain that the chances of client disagreements are extremely low, never begin a job without a clear written agreement on pricing and terms. It's always better to have more in writing rather than less.

A preproject written agreement can accomplish various goals for both the designer and the client. It is an excellent means of establishing your working procedures, pricing and scheduling standards. It generally introduces the client to your working style, answers questions about how you handle projects and helps you define your creative, production and billing processes. If you take the time to carefully create the document, it can also act as a strong promotion piece to communicate your professionalism, skills, capabilities and experience.

In some cases, the client will be a step ahead and may request a written agreement from you. They may even have their own form of agreement, especially if they are a larger company with formal accounting practices and procedures. You will want to review these agreements carefully to make sure you aren't committing to something you can't deliver. Make sure you agree with any requirements that are stated. If you are unclear or uncomfortable about anything, feel free to ask advice from your mentor or someone in your network who is experienced with these types of agreements. Whether initiated by you or the client, most clients will expect and respect the professionalism of a written agreement, proposal or contract. So let's look at some details related to written agreements and answer questions like: What format is appropriate in various situations? What should be included in the document? How important is a presentation of the document? How much detail is necessary for you and for the client?

DIFFERENT FORMS OF WRITTEN AGREEMENTS

Preproject paperwork comes in various forms for different types of situations. Depending on how formal your business (part-time freelancer versus multiple-person firm, for instance), the type and size of job and the requirements of your client, you can use different formats. Cam Foote of Creative Business, identifies four different forms of preproject paperwork: contracts, estimates, letters of agreement and proposals. It's important to understand when, where and how you should use them.

Standard Legal Contracts

There are various standard legal contracts available—just look online. Some great resources are www.aiga.org/content.cfm/professional-resources or www.designerstoolbox.com. Although all signed agreements are equally binding (differences are generally in how specific the contract lays out requirements, scope, schedule, etc.), it's important to find one that is well-written, clear and from a source you trust, such as AIGA. The biggest advantage of standard legal contracts is that they can save time, effort and legal fees, while providing a good level of detail. Because this type of contract can be long and legalistic, some clients find them daunting and intimidating. But it can be especially important to protect yourself in the case of long-term or very-large-dollar projects. Projects with new or difficult clients often warrant a longer, more specific contract.

Contract Customization

Some standard contracts allow for customization. Customized agreements provide more specific detail regarding the job, such as project scope and a specific detailed schedule, and generally make the client feel more comfortable, since they aren't receiving a form letter. The one used by many designers, and from a trusted source, is the AIGA Standard Form of Agreement for Design Services. You can download it from the AIGA web site (www.aiga.org/content.cfm/standard-agreement), which describes the agreement, "It does not take a one-size-fits-all approach, and it is not an extensive preprinted document where you simply fill in the blanks. Instead, this agreement acknowledges that most design firms develop their own custom proposal document for each project and are looking for an appropriate set of terms and conditions to attach to it. When put together and signed, the custom proposal document and its attached terms and conditions comprise the binding agreement with the client. ... The first two modules, Basic Terms & Conditions and Intellectual Property Provisions, should be used for all design assignments." There are three additional modules that can be added when appropriate, one focused on print, one interactive and one environmental.

One-Page Estimates

For most jobs under three thousand dollars, a simple one-page estimate will work well. They are quick to prepare and give the client what they need to initiate paperwork on their end, such as a purchase order. The document should include an estimate of cost, what is specifically included in the project (letterhead, envelope, business card, for instance) and a simple schedule and terms (how many revisions the estimate includes, hourly rate above that, etc.). It is also good to include a line for an approval signature so you don't forget to have it signed.

Letters of Agreement

For jobs between three thousand and twelve thousand dollars, a little more detail is appropriate, since there is more at stake for both you and your client. Letters of agreement are generally two to three pages long and have a more specific listing of work to be accomplished, pricing of parts of the project, a detailed schedule and terms and signature line for approval. This higher level of detail will force you to organize yourself and the project.

When you are working with a new client, it's best to enclose the letter of agreement in some type of presentation folder with information about yourself and your work, such as a brief bio or capabilities brochure, a current client list and samples of similar work. This will communicate your professionalism and experience, and build respect and confidence.

LEGAL ISSUES WITH WRITTEN AGREEMENTS

CAM FOOTE , "CREATIVE BUSINESS" NEWSLETTER (WWW.CREATIVEBUSINESS.COM):

There is seldom as much actual legal protection in (written agreements) as most of us would like. The reason is our "product"—creative executions—is unique, hard to define and subjectively evaluated. This provides so many potential loopholes that a client desiring to find one usually can, especially if they have legal staff on retainer. Also, enforcing an agreement through the court system often takes more time and money than many small design firms can muster.

So while most agreements should be in writing, they can't be counted on for anything other than rudimentary legal protection. Written agreements are legally powerful only in very clear violations involving substantial sums of money. Otherwise, what they mostly provide are details that reduce misunderstandings, as well as a point of reference from which to appeal to a client's conscience.

The reason for mentioning the limitations of written agreements while simultaneously encouraging them is to discourage you from spending an excessive amount of time on their preparation.

Proposals

Most larger jobs, above twelve thousand dolloars, require a longer and more detailed proposal. It's important to describe the schedule for the project, the scope of the work to be completed and an estimated cost. Especially for complex jobs, it's important to segment the project into phases to communicate that the work process is organized and understandable using headings such as: 1) orientation/research, 2) concept development,

3) design development, 4) execution/production and 5) delivery/debrief. For long jobs, the designer will probably bill after each phase of the project. Proposals generally contain some or all of the following sections:

- cover with project title, name of firm, name of client and date

- table of contents

- summary of the client needs, including background information, client project goals and an analysis of current situation, competitive and industry challenges, and requirements

- a definition of the project engagement, including objectives, project scope and deliverables

- the approach to the problem, including process methodology, schedule, deliverables and milestones

- total fees and expenses for various phases of the project with a billing plan

- information about the design firm, including philosophy, overview of services, client list and staffing

- conclusion, next steps and project handoff information

- signature lines for decision makers

- any appendices (references, case study examples, etc.)

- basic terms and conditions (AIGA Standard Form of Agreement for Design Services)

- intellectual property provisions (AIGA Standard Form of Agreement for Design Services)

- supplemental terms for print, interactive or environmental (AIGA Standard Form of Agreement for Design Services)

PRICING

Determining what to charge for your work is often a quite difficult, and sometimes painful, process. Most designers are truly passionate about what they do, and they don't like the idea of putting a number on it. It's important to think about this from the perspective of the client. Your time and skills are worth the money you charge for them. If you charge too little, then you are communicating that design isn't worth much and that's not the message you want to send. So it's extremely important to confidently charge competitive rates and to understand what each type of project is worth. It can be complicated at first, but if you develop some standards for yourself, you will be able to determine your pricing quickly and consistently. Remember, you are pricing your work—not your own self-worth. Separate the two in your mind, or you'll drive yourself crazy.

There are two main ways you can charge for your work: an hourly rate or a flat rate per job, such as a set amount for a logo design or a poster. There are varying opinions about which strategy is the best one. I like to evaluate each situation independently. I use both methods, generally depending on the size of the job, and I base much of my pricing on the updated *Graphic Artist Guild Handbook: Pricing and Ethical Guidelines*. This valuable resource provides standards for pricing various categories of jobs, such as brochures, web sites, logos, etc., and also gives you guidelines for figuring jobs based on the size of the company. The important point is that each designer figures their pricing a bit differently, which is why it's so important to communicate it clearly to clients.

In *The Designer's Guide to Marketing and Pricing*, Ilise Benun and Peleg Top discuss the problems with charging an hourly rate. "Many designers price by the hour, and for all the wrong reasons. First of all, it's easy to price your services by the hour. It's clean, it's orderly and it doesn't require much math. But it is not to your benefit, especially in the long run. ... A logo might take you five hours today when, two years ago, it may have taken twenty. You get better—sometimes a lot better—with time. But if you charge by the hour, as you get better, you earn less. ... Also, design is a creative process. Not only is there no rule about how long it should take; there is a certain amount of inspiration involved. You probably don't know how long it will take for your best ideas to come. They could come right away, or they could take a while. Should you be paid based on how long it takes for your ideas to come together? Is that how you should determine how much money you earn?"

At the same time, in order to know how much to charge for a logo design, for instance, its important for you to understand approximately how long it takes you to do such work. Early in your career, it's important to keep track of your hours, however annoying. On a half-hour basis, keep track of what you do during the day. This will be an excellent time management exercise as well. You'll be surprised how you spend your time. This becomes important information for you as you determine your price for the logo design, in this example. Your time, along with other information, figures into the overall project fee.

APPLICATION: DETERMINING THE VALUE OF YOUR WORK

Assess each variable and determine how or if it affects your pricing.

VARIABLE	RELATED NOTES	EFFECT ON PRICE
SAMPLE		
Location of studio	Cost of living and studio overhead is high	Increases price
Location of your studio (big city vs. rural area)		
Location and size of the client		

VARIABLE	RELATED NOTES	EFFECT ON PRICE
The timing (rush vs. nonrush jobs)		
What the market will bear (economic changes)		
How many meetings you anticipate		
How busy you are (Do you need work?)		
Complexity of project requirements/time commitment		
Requirement of working with others		
Your experience level and reputation		
Amount of overhead (employees, facilities)		
Travel and research expenses for the project		

REAL WORLD ADVICE: CALCULATING YOUR HOURLY RATE

PAUL GHIZ, GLOBAL CLOUD

Option 1: Each year, I review what my hourly cost of doing business is by looking at all of my expenses from the prior year divided by 1,920 working hours divided by the number of employees and then build in my profit margin to calculate what the hourly rate will be. Example: $1,000,000.00 in operating expense [rent, utilities, connectivity, hr benefits, etc.] / 1920hrs = $520.83 / 20 employees = $26.04/hour/employee just to break even. Then you can build in your margin to determine what your hourly rate is ($26.02 x 2 = $52.04, rounded up $55/hour)

Option 2: Take your top three highest paid employees and come up with an average hourly cost of doing business and then build in your profit margin. Example: $80,000.00 + $75,000.00 + $70,000.00 = $225,000.00 / 3 = $75,000.00 x 1.35 (for benefits) = $101,250.00 / 1920 hours = $52.73/hour X 2 = $105.47, rounded up to nearest increment of $10 = $110/hour

When first starting out, you often have very low rates, such as option 1, because you are trying to build your portfolio and be very price competitive. As you mature and grow, you can begin using a higher, value-based rate like option 2, which is what we use currently.

Handling Revisions

It's very important to establish set parameters for revisions from the beginning of the project. The client should know how many revision cycles are part of the cost of a project. If you are charging hourly, obviously this is easy because you just charge the client for more time. But if you are billing a flat rate for the entire job, you need to work in revisions as part of the cost.

There will always be revisions—sometimes, just minor refinements and sometimes, a complete overhaul. And you can't predict it. That's why it's important to indicate that the fee includes "one round of revisions," for instance. If there are additional revision cycles, it's best to handle those on an hourly basis, since you can't predict how many changes will be needed. There's nothing more frustrating than getting caught in endless revisions with a client and risking not being paid for them because you didn't confirm your policies in the paperwork up front. It's important to be prepared and have a clear understanding with your client.

Varying Rates

Some designers charge the same amount for every part of the process—concepting, research, design development, production, etc.—while others charge varying rates. Concept and design development would normally be charged at higher rates because they require a high level of the brain work and creativity. Production work, including managing the project through the printing process, would normally be charged at a lower rate.

The advantage of a single price is obvious: It's simple to figure and you are communicating that every part of the process is of equal importance. The advantage of the varying fee structure is that you can usually charge a bit more for concept and design development, since it's easy to convince the client of the increased value of this part of the process.

Markup

In *The Designer's Guide to Marketing and Pricing*, Ilise Benun and Peleg Top make a good case for adding "markup" to your fee structure. "Markup is the amount added by a seller (you) to the cost of a commodity to cover expenses and profit in fixing the selling price. It's like a broker fee that you take for facilitating a process. It is standard business practice to add a markup on anything that you have to oversee and coordinate, including printing, mailing lists, fulfillment and copywriting.... Standard markup in the design industry is 10–30 percent, depending on several factors, including who the client is, the size of the company, where you are located and what they would pay for the services or products if they procured them directly."

Rush Fees

Many designers get in the practice of charging clients a rush fee for jobs with an especially tight time frame. You will need to determine what that means for you personally, and of course, the type and complexity of the job will also affect that decision. Getting into the practice of charging rush fees can be important in establishing a professional status with your clients. Rush fees are generally 50–100 percent markup of your standard fee. Rush jobs can be lucrative if you have the right attitude and can handle the additional pressure.

When to Be Paid

Many designers bill their clients several times over the course of a project, instead of waiting until the end. There are many advantages to setting up your billing in this fashion, especially for longer and larger jobs: It breaks up the cost for the clients so the overall fee isn't overwhelming; it gives you much needed money along the way; and you aren't gambling the entire fee (if the bill for the first third of the project isn't paid promptly, then you have some warning that there might be future issues with payment). Some designers set up the payment schedule based on time (charge after so many weeks into the project), others based on the point in the project (charge after the conceptual phase, the design phase, etc.), others ask for a percentage up front (a deposit), while for short jobs, most wait until the project is complete to invoice.

REAL WORLD ADVICE: PRICING

JENI MOORE, CREATIVE DIRECTOR, PLUM DESIGN

I bid jobs by the hour—concepts, revisions, production, print management. I don't absorb print costs because I've found that companies can take a long time to pay, and I don't want to be stuck with the bill while they drag their feet. I have to mention that accounting sucks; I'm sure I'm not alone in that opinion. I hate estimating and billing. Both take up so much of my time that I had to up my rates in the first year just to cover all that extra time I spend/spent doing admin stuff. I will say that I've heard more than once that I'm expensive. But, I'm fast. And I tend to get it right from the beginning, and after that initial cringe, I can usually prove it's worthwhile.

PAUL GHIZ, FOUNDING PARTNER, GLOBAL CLOUD

Pricing can be tricky because clients place different levels of value on your services, and many times, you have to modify your pricing up or down based on the client's perspective and expectation. It often becomes an exercise on a case-by-case basis, especially when you are first starting out and need to build your portfolio and pay the bills. As your firm matures, you can begin standardizing your pricing based on different services offered or different packages offered, at which point, less time is spent on negotiating a price each time. Standard pricing may be based on hourly rates or as lump sum project costs, which by the way, can become more risky for you if the client or project is not managed well. Hourly rates can be determined by understanding your costs of doing business, researching your competitors' rates and understanding what the market will bear over time. Value-based billing comes into play as your reputation and brand equity is known in the marketplace.

EILEEN COREY, COREYOGRAPHY

Over the years, I have approached pricing as a balance of what it takes hourly to get the job done and what it is worth to me or to the client to get the job done. I always start by asking whether my client has a budget for design and production and then evaluate my time investment and what I will gain from the job against that. (Will the job result in a great sample/portfolio piece? Will it nurture a great client relationship? Those can be worth more than dollars over the long run.) If what makes sense to me is less than their budget, I tell them so and encourage them to use the overage in production or to plus other budgets (photography or illustration).

JENNY LANICCA, CREATIVE DIRECTOR, DELICIOUS DESIGN

A few years ago, when I started freelancing with a small design shop in Santa Monica, I was making 30 dollars an hour and being billed out at 175 dollars an hour. After about a year of this, I realized I was handling entire projects, and if I could go on my own, I could raise my rate considerably while still being affordable to large companies. From the client's perspective, a freelancer costs much less to employ than a full-time employee, even if the freelancer has a higher hourly rate.

I try to stick to an hourly rate that is competitive to what a small firm would charge for the same work. Since it is hard to bill a forty-hour week, once you account for all the nonbillable tasks, like finding new work, correspondence and other things that need to be done in order to keep the business going, the hourly rate needs to be high enough to offset the nonbillable time and also high enough to make up for paying for your own benefits and taxes.

KEN BULLOCK, ART DIRECTOR/DESIGNER, BULLOCK STUDIOS

Generally speaking, the model Bullock Studios has adopted is a single-rate model. This means that we bill the same rate regardless of the type of work we are doing, print, web, multimedia or photography. When quoting a project, we estimate the hours to produce the project and display cost all broken down into the separate parts and deliverables. Other services, like stock photography, printing, voice over and music (for multimedia), are all listed with the estimated cost and then totaled together at the bottom to give them an overall cost.

Setting expectations is very important. Most clients have little stomach for inflating costs or increased schedules. Our standard policy is to include our terms and conditions with every quote. Things we typically include in our terms and conditions are:

- the payment terms—when and what percentage based on project milestones (i.e., payment to start, on delivery of high comps and delivery, etc.)

- changes to schedule and scope and the associated costs of each

- written approvals from client to proceed or make changes that effect cost and schedule

- client responsibilities to provide content (artwork, text), timely feedback and reviews

- rights to the final designed piece.

RESOURCES FOR PRICING AND CONTRACT INFORMATION

- Information about the "Creative Business" newsletter and resources: www.creativebusiness.com

- Graphic Artist Guild *Handbook: Pricing and Ethical Guidelines*: www.gag.org

- AIGA Standard Form of Agreement for Design Services: www.aiga.org/content.cfm/standard-agreement

- IRS information for small business/self-employed: www.irs.gov/businesses/small/article/0,,id=99921,00.html

- Web site with resources such as contracts and forms: www.creative-public.com

- Resources including contracts and business form templates: www.designerstoolbox.com

CHAPTER 20
INTELLECTUAL PROPERTY BASICS FOR DESIGNERS

This chapter was contributed by Todd H. Bailey,
Attorney at Law, Frost Brown Todd LLC.

Understanding your legal rights is very important, especially when you are working on your own. Most designers don't even consider many of these issues as they begin a business and start creating solutions to answer the design problems of their clients. Having a general understanding of intellectual property issues is important in protecting yourself and your work.

Be focused on how to best protect the value of your hard work as a graphic designer. Legal protection of your original designs is extremely important. This applies to your work as a student and as a professional designer. In fact, without effective protection in place, other people can take your designs and use them and have no obligation to pay you either for your designs or for the use of your designs.

This chapter will give you a good understanding of what different components of your design can be given legal protection. It will also show you how to develop a way to analyze your original design in order to try to get the best overall legal protection.

Do not be concerned that we are getting involved with legal stuff that only lawyers should handle. The simple fact of the matter is that you can get enough information about your legal rights so that you can then work efficiently and effectively with a lawyer whenever that is necessary.

The goal here is to make sure that you do not do something that reduces the business value of your original designs. In this age of easily transferred digital content, graphic designers must have a good, solid approach for the protection of their intellectual property rights (we will call these IPR), which are the creative work of the artist. Given the ease with which digital content can be stolen by infringers, the valuable creative work of the artist is often at risk.

Intellectual property is a type of personal property, also called intangible property. It is as valuable, or maybe more valuable, than other types of property. It becomes protectable property when, in the hands of the designer, an idea becomes a reality through expression—that is, when the design can actually be seen by someone. IPR attach at the moment of expression, but do not protect the underlying idea or concept. The various steps that are necessary in order to protect the property interests contained in that tangible expression are at the heart of this IPR chapter.

Of course, the graphic designer can maximize the value and commercial return from that creative work only if the property is properly protected. This chapter will provide the fundamental steps for constructing a protection strategy. A properly planned IPR strategy will allow the designer to get the greatest amount of money or other value from the new designs.

TYPES OF IPR OF INTEREST TO A GRAPHIC DESIGNER

There are three fundamental types of IPR that we'll examine in this chapter: copyright, trademark and trade secrets. Copyrights have only limited time period during which the artist or inventor may prevent other people from using the designs. The other types, trade secrets and trademarks, can have value for extended periods of time and, in fact, can last forever if they are handled properly by the designer.

After the time period allowed for a copyright ends, the creative and original design that is represented in the copyright is then made available to the public and may be used by anyone. The origin for this limited period of exclusive ownership for the artist is found in Article I, Section 8, Clause 8 of the U.S. Constitution. The authors of the Constitution understood that artists and inventors needed to be protected. The founders knew that this would be central to the commercial and competitive success of this country.

Unlike copyrights, trademarks have a potentially limitless lifetime, so long as they continue to be used in the business world. Trademarks work as "source indicators" for a specific product or service. What this means is that when someone sees a trademark, they then automatically think of who made the product or service being sold along with the trademark. The marketing, advertising and intellectual property lawyers call this the "call to mind" test. Everyday examples include the name "Coke," the shape of the Coke bottle and the slogan Coke uses.

Graphic designers will often create two- and three-dimensional designs, including creative and original contributions to such items as the design of web sites, packaging, logos, etc. When a trademark design goes beyond just a two-dimensional logo, then it becomes "trade dress." Trade dress is a specific type of trademark that is protectable under the law if it acquires a "secondary meaning" in the marketplace through advertising and commercial success. Trade dress protection can last for as long as trademarks.

The final category of IPR is trade secrets. These rights, for a graphic designer, are best described by having you think about your own specialized insights, information or techniques that give you a competitive advantage in the market and that make you a better designer. This type of information must be the kind of information that is not generally known within the professional community of designers.

Trade secret IPR have value so long as the designer uses reasonable means to keep them a secret within the designer's own studio and away from the public or competitors. These IPR can include the names of the designer's customers, potential customers or clients, and such things as design software that you develop on your own, as long as you do not share it with other people. Trade secrets even include "negative information," which is that operating knowledge about how not to do something because it is too inefficient, yields inconsistent results, is too expensive, etc.

Trade Secrets Are Stem Cells for IPR

Most new designs start with an idea or a concept. Then the design begins to develop, unfold and take form. Sometimes, it is a "eureka" moment when you first see the design in your own imagination. However, sometimes the design takes a while to go through its various stages before it is final. What you need to remember is this: After the moment of initial conception of the idea for the new design and its expression in some tangible form until the design is shown the client/customer, and/or is then displayed publicly and/or used in business, the design is a trade secret.

Under a law known as the Uniform Trade Secrets Act (as used in virtually all of the fifty states), the designer is required to make reasonable efforts to keep the design a secret. Usually it's not possible to avoid showing the design to anyone. So one option is for all employees and associates of the designer to sign what are called nondisclosure agreements. These confidentiality agreements could require such things as no displays at shows or conferences, on the web site, to visitors in the studio, during a client presentation or in responding to a request for proposal, etc., unless or until the new design is otherwise protected by other ways (such as by common law copyright). If the design is shown to anyone outside of the studio, and the designer wishes to protect the design, it is necessary for the designer to have those people sign confidentiality or nondisclosure agreements—this includes your own customers as well.

For example, if the designer believes that a preliminary design must be shown to a limited number of people outside of the studio in order to respond to a request for proposal or to get money for a project, then the designer should first get a signed confidentiality agreement or nondisclosure agreement from everyone who will see the new design.

TRADE SECRETS

WHAT CAN BE PROTECTED?

Information, that:

1. is not generally known by or available to competitors;
2. has independent economic value as a result of being confidential; and
3. is treated as confidential (i.e., the owner takes steps to maintain the secrecy)

RIGHTS OF OWNER

Exclusive right to use and/or license the trade secret

Note: The trade secret owner may not stop another's use of the same or similar information acquired by the other by lawful means, such as by independent development, research or reverse engineering.

OWNERSHIP

Ownership may be agreed by contract. Otherwise, a nonemployee developer of a trade secret will own it. An employer may own the trade secrets of its employee if developing the information is within the employee's regular job duties.

HOW RIGHTS ARISE

In order for information to be a protectable trade secret:

1. Owner must take reasonable measures to protect its secrecy.
2. It must have independent economic value.
3. It must provide a competitive advantage.
4. It must not be generally known.

NOTICE

Not applicable.

DURATION OF RIGHTS

Protection continues indefinitely as long as the information remains secret.

INFRINGEMENT

There is no "infringement," but rather, "misappropriation."

Misappropriation includes: (1) acquisition of a trade secret of another by a person who knows or has reason to know that the trade secret was acquired by improper means; (2) disclosure or use of a trade secret of another without the express or implied consent of the other person by a person who did any of the following: (a) used improper means to acquire knowledge of the trade secret; (b) at the time of disclosure or use, knew or had reason to know that the knowledge of the trade secret that the person acquired was derived from or through a person who had utilized improper means to acquire it, (c) knew or had reason to know that it was a trade secret and that it had been acquired by accident or mistake.

TRANSFERS

Trade secrets can be sold or licensed.

In order for the rights transferred to be of value to the transferee, the terms of the transfer must obligate the transferor to maintain the secrecy of the information. Certain licenses may be implied.

COMMON LICENSE TERMS

• definition of subject matter of the license, e.g., identification of the licensed trade secrets

• method of royalty calculation and payment and procedure for reporting/auditing

• exclusive or nonexclusive; right of licensee to sue others for infringement

• geographical and/or distribution channel limitations

• nature and scope of use

• duration—initial and renewal terms

• definition of material breach, provisions for termination and remedies for breach

• representations and warranties that the licensor owns the rights that it is purporting to license and has the right to license them; indemnification—agreement to defend and/or hold harmless against suits by others claiming rights in same trade secrets

- provision for maintaining confidentiality

- ownership of improvements developed by licensee

Copyright Registration—The Next Step

Another way to protect IPR is for the designer to mark the design with "©," the artist's name, year of creation and add the words "all rights reserved." This gives what is called actual notice to the world of the common law copyright what the artist has with respect to the design. Then, as the next step, the artist can pay thirty-five dollars and file a Copyright Registration along with two copies of that work with the Copyright Office in order to get what is called constructive notice. After registration of the design, the designer will be allowed to file suit in Federal Court against infringers and will be eligible to recover what are known as statutory damages and attorney's fees from the infringer if the lawsuit is successful. All of the registration steps to obtain a copyright registration can be done quite easily by following the simple instructions on the web site found at: www.USPTO.gov.

Authors of original works enjoy protection under both the common law and the United States copyright statute. Because the copyright law is a very powerful source of legal remedies for the designer, registration under the statute is both wise and necessary in order to expand the protection of IPR associated with copyrights.

The scope of copyright protection can be quite broad. Except for limited uses, which are permitted under the sometimes hotly debated fair use categories, like limited copying for educational purposes, use in criticism of the work, preparation of a very small number of copies that do not deprive the artist of commercial value (determined by number of copies made and/or the amount or the significance of the portion of the work taken by the alleged infringer), the artist has the right to control all uses of the graphic design.

Copyright includes control over the creation of what are called derivative works. Derivative works cover modifications or adaptations of the original design made by other artists who use protected elements of the original design without permission and do not sufficiently transform it so as to create a new, original work. The original designer gets the legal right to make the designs that derive or come from the original design. However, another designer who changes the design to a significant extent, has not infringed on the original designer's copyright. There is some limitation to the scope of the copyright. There is not a clear line between "derivative" versus "transformative," but generally speaking, the Courts wish to protect the IPR of the original artist.

Copyright protection and infringement do not extend so far as to exclude the designs of another artist who entirely independently came up with a substantially similar or even identical design. If the second artist truly had no access to the first artist's work, then a work that might otherwise be infringing will not actually infringe. As we discussed in the introduction, in this age of secretly accessed and easily portable digital content, it is difficult to show that someone has not had access to another artist's work (that is, "prove the negative"). With the advent of the Internet, along with reliance on powerful search engines and data aggregators, virtually all design content is both accessible and anonymously transportable.

In order to provide some basis to prove access by the alleged infringer, some web designers and artists insert digital fingerprints and watermarks into their designs to permit easier identification and tracing of infringers who steal the original designs of the artists. This means that the designer's IPR strategy should be in place at the beginning of the design process by including design features or elements that can be digitally traced and identified.

Unless the work is created as a part of the designer's regular employment within the scope of his/her job, (thus becoming a work for hire), or is otherwise specifically commissioned and then transferred in writing, the artist retains the rights to the work. Copyright law also has what is called the statute of frauds requirement, which means that ownership rights in a copyright can be fully transferred to a new owner only by doing so in writing. The document which says that ownership transfers must be actually signed by the original author or designer.

Designers can also transfer limited rights in their copyright works. This is usually done by the designer agreeing to a license. For example, the artist can sign what is called a limited or restricted license, permitting use of the design for a specific medium (e.g., print or electronic media), for display only on a designated web site for a limited period of time, for use in publications distributed in particular countries, etc. These licenses can be exclusive, which means that no one else will be able to get the same license; they can be nonexclusive, which means that other licensees can also negotiate for the same rights under the license; or they can be whatever else the designer agrees to in the terms of the contract or license agreement.

The artist has great flexibility in how to permit others to use his or her designs. As you see from this discussion of copyright, the laws for IPR give you, the designer, lots of options for the commercialization of the work.

Let's discuss some other copyright issues. There are various types of works that can be of concern to the designer. A collective work, for example, will have two separate copyrights. Each separate design included in the collection retains the specific copyright of the individual original artist, but each design is now displayed in conjunction with the works of other artists, e.g., in a book on graphic design. The author of the new book has created a new design and has a separate copyright in the original arrangement and display of the compilation or collective work, but the original copyright still resides in the original artist for the individual design that was contributed to the book. Permission must be obtained from each contributing artist in order for the designs to be legally included in the collective work.

There are also joint works where each contributing artist has been involved in developing the overall final design. Such a design is considered to be a unitary whole. Each designer has an individual and equal copyright ownership interest in the entire finished or completed work to which they contributed. For this to occur, it is important that there was intent to create a joint work. Each such contributing artist also has the right to commercialize the overall design without the permission of the other contributing artist because the law of copyright says that each has what is called an undivided ownership interest in the entire design. Since this can create significant difficulties for the designers if they cannot agree later on how to use the design in their business activities, it is best to reach a written agreement on these matters in advance of the collaborative design process getting started.

COPYRIGHTS

WHAT CAN BE PROTECTED?

An original work recorded in or on a tangible medium

- Copyright protects the particular expression of an idea, but not the idea itself.
- Words and short phrases may not be protected

RIGHTS OF OWNER

Exclusive right to reproduce, distribute (and in some cases to display, perform or use) the work and prepare new works based upon the original work.

OWNERSHIP

Generally, initial ownership vests with the individual who created the work. In certain situations, the employer of the creator is the owner.

HOW RIGHTS ARISE

A copyright in an expressive, original work that arises at the moment it is created and is fixed in a tangible form.

Federal Registration: Registration with the U.S. Copyright Office is a prerequisite to filing a lawsuit seeking to enforce a copyright or seeking remedies for copyright infringement. Registration prior to the infringement is necessary for certain remedies to be available.

NOTICE

Mark all copies of the work with copyright claim, e.g., © 2009 artist's name all rights reserved.

If the copyright owner has failed to give notice of the copyright claim by using such a signal, the defendant in an infringement suit may be able to limit damages by proving innocent infringement.

DURATION OF RIGHTS

Individual author: life + 70 years; Owned by the employer: shorter of 95 years from publication or 120 years from creation

INFRINGEMENT

It is copyright infringement to engage in any of the acts in which the copyright owner has exclusive rights.

To prove copyright infringement the owner must prove: (1) ownership of a valid copyright, and (2) copying of elements of the work that are original. To prove copying (particularly where exact reproduction in some form is not apparent), the owner must prove (a) that the defendant had access to the work, and (b) that the defendant's product is, or contains portions or components, that are substantially similar to the work.

TRANSFERS

The owner can assign (sell) a copyright in a work.

To be effective, an assignment of copyright (other than by operation of law) must be evidenced by a written document signed on behalf of the assigning copyright owner.

The owner can license the copyright (permit exercise of some or all of the exclusive rights).

Certain licenses may be implied.

COMMON LICENSE TERMS

• definition of subject matter of the license, e.g., identification of the copyright protected work and any copyright registrations

• method of royalty calculation and payment and procedure for reporting/auditing

• exclusive or nonexclusive; right of licensee to sue others for infringement

- geographical and/or distribution channel limitations

- nature of use and/or reproduction of the work

- duration—initial and renewal terms

- definition of material breach, provisions for termination and remedies for breach

- representations and warranties that the licensor owns the rights that it is purporting to license and has the right to license them; indemnification—agreement to defend and/or hold harmless against suits by others claiming rights in same work

- ownership of copyrights in derivative works

Trademarks and Trade Dress as "Source Indicators"

The purpose of a trademark is to operate or function as a source indicator. Trademarks get their value from their use in commerce and business. When a consumer or mere observer sees the trademark for a product (e.g., "COCA-COLA®") or a service (e.g., "Federal Express®"), the trademark "calls to mind" the quality and characteristics of the product/service offered under that brand. Trademarks are evidence of sponsorship or affiliation with the manufacturer and distributor of the product/service.

Trade dress is a type of trademark. Whereas trademarks are the "logos," the specific words and associated type face/font size and script, colors and graphics (e.g., the concentric circles and specific colors used with the "Tide®" logo on detergent bottles) used to make the "brand," trade dress is broader in scope and presents interesting additional opportunities for the designer. Trade dress covers the total image and overall appearance of the product or the delivery of the service, including features such as shape, color, texture, graphics, sounds, smells, size and particular sales techniques. For example, the shape of the Coca-Cola bottle is protectable trade dress.

Trade dress is only protectable if it is distinctive and nonfunctional; that is, the parts of the design that are claimed as trade dress do not serve a utilitarian or functional purpose. The key for the graphic designer is to understand how to best approach the description of the aspects of the design in order to best describe and capture the distinctive and nonutilitarian aspects of the design for trade dress protection. As mentioned earlier, trademarks, including trade dress, have value only because of their use in commerce.

In order to register a trademark, you must describe the use of the mark in commerce. Periodic updates of the registration must be filed with the USPTO describing continued use of the trademark in commerce. If this is not done properly, the registration may lapse and the trademark will be declared abandoned. At that point, someone else may obtain rights to the mark.

Trademarks vary in their strength, power and effectiveness when they do their work as source indicators. The weakest marks are "generic" marks, which simply refer to a category of products/services e.g., "Book Store." These have no power and receive no IPR protection. Next are the "descriptive" marks, which provide some additional, nonspecific information, e.g., "Smith's Good Used Book Store." These are followed on the ranking of stronger trademarks by "suggestive" marks, e.g., "Thoughtful Place Books." Next are "arbitrary" marks where a preexisting, but totally unrelated work is used as the brand, e.g., "Delta River Books." Finally are the "coined" or "fanciful" word where a new word is made up as the mark, e.g., "Xyon Books."

There are two different places where trademarks are registered with the Patent and Trademark Office. They are referred to as the Principal and Supplemental Registers. Trademarks that are considered to be suggestive, arbitrary or fanciful may be on the Principal Register. If a descriptive mark is used, it is considered to be a weak mark and will only qualify for registration on the USPTO Supplemental Register. After use in commerce for several years, plus advertising and demonstrated sales success, the mark acquires secondary meaning in the marketplace. Secondary meaning tells us that the mark has acquired power in the market and now works as a source indicator and may now be eligible for the Principal Register. The best way to establish secondary meaning is through advertising, use in commerce and demonstrating consumer recognition of the trade dress based on surveys.

TRADEMARKS/TRADE DRESS

WHAT CAN BE PROTECTED?

Name(s), word(s), symbol, logo, product design or package design that is distinctive and serves to indicate a particular source of products or services, i.e., it serves as a brand designation

- A generic word for the product itself cannot be protected as a trademark for the product, e.g., "apple" cannot be protected as a trademark for apples.

- A purely descriptive term cannot be protected as a trademark merely by adoption, e.g., "RED" cannot be protected as a trademark for red apples merely by adoption; other conditions must also be met.

RIGHTS OF OWNER

Right to prevent others from confusing or deceiving consumers by using confusingly similar trademarks

OWNERSHIP

First user of the trademark has superior rights to use the trademark in connection with particular goods/services (subject to possible geographical limitations).

HOW RIGHTS ARISE

Trademark rights arise through use of a distinctive mark on or in connection with identifying, marketing, selling or promoting goods or services (rights automatically arise from use, in relevant geographic market).

Federal Registration: Nationwide trademark rights can be acquired by applying for registration of the mark with the United States Patent and Trademark Office. Registration allows for certain additional remedies and presumptions.

NOTICE

TRADEMARK® (registered marks) or TRADEMARK™ (unregistered marks).

If the mark owner has failed to give notice that mark is federally registered by using such a signal, in an infringement suit no profits or actual damages can be deemed to have accrued until the defendant was given actual notice of infringement.

DURATION OF RIGHTS

Protection continues indefinitely as long as (1) use continues; (2) the mark does not become a generic term (examples: cellophane; aspirin).

INFRINGEMENT

To prove trademark infringement the trademark owner must prove (1) ownership of a valid trademark; (2) defendant's use of confusingly similar words, symbols, trade dress or a combination of the same, in connection with the sale, offering for sale, distribution or advertising of any goods or services, in a manner that is likely to cause confusion, mistake or deception among consumers.

TRANSFERS

The owner can assign (sell) trademark as long as all goodwill is assigned along with the mark.

The owner can license use of the mark but must exercise control over the nature and quality of the licensee's goods and services.

COMMON LICENSE TERMS

- definition of subject matter of the license, e.g., identification of the licensed trademarks and any trademark registrations

- method of royalty calculation and payment and procedure for reporting/auditing

- exclusive or nonexclusive; right of licensee to sue others for infringement

- geographical and/or distribution channel limitations

- nature and scope of goods/services with which the trademark may be used

- duration—initial and renewal terms

- definition of material breach, provisions for termination and remedies for breach

- representations and warranties that the licensor owns the rights that it is purporting to license and has the right to license them; indemnification—agreement to defend and/or hold harmless against suits by others claiming rights in same trademark

- quality control provisions

- requirements as to nature and manner of reproduction, appearance and use of mark, logo on products, packaging and marketing materials

PART SEVEN

PRACTICING PRODUCTION BASICS

As a designer, your work is not a "one-off." Your pieces will be mass-produced into the hundreds, thousands or even more and distributed to a wide audience. You will need to work with professional printing and paper companies to bring your design visions to life. It's extremely important to understand what's possible, what's available, what's impractical and what's impossible. If you don't have at least a basic understanding of printing and paper, you won't be able to communicate your design vision.

It's not about being an expert; it's really about an attitude of continuous learning. Depend on the printer, respect their knowledge, ask for their suggestions and look to them for education about printing and new technologies. Thomas H. Gilmore, Director of Brand Strategy for RGI Design, puts it this way, "Ongoing knowledge of the newest product offering, services and available technology will enable a designer to achieve success when producing artwork for print. Paper and printing company account representatives are wonderful resources for better understanding the latest production techniques and processes, providing valuable insight to the designer."

CHAPTER 21
WORKING WITH PRINTING AND PAPER COMPANIES

You've created a beautiful design that your client loves, and now you need to work with a paper company and a printer in order to deliver the ten thousand copies that the client needs for their promotion. Depending on your choices, your design will either shine or sink. The importance of this final execution/production phase should not be underestimated. The wrong paper, binding or printing can completely ruin the communication of your idea and the beauty of your design.

Let's talk about how to find the right printing and paper representatives and establish a positive working relationship with them. If you don't connect with the right people, you'll run into trouble all along the way. In addition, it's important to understand how you should communicate what you need. Without the proper information your reps, however good they are, will not be able to do an excellent job for you.

CHOOSING THE RIGHT PRINTER

What are the criteria you should use when choosing a printing company? You need to weigh the characteristics of the printer with the size of the job and its budget. For instance, if the job is high-end with a large budget and a client with high expectations, then you will weigh the need for high-end quality above that of price. However, if you're doing a job for a nonprofit that would like a nice piece but has to strongly consider budget, then the price will become a much more important factor.

• **Knowledge of design and design software:** You and the printer will need to communicate—meeting half way with your communication. If you know a little about printing and they know a little about design, then you'll be in good shape. Are they up-to-date on your design software? Do they have the same version? If not, how do they want the file? For a printer, the file you give them is as much about communication as giving them written or oral instructions. The digital file either clearly communicates through its concise construction, or it confuses due to its sloppy craft.

• **Capability and depth of knowledge of printing processes:** What type of equipment does the printer have? Does the size and quality of the presses match the needs of your job? Does the printer have special capabilities that you might need, such as foil embossing or perfect binding? If not, do they farm that out to someone else? What are their standards for production? It's very important to consider the level and size of the printer in relationship to the job complexity and budget. A small printer down the street might be great for that simple letterhead job, but wouldn't be a good match for a complex, six-color brochure with embossing and die cuts.

• **Quality of samples and experience:** Ask the printer for samples of the work they've recently done. What types of processes are included? Do any of the pieces have the same processes you need for your job? This is the printer's portfolio; examine it for quality, consistency and innovation.

• **Service recommendations:** Ask other designers for recommendations. This can be golden information that's difficult to get any other way. Work with your network to build a good pool of dependable printers at various levels for all your printing needs.

• **Price:** Obviously, the budget for the job will almost always be an important factor in your decision, but it isn't good to choose by price alone. Make sure you are comfortable with other criteria in relationship to the price. Look at the bigger picture.

• **Location:** If you want to do press checks with this printer, then the location is important. It's also good to visit the shop and get a tour to see their equipment. Is the printer close enough for convenient visits? Sometimes, press checks can take days and you will be traveling back and forth for frequent checks on different runs. If the printer isn't near your home or office, is it going to be a problem to stay overnight at a hotel and be away from the office for extended periods?

• **Dependability and timeliness:** Deadlines are very important, and it's key to work with a printer you know you can depend on to deliver a high quality product by a specific date. With many jobs, there's little to no leeway in the schedule, and the printer is the last one in the process, so they can be crunched for time. Are they good under pressure? How will they troubleshoot if problems arise? Did the recommendations you received indicate any dependability issues?

APPLICATION: FINDING THE RIGHT REPS

• **Ask for samples of similar projects.** How do they look? How long ago were they printed? Would your job be printed on the same equipment?

• **Ask if you will be working consistently with a particular rep.** You want to be able to establish a relationship and build trust. Who is that person? What are their qualifications? Have they worked on projects similar to yours before?

• **Set up regular meetings with the rep to review your jobs in process and get ideas for paper and printing techniques.** What questions will you ask to make sure your project is on the right track? How will they address problems that arise?

• **Get references.** What advice can they give you about your paper rep? What questions will you ask?

PROVIDING COMPLETE INFORMATION

Working with printer and paper representatives is all about communication. It's very important to provide complete and accurate information when ordering paper or printing services. If your instructions are confusing or incomplete, you gamble the quality of the job and you'll strain your working relationship with the rep.

Ordering Paper

Ask your paper rep or printer for a sample job printed on the paper you've selected. You may be surprised how different things look on various papers, especially photographs. There are many factors that should be considered when selecting a paper stock:

Color
- How much contrast do you need for readability of text and images?
- What aesthetic quality can the paper color bring to your design? Do you want a sharp, bright white or a softer off-white?

Weight
- How large is your document (overall size and how many pages)?
- Does the piece need to be folded? How many times? Will you need to have the paper scored so it folds more easily?
- How flexible do you want the piece to feel? You don't want it to be too flimsy or too stiff.

Opacity

• Is it important that the paper have minimal "show-through" from one side to the other?

• Are you printing on both sides?

Finish/Texture

• Do you want the paper to be highly smooth, have a rough texture or be somewhere in between?

• How do the aesthetics of the paper choice match your overall design concept?

Coated or Uncoated

• Coated papers have a better ink holdout for a crisper image quality. How important is image contrast and sharpness to your design? Would you prefer a softer look to the images?

• How "shiny" do you want the paper to be? Highly glossy? A smooth matte?

Sustainability

• Are you considering the recycled content on the paper?

• How does your paper choice impact the environment?

• Is your client concerned about the sustainability of your choices?

Special features

• What about deckle edges or special textures? Metallic or translucent papers?

• How would specific, special paper features affect the aesthetics of your design or enhance your overall concept?

Type of Printer

• Will your budget and time frame afford high-end, commercial printing or do you need to stick with a quick turnaround color copier? The printing device will affect the type of paper you can select.

Cost

- What will fit into your budget?
- Perhaps you love a very costly paper: Are there similar choices that are less expensive?

End Use

- Once the job is printed, will it need to be imprinted by another type of printing device, such as a laser printer (stationery, for instance)?
- Will your piece need to be mailed? What are the postal requirements?

Common Sizes

- Can you reduce cost and waste by effectively using the standard paper size? If you are designing an envelope, can you use a standard size to reduce the converting and postal costs?

Swatch books, which are books that show samples of different paper stocks, are a fantastic resource, and it's important to build a good library for reference. Your paper representative can assist you with this. Read these books carefully and make sure you understand how they are organized and what information they are presenting. There should be a chart that outlines the weights, finishes and colors that are available in that particular stock. There may also be notes about the percentage of post-consumer waste, grain direction or other paper qualities.

When you order paper make sure to include the following information:

- weight (80#)
- color (Soft Coral)
- brand name (Gilbert Oxford)
- finish (Antique)
- grade (Text)

If your job has an especially tight budget, or perhaps you're doing a pro bono job for a nonprofit and they need to keep their costs down, ask the paper or printing rep if there's any leftover paper stock on hand.

COMMON PAPER TERMS

FROM *PAPER BASICS*, MOHAWK PAPER MILLS, 2003

- **acid-free:** prevents internal chemical deterioration of the paper over time
- **basis weight:** five hundred sheets (one ream) of a standard basic size
- **brightness:** percentage of light reflected from the paper's surface, not necessarily related to whiteness or color
- **caliper:** paper thickness (in thousandths of an inch)
- **cast-coated:** high gloss coated paper made by highly polished drums
- **deckle edge:** the rough edge on handmade and some machine-made papers
- **digital papers:** designed for specific processes such as laser printing
- **double-thick cover:** laminating two pieces together; can be two different colors, also referred to as "duplex"
- **felt:** carries the paper from the wire to the dryer section, can give a texture to the paper
- **formation:** uniformity and distribution of the fibers within a sheet
- **grain direction:** fibers orient themselves in the direction of the paper machine; important for folding
- **ink holdout:** capacity to keep ink on the paper surface; better ink holdout results in sharper printed images
- **laid:** linear pattern applied by the dandy roll, often used in stationery papers
- **linen finish:** embossing, on or off the paper machine, by a patterned steel roll
- **opacity:** percentage of light passage through a sheet of paper; very important for avoiding ink show-through
- **recycled:** 30 percent post-consumer waste for uncoated, 15 percent for coated
- **smoothness:** flatness and surface quality
- **vellum finish:** natural or machine finish, "antique" or "eggshell"
- **watermarks:** designs formed by the dandy roll; thins the paper; very popular in stationery papers

- **wire side:** side of the sheet that rests on the paper machine wire; "felt" is the opposite side

REAL WORLD ADVICE:
RELATIONSHIPS WITH PRINTING AND PAPER REPS

ERIK BORRESON, SENIOR GRAPHIC DESIGNER, MARSHFIELD CLINIC

A good printer can be your best friend, as a bad one can be your worst enemy. They are the last stop before the product hits the client's hands. Know your printers, know their strengths and weaknesses. See if they have experience in a special technique you are interested in using. Get assurance that they can deliver the printed piece by the due date.

JEFF FISHER, ENGINEER OF CREATIVE IDENTITY, JEFF FISHER LOGOMOTIVES

I have print and paper reps with whom I've had relationships of fifteen to twenty years. Print reps have been lifesavers, guiding projects with unreasonable deadlines through the process on time. Paper reps have overnighted paper samples to me, created folding mock-ups, found existing project dies and even met me in the parking lot minutes before a presentation to make me look good in the eyes of a client with unrealistic expectations.

I was once told that I must work with a specific printing rep on a project, and I was not too pleased about being told what to do in the situation. However, this individual became an incredible resource and ally. Those are the individuals a designer wants in their corner on a regular basis. It's also very important for the designer to show how much they value the efforts of such individuals with a handwritten thank you note or some other form of appreciation.

A major pet peeve I have with designers is that so many have a problem with asking printers the necessary questions before executing all major work on a client project. Contact the specific printer being used and ask the question to avoid costly mistakes, time delays or other problems.

MARK HAMILTON, ASSOCIATE DIRECTOR FOR MARKETING AND CREATIVE SERVICES, COLLEGE OF ST. ROSE

Working with printers is rather similar to working with clients. It is very much about relationships. It is not only an investment of time and money, making your investment is a result of many principles and values including:

- Commitment to quality: The old saying, "you get what you pay for" rings so true in printing. If a quote seems too good to be true, then it is. Select a vendor based on reputation, samples, references, attention to detail and personal satisfaction.

- Honesty and Confidence = Customer Service

- Capabilities: All printers are not the same. Printers may have the same equipment, but equal value is never a guaranteed outcome. Different people, with different attitudes and standards, may deliver vastly different results. A printer's role is to be your problem solver.

STEVE REIST, WEST-CAMP PRESS

It's very important for the designer to get to know the prep people—preferably by name. Take the time to go to the shop and learn as much as you can. Communication is key.

To ensure the job goes smoothly, call the printer from the beginning of the job. Make sure the files will work. Communicate early in the process to avoid problems before you get to deadlines. Avoid redesigning and reworking.

Paper is very important early in the job. A house sheet can work well because it's cost effective and the printer knows how it prints. ... Really consider the weight of the paper, especially if the job is supposed to be sent through the postal system. Postal regulations change constantly, and printers are great resources for understanding and recommending solutions to postal issues. For instance, at West-Camp, we have a person who's devoted to knowing the latest postal regulations.

CINDY HURLEY, MIAMI UNIVERSITY INFORMATION TECHNOLOGIES SERVICES, PRINT CENTER

• Contact the printer before designing to ask how they would like the file to be delivered.

• Be specific with specs and instructions; provide samples.

• Make sure you understand the terminology used by printer. If unfamiliar with the terminology, such as bleeds, yields, signature, saddle stitch, etc., ask what it means.

• Plan well in advance and contact the printer to ask for the turn around for delivery on a project. Add another week for proofing and corrections to the project schedule. Proof, proof, proof if the project is large and expensive.

• I would recommend showing the printer a sample of the piece being printed and ask them for several paper recommendations. Ask for proofs on the recommendations made so that you can make a decision based on the completed output. Papers can make the piece, and the printers have the most experience with what designs look best when put on paper. They will also know that you want to avoid papers with textured finishes if you are printing small quantities on digital equipment, which print better on smooth papers. Offset equipment used to print large quantities print better on textured papers, but not on smooth papers.

- Give the printer the time it requires to turn an order around so they can take the time to follow their own quality control procedures for quality assurance. When jobs have to be turned around quickly, there are shortcuts that have to be made to those procedures and the quality in the completion of that order is compromised.

BARBARA BERNE, HAMILTON GRAPHICS

A new graphic designer should establish a relationship with their printer, arrange a walk-through of the plant and learn the processes involved from file input to output to plate to bindery. Learn what programs and file types are compatible with the printer's devices, the correct way to set up jobs, define colors, etc. Talk to your printer about stock. Most printers have their prepress guidelines published on their web sites. They should be read.

Most frequent problems include:

- no bleeds
- not having everything needed for output (fonts, all placed graphics, etc.)
- low resolution graphics
- colors defined improperly—spot or process
- lack of initial communication, requiring e-mailing or phone calls to answer questions
- graphics created as raster images, where vector would provide better image quality
- documents created in office software like Publisher or Word
- unrealistic turnaround expectations, like large quantity four-color printing with die cutting and folding expected in a day

Things a printer really appreciates:

- all specs and contact information supplied

- a printout of the FINAL version, to check the output for font issues, typewraps, missing graphics, etc., and confirm that it backs up and folds properly
- making sure your document has been proofread and signed off on by the powers in charge before you give it to a printer (A proof is not an opportunity to rewrite a brochure or redesign pages.)

JIM HARDY, BAESMAN PRINTING

Visit a couple of commercial printing companies, ask questions, learn about the process and understand what goes into the production of a printed piece. Have ideas or samples that the printer can show the full process of how they were produced.

- Talk to the printer and paper companies about your ideas before presenting to the client.
- Be willing to adjust your idea to compensate for what can feasibly be done.
- Allow enough time to complete the project including the printer's time frame.
- Understand the client's budget before specifying a paper.
- Always make sure the images are linked as well as furnishing all the fonts used.
- Have regular meeting with printers. Make them keep you informed; they should already do that.
- Communication is key: Always be willing to have open dialogue with the printers.

JIM SHARP, A & B PRINTING

Consult with them about the types of projects they are capable of producing well; just because they are a print house doesn't mean they do all print projects well. Communication will help you determine what type of work they are well suited for.

Project preparation is huge! It is important to know and understand the production needs of your project. A lot of additional funds can be put into a project by not properly preparing to go to print. It is important to meet and discuss with your print house about how they need to have files prepared. This includes being aware of bleed allowances, pagination (readers or printers spreads), and how will the job be produced, such as four-color process, spot color only or process and spot together.

Designers have many ways to stay up-to-date with the changes in the printing industry today. The Internet is a constant buzz of forums and user groups and blogs that are always spewing the latest in industry changes and direction. Attending trade shows and seminars put on by leaders in the industry is another way to stay current.

Paper is the base of every print project, so it's important to know the characteristics of the paper you are specifying for a project. There are many things to consider when selecting paper for a specific project: ink coverage, folding, scoring, etc. Does the paper you have specified for the job fold well when printed, or does it crack severely, leaving an undesirable edge? Paper cost is another important factor to consider from many angles. How readily available is the stock you have chosen? Is it a mill order item or is it available in a time frame to meet your delivery deadline? These are typical things to consider.

CHAPTER 22
PRINTING PROCESSES

UNDERSTANDING PRINTING

The most well designed piece is a failure if it can't be correctly output and printed. Professional printing (in large quantities) is very different from the printing that you may be accustomed to using in your home, office or university computer lab. Digital printing, such as laser printing, is good for small quantity jobs, jobs that don't require high quality or specialized papers and jobs that aren't large or require special binding or finishing processes, such as die cutting. For high quality printing in large quantities (several hundred and up), a professional printing company is required. Offset lithography, which we will discuss later, is the most common form of printing done by professional printers.

Printing Processes
Let's start by getting an overall view of the various printing processes. Some were quite popular in the past and are now rarely used, while other methods are up and coming.

• **Letterpress printing:** In letterpress the image or type to be printed is positioned above the base on which it rests. It is inked, and paper is pressed against it to transfer the image. (This is also called relief printing.) This process is over five hundred years old, but it is still used in a very limited way. It can be costly, but produces high quality. Some of the main uses today include processes that don't actually use ink, such as scoring, blind embossing and die cutting.

• **Gravure printing:** Gravure is the opposite of letterpress: The image is printed from a recessed surface instead of a raised surface. This process has a long history, like letterpress, and is also referred to as intaglio. Gravure is especially excellent for photo reproduction. It can be a very expensive form of printing and is generally used only for publications and magazines with very high runs. Roto-gravure is the web-fed (continuous rolls of paper) gravure machine.

• **Screen printing:** Screen printing is also referred to as silkscreening or screen process printing. In this process, a fine, porous screen is mounted on a frame, and a stencil is cut (manually or photomechanically) for the lettering or design to be reproduced. The stencil is placed over the screen and thick ink is pushed through the open areas in the screen and onto the paper. Screen printing is capable of producing a wide range of sophisticated imagery and is known for very vivid color and ink opacity. This process is commonly used for posters, T-shirts, banners and packaging. One of the great benefits is that you can print on just about anything—bottles, textiles, metal, etc.

• **Laser printing:** As previously stated, laser printing is good for producing limited number of copies and is a similar process to Xerography. This is a very hot process at smaller sizes (i.e., 12" × 18"), so paper types are limited. There is also a limited quality level and color matching, but this can be a very cost effective option for low quantities.

• **Offset lithographic printing:** Offset has become the preferred method of printing. Eighty to ninety percent of printing today is offset. Lithography or planographic printing means "printing on one surface," and the process is based on the concept that "oil and water don't mix." A printing plate with a planographic image is clamped onto the plate cylinder. Dampening rollers coat the plate with water; ink rollers ink the plate (the ink adheres to the image area only), and the image is offset to the offset cylinder and then transferred by the impression cylinder onto the paper. Offset is comparatively inexpensive and produces good quality, but it's necessary to print a fairly large quantity.

• **Commercial digital printing:** Digital printing processes are becoming more and more commonplace in printing facilities and may replace traditional offset technologies in the near future. Digital printing combines the power and flexibility of digital imaging with the quality of offset and is an offshoot of offset technology that incorporates lasers, ink and direct digital input.

APPLICATION: TAKING A FIELD TRIP

Call a local printer and ask to take a tour of their facilities. While you are there, ask the following questions:

What types of printing presses and equipment do you have on site?

Can I meet the press people I may be working with in the future?

Do you also have binding and finishing equipment, and may I see it?

What new developments are on the horizon for the printing industry?

What resources do you recommend for learning more about printing?

In the future, how can I work with you in an effective manner?

DIGITAL PRINTING VS. OFFSET PRINTING

Digital printing is becoming more and more common and is competing with traditional offset lithography. Advances in technology have taken a very limited resource—that's been hindered by poor color matching, limited sizes and paper choices—and have extended it. The printing industry will convert to digital as more technical issues are resolved.

REAL WORLD ADVICE: DIGITAL AND OFFSET PRINTING

CYNTHIA PINSONNAULT, PINSONNAULT CREATIVE (WWW.PINSCREATIVE.COM)

Advantages of Digital:

- shorter turnaround

- every print is the same, more accurate counts, less waste and fewer variations due to not having to balance ink and water during press run

- cheaper low-volume printing (While the unit cost of each piece may be higher than with offset printing, when setup costs are included digital printing provides lower per unit costs for very small print runs.)

- option for Variable Data Printing (This is a form of customizable digital printing. Using information from a database or external file, text and graphics can be changed on each piece without stopping or slowing down the press. For example, personalized letters can be printed with a different name and address on each letter. Variable data printing is used primarily for direct marketing, customer relationship development and advertising.)

Advantages of Offset:

- high image quality

- works on a wide range of printing surfaces including paper, wood, cloth, metal, leather, rough paper and plastic

- the unit cost goes down as the quantity goes up

- quality and cost-effectiveness in high volume jobs (While today's digital presses are close to the cost/benefit ratio of offset for high quality work, they are not yet able to compete with the volume an offset press can produce.)

- Use of computer-to-plate systems (Many modern offset presses use computer-to-plate systems as opposed to the older computer-to-film work flows, further increasing quality.)

Still not sure which is right? Use these factors to help decide:

- Quantity: Offset printing has a front-end cost load. Short runs have a high unit cost. But as quantities increase, the unit cost goes down with offset printing. Very short runs can be much more cost effective with digital printing; while larger quantities are likely to have a lower unit cost with offset printing.

- Printing medium: Do you need or want a special paper, finish or unusual printing surface, or unique size? The options are increasing continually for digital, but offset printing still offers the most flexibility.

- Color: Digital presses use four-color process printing. If you need only black ink, or one or two ink colors, offset printing may offer a more cost-effective solution. If you need four-color printing, digital may offer advantages in lower up-front costs.

- More on color: If you're planning to print using the Pantone Matching System, offset printing will give you the best match, since it uses actual Pantone ink. Digital printing simulates the color using a four-color matching process, so some digital printers may offer less accurate color matching on projects.

- Turnaround: If you need it fast, digital usually offers quicker delivery.

- Proofing: Digital offers accurate proofs since you see an actual sample of the printed piece. Accurate color proofing for offset printing can be expensive.

- Customization: Without question, digital printing offers the most affordable way to customize marketing materials, direct mail pieces, letters, etc."

GENERAL COLOR PRINTING OPTIONS

• **Spot color:** one ink color that is applied to portions of the printed sheet, as compared to flood or painted sheet where the entire sheet is covered with a color. This term normally refers to Pantone colors where a specific color ink is chosen to print solid areas, as opposed to optically mixing color using small dots.

• **Duotone/tritone:** a photographic reproduction using two (duo) or three (tri) colors (one normally being black) that separates the highlights from the midtones from the dark tones into different printing plates to emphasize the value depth in the image. For instance, you might have black printing for the dark to midtones and brown printing for the midtones to light tones.

• **Full color or four-color process:** a printing process that uses four ink colors (black, magenta, cyan and yellow) to reproduce full-color images and colored text. The images are separated into four different printing plates (C, M, Y, K) using small dots. Once the dots overlap when printed, the color optically mixes to create the color image. This is a less expensive way to reproduce a wide range of color, as opposed to having a Pantone number for every color you need to print.

• **Five or six color printing (four color plus spot colors):** This is a mixture of four-color process printing and some specific Pantone colors (for instance, a company's corporate color). Typically, printing costs increase with each additional color and "press pass."

SPECIAL PRINTING PROCESSES

There are many special printing and production processes and it's important to know your options. These choices go beyond normal ink, whether Pantone or process. The budgets for the vast majority of printing jobs won't allow you to use many of these processes—they can be expensive. But there may be that well-funded job here and there that will allow you to use a special foil, embossing or engraving. Other choices are fairly commonplace and functional, such as scoring.

• **Engraving:** A printing process using a plate, also called a die, where image and/or type are cut into its surface. The plate is inked and paper is pressed onto the plate transferring the ink from the plate recesses onto the paper. The plate and paper are put through a high-pressure press that leaves an impression on the paper. Engraving is used rarely today and can be quite expensive.

• **Embossing:** There are various forms of embossing, such as standard, blind, deboss and foil embossing. Standard embossing is when an image or type is pressed into the paper so that it protrudes from the surface, creating a raised area. Debossing, as you might guess from the name, is the opposite—the image or type will be an indentation. A blind emboss, or deboss, is when the image or type is not printed with ink or foil. Lastly, a foil emboss is when an image or type is both embossed and foil stamped.

• **Scoring:** Scoring means to crease paper along a straight line so that it folds accurately and easily. It seems like a small thing, but scoring can be very important to the overall quality of your printed piece. If you are printing on heavy paper, such as a cover, and you want to fold the paper, then scoring is a must. If you don't score the paper, the fold will probably splinter and it will not be clean. Scoring is even more important if you have ink coverage over the top of the fold.

• **Thermography:** This is a method of printing using colorless resin powder that takes on the color of the underlying ink. This method attempts to give the impression of engraving, but is much less expensive. The colored resin looks like raised printing on the surface of the paper.

• **Varnishing, clear coat or aqueous coating:** Varnishes and coatings are applied to the surface of the paper following the printing of ink to give protection and a desired finish to the paper. There are a variety of surface choices, such as matte or glossy. Varnishes and coatings can be applied "in line" on the same printing press as the ink, or "off line" on a separate press. The in line process generally results in a more subtle finish.

• **Die cutting:** Die cutting involves cutting irregular shapes off the side or out of the center of the paper. Normally die cutting is done with thicker paper stocks that can hold up to the structural weakness caused by the hole in the paper. The cuts are made with a die, which is a device for cutting, scoring, stamping, embossing and debossing.

• **Metallic inks:** Metallic inks can be used much like normal inks. Metallics have powdered metal or pigments that simulate metal mixed into them. This gives the ink a shiny appearance. Metallic inks come in a wide variety of colors.

CHAPTER 23
PRE- AND POST-PRESS PRODUCTION

PRE-PRESS INFORMATION

It's key to set up a strong relationship with your printer. They are your partner in completing a successful project. First and foremost in that process is becoming adept at supplying clear, concise and complete files to the printer for output. Clear communication is paramount. The pre-press portion of the project is critical in setting up your job for timely and quality delivery. If you set up the digital files improperly, if your specifications are confusing or if you give inaccurate information, you are creating a situation where your job may be delayed or you may not receive what you expect.

Sending Jobs to the Printer
1. Check your spelling. It's very important that you print out your files and read them for errors. Better yet, have someone else read them too, as you've probably gotten too close to the information and will no longer recognize errors that would be obvious to a fresh set of eyes. You should never depend solely on the spell-check function in your software. You should run the spell-check to pick up blatant errors, but after that, you should read through for more subtle errors. Additionally, most people

are more meticulous proofreaders if they read from a printed file, as opposed to on screen.

2. Delete unused colors from your files. As you are experimenting with a file and coming to final color choices, it's common to have stray colors that you are no longer using in the final design. Or perhaps your job is four-color process (CMYK) and you have unused Pantone or RGB colors in your file. It's very important to clean up the final file by deleting all unused colors. There is no reason to have a sloppy file that may be confusing and misleading for your printer. This could delay your job or cause a mistake.

3. Define colors correctly. If your job is to be printed with Pantone colors (spot color), it's important the colors are selected as Pantone. In addition, there are many different forms of Pantone. For instance, don't mix Pantone "C" numbers (coated) and Pantone "U" numbers (uncoated). These two choices are intended to be printed on two different types of paper (coated and uncoated), and the colors may shift unexpectedly if they aren't selected appropriately. If you're doing a process color job, the colors in the file should all be identified as CMYK mixtures. Also, don't use RGB or web colors for print work—these are intended to be mixed using red, green and blue primaries, not CMYK. When moving from program to program (Photoshop to Illustrator to InDesign for instance), it's very important to match the color names/types throughout. If your logo is in Illustrator and you pull it into InDesign, make sure the color designations are exactly the same, otherwise the colors may print differently.

4. Define colors and resolution of photographic images correctly. Make sure Photoshop and other photographic images match your Pantone or process choices as well. If your photograph is set up as RGB and you are printing in CMYK, you will probably get an unwanted color shift. Or perhaps you're printing in two-color Pantone and duo-toned photographs. Make sure the photographs aren't set up using CMYK, but the correct Pantone colors. In addition, make sure your images are set up at the proper resolution for the type of printing you are doing. If you are working with a high-end commercial printer, they will probably prefer images at 150–300 dpi, as opposed to lower resolution for digital color copies. Ask your printer for screen resolution recommendations.

5. Build bleed into your file. If your design has ink color that runs to the edge of the paper, you need to create a bleed into your file. The bleed needs to run about ⅛" beyond the edge of the file. Presses can't print exactly to the edge of the paper so some "slop" is required; the final will be trimmed.

6. Make sure all images are in appropriate file formats. For printed work, don't use GIF or JPEG formats—they are intended for web work. Use EPS or TIFF files. Replace any low-resolution images with high-resolution for high print quality. Some designers set up their files with low-resolution images, so the files load, process and print more quickly as they are working on the job. In this case, it's important that these low-res images be replaced with their high-resolution counterparts before the job is sent off to the printer.

7. Convert fonts to outlines where possible. Converting all fonts to outlines/paths will save time, possible errors and copyright issues (see Chapter 9: Key Ethical Guidelines). If you use true fonts instead of outlines, then check the accuracy in the proof and make sure that nothing defaulted to an incorrect font. You can also save your file as a PDF file imbedding the fonts. Many printers prefer this option.

8. Collect for output. Once you're done with the steps above, you can collect for output. This is an automatic feature that puts the main file, all picture/image files and fonts together in one neat folder. It's good to put the word "final" on the folder for clarity.

9. Be as neat as possible. When organizing your files, make sure everything is organized and clear. This will make for a much better relationship with your printer and the chances for errors will be greatly reduced.

10. Print a composite proof at 100 percent. Open the final document and print the file at 100 percent to make sure everything works properly. Supply this proof so the printer can see what the final is supposed to look like.

11. Create a mock-up. If you're doing a brochure that folds, or a document that needs folding and binding, make a mock-up to again ensure that the printer is clear about folding requirements.

12. Print color separations of files. Printing out the color separations will ensure that you aren't using any unwanted colors.

13. Burn the job to a CD. It's best to burn a CD with only your final job on it, as unneeded files may cause confusion and miscommunication.

14. Put any additional instructions in writing. Include instructions such as the quantity to be printed, any special folding instructions, etc. Try to anticipate any questions the printer may have; try to make his/her job easy. Remember that you are establishing a relationship with the printer with the hope that you will work together many times. The easier you make the printer's job, the harder they will work for you.

APPLICATION: SENDING JOBS TO THE PRINTER— A FINAL CHECKLIST

☐ All electronic files including any supporting files, images and/or fonts (if necessary).

☐ Anything that needs to be scanned by the printer (transparencies, for example).

- [ ] A laser printout of the project to show the printer what it should look like. If it's a folded piece, then trim and fold a sample to clearly represent your final vision. Think of this as a mock-up or prototype.

- [ ] If it's a spot or process color job, then it's very helpful to test your file setup by printing separations to ensure that you don't have any stray/unnecessary colors or separation issues.

- [ ] If this job is a reprint from a previous job (you need more copies of a successful piece), then include a sample from the previous print run. This will help the printer match that job.

- [ ] Include any instructions in writing, such as paper choice, quantity, trim size, scoring, etc.

PROOFING PROCESSES

You should always ask for a proof of your job, even if it's a fairly simple piece, as they may not be provided automatically. Mistakes can easily happen, and this is your chance to check accuracy before the piece goes to press. Additionally, for medium to large jobs, you will want the client to sign off on the proof. They are paying for the printing, and you want to ensure they are satisfied. This will also help to cover you, as the designer, if there are errors. The more eyes looking at the proof and signing off on it, the more chances there are to catch mistakes and the more dispersed the responsibility if there are errors in the final produced piece.

Try to avoid making changes at the proofing stage because it can be expensive and might add time to the schedule. Carefully review the job before it goes to the printer. Take every precaution to ensure a clean job that has little to no errors.

APPLICATION: CHECKING THE PROOFS

☐ Are the images in the proper orientation? Are all the images cropped properly?

☐ Are there any unwanted marks, either from the digital files or from the films?

☐ Is anything missing—images, logos, text?

☐ Are all the fonts correct? Did anything default due to missing fonts?

☐ Are all elements aligned properly? Are the margins the correct size?

☐ If it's a multiple-paged piece, are the pages in order and is everything right side up? Check the page numbers.

☐ If it's a color matching proof, are you happy with the color? Flat color? Color images?

☐ Check the color placement: Are the colors in the right places?

☐ Look carefully at the crop marks and/or ask for a trimmed-out proof: Is anything getting cut off that shouldn't?

☐ Are all die cuts, embossing or special processes done properly?

PRESS CHECKS

Once you've sent your job to the printer and have proofed it, as discussed in the previous chapter, the job is ready to be printed. In order to ensure that your job is looking right coming off the press, you will want to do a press check. Not every job calls for this. You may have a well-established relationship with your printer and they know your needs and expectations. Or maybe the job isn't very complex and you're sure the printer understands what you're looking for. In cases like these, you might not need to do a press check, but for many jobs, it gives you that last bit of quality control before the piece goes off to your client.

REAL WORLD ADVICE: SUCCESSFUL PRESS CHECKS

**DERALD SCHULTZ, MEDIARAIL DESIGN, INC.,
ARTICLES EDITOR FOR CREATIVE LATITUDE**

When you are asked to inspect the first press sheet, you could approve it and the press check is over. But, there are a number of things to check off your list beforehand. Do not feel pressured to sign off or make a decision quickly. It should take you at least five to ten minutes of inspection and questions before you make your decision.

Color: Compare the press sheet with the digital proof to make sure the colors are vibrant and true. If you want to further enhance or reduce a color, be sure to ask if other areas on the sheet will suffer to achieve it. Inspect solid color areas and central items to the job such as a main image. Are there pinholes in them? If so, circle them on the press sheet as an indication that they need to be eliminated.

Registration: Look at the crop marks at the corners of the sheet and the marks at the center of the sheet. They should be aligned with no individual color hanging outside it. The press person will have a loupe or magnifier to take a closer look. Remember, printing is not a perfect science, but registration should be very accurate.

Alignment: Check that colors are butting up next to each other without overlapping too much or having white space between them. This could happen even if the sheet is properly registered.

Sharpness: Look for detail in the photographs of the proof and compare them to the sheet. You should be able to see the same clarity and detail, especially in the highlight and shadow areas.

Nonimage Areas: Make sure there are no ink spots or slight color hues in the white areas of the sheet. This can be caused by a lack of fountain solution in nonimage areas that is used to repel ink.

Text: Inspect the text to make sure it is crisp and that there are no broken characters. If the text is a color other than black, make sure there are no other colors hanging out.

Press checks can be a great learning tool for any designer, and the added experience creates a greater value for you, your clients and the printer. Use it to build lasting and profitable relationships with both of them. If you go into a press check prepared and communicate clearly and concisely, everybody wins.

POST-PRESS BINDING OPERATIONS

If your project has multiple pages, then you'll need to determine the most appropriate binding technique for your design.

• **Saddle stitch:** In this process, folded signatures of paper are placed over a "saddle" and then stapled through the fold. Saddle stitch is one of the most common, simplest and inexpensive binding methods. It's good for brochures or pamphlets, because the staple can only penetrate and hold a limited number of sheets. This is considered a fairly informal style of binding.

• **Perfect binding:** In this process, the binding edge of the stack of paper is glued together and a tape or cover is placed over the pages to create a spine, like in a paperback book. This is an inexpensive form of binding, but may not endure a lot of bending and opening of the book. The glue tends to break down over time, so this isn't a good solution for jobs that need to last a long period of time.

• **Spiral binding or wire-o:** This binding method is also inexpensive. The plastic or wire material comes in various colors and can become an interesting design element if thoughtfully integrated into the overall piece. A substantial gutter area (about ½") needs to be left for the binding allowance since it cuts into the pages of the book.

• **Sewn binding or side stitching:** Sewn binding can look like perfect binding at first glance, but when you look into the fold of the signature, you'll see stitching. The stitching holds up over a longer period of time, although it is more expensive to produce. Sewn bindings are often used for jobs that require a longer shelf life, such as academic journals that are intended to be kept and archived in a library, as opposed to consumer magazines that will end up in the recycling.

• **Edition or case binding:** This process is used for high-end books that are intended to have a long shelf life. It can be expensive, but necessary and desirable for certain types of projects. In this process, the signatures are sewn together and then a hard cover is attached. This binding method will give a very formal appearance to the project.

PART EIGHT

EMERGING DESIGN PERSPECTIVES

One of your biggest responsibilities as a professional will be your personal engagement in the field to ensure its enhancement, growth and development, both independent of other disciplines and in collaboration with them.

Richard Grefé, Executive Director of AIGA, writes about the future of design in his article "2015: A Design Odyssey," "Designers are gifted with a special ability to see and communicate with clarity what others may not even understand. Designers are the intermediaries between information and understanding."

This section presents three of the most important emerging directions impacting design today: digital marketing, universal design and sustainability. Topics like these are creating paradigm shifts for designers and their clients. They require new ways of thinking about problems and implementing solutions. They require a new perspective on the audience/user—one that asks them to participate in the creation process, instead of being an outsider.

CHAPTER 24
TRENDS IN DIGITAL MARKETING

This chapter is adapted from a presentation by Marketing Professors Jim Coyle and Glenn Platt, Miami University, Oxford, Ohio.

THE POWER OF THE NETWORK

To understand digital marketing it's important to think about how technology impacts your life as a designer, as well as the impact on your clients and their target audiences. How does our connectivity—the growing network in which we interact—influence how you approach your problem solving and your relationships with your viewing audience?

These networks are important to designers and marketers for various reasons:

• **Information.** They allow marketers to gather large amounts of information about consumers, such as details about cell phone or internet usage, and process them very quickly. In addition, they derive value from having such information. For example, Amazon makes recommendations that get better as they gather more information.

• **New markets.** Networks change the way marketers connect to us by creating new markets. There are new markets that are available simply because of the advent of new technologies—there are new products, new designs and new services.

• **New channels.** You've got the screen of your TV, you have your screen on your desk or your laptop and now you have a little screen you carry in your purse or pocket, referred to as the "third screen." As a result, networks impact how messages are sent and how we design communications.

The beauty of networks is the availability of what Chris Anderson calls "The Long Tail." If you take the distribution of everybody on the planet, the whole Internet world, there is a "long tail" of distribution that provides the ability to market to very narrow targets. The individuals in these narrow markets are now able to find each other through this network and coalesce into a group that marketers want to target and designers need to connect with. New technologies make all of these new small markets worthwhile. This is a very different model than marketers and designers had previously, where they needed to have a large enough group to make the financials feasible.

As a designer, you need to be aware of these changes in technology and the growing importance of networks. That awareness should translate into action as you take advantage of these developments to market your own work and the work of your clients. The network can allow you to:

- collaborate with an international pool of designers, while focusing in on specific individuals with similar interests and needs

- cost effectively market your design work and philosophy to a broad audience of prospective clients

- target particular clients that match your business needs

- focus in on specific target audiences to meet your client's marketing needs

- gather data about your clients or their target audiences

- design innovative interfaces to engage clients and their audiences

E-MAIL ADVERTISING

Effective e-mail marketing is created by developing an e-mail plan and strategy that is targeted to what someone needs and wants. Marketing works best when you are showing a person something that's relevant to him, either a purchase or information of some sort. Permission-based marketing takes advantage of the relationship that the marketer has with the individual receiving the e-mail. There are various types:

• First there's direct e-mail. In this case, specific permission isn't given, but the e-mail, which often looks like a web ad, is targeted to a list that identifies a particular demographic as reasonable targets.

• Permission-based e-mail can be either unsponsored or sponsored. For instance, there might be a newsletter on alternative music and you have subscribed because you want to know the latest alternative music news. Perhaps it's brought to you by a sponsor, such as a specific band. So in this case, the relationship with the particular band is indirect, rather than the direct mailing list.

• Retention-based e-mail is a type of permission-based marketing, such as a newsletter. By signing up, you are saying "I want to hear what you have to tell me." Its focus is to establish, encourage and promote a relationship, rather than a sale.

Savvy one-to-one marketers and designers have learned that the more they allow the customer to be in control, the better they are equipped to take that data and insight and use it to deliver e-mail offers and information that are specifically relevant in both content and design. If the target shares their specific needs, interests and preferences, then the marketer can promise that they will only communicate when there is a specific reason to do so. The e-mail channel is a great way to complete the job of customer acquisition started by brand marketing tactics such as print, broadcast, tradeshows, public relations, blogging and search.

According to Glenn Platt, Professor of Marketing at Miami University, "Scotts Miracle-Gro does so well with 'Lawn Care Update,' which is their e-mail newsletter that consumers subscribe to. They practice a very simple mantra as it relates to e-mail and it goes like this, 'As it relates to e-mail, our job is to serve, not to sell.' They serve the customer best by delivering information that is relevant to the climate in which they live, the type of grass they are growing in their lawn, the size of the lawn. They have an understanding of what weed or insect problems the customer may be most prone to experiencing, and they provide the information that enables the consumer to make wise choices based upon which products they use to treat for that time of the year."

SOCIAL NETWORKS

Before the Internet, research suggested that in order to spread the word, the marketer would identify a few people with extraordinarily large networks and that these people would then pass along the marketer's message to their network. Now people like you and me, people with small to moderate size networks, are just as willing to share information with those networks.

According to Jim Coyle, Assistant Professor of Marketing at Miami University, "Marketers know that consumers are talking about brands online. In Facebook, MySpace and other online social networks, consumers are actively making recommendations about things that they love and panning things that they are disappointed with. Facebook created a new program through which marketers could become a part of the rating process and other online activities."

If marketers put together content that is engaging, then consumers are often more than willing to share that content with their social network. This is referred to as a "viral campaign." What makes a viral campaign effective?

- The brand should be central to the creation. We have all seen thirty-second spots that we thought were terribly funny, but if you can describe the campaign and execution without mentioning the brand, it has failed to create an impression of the brand.

- It should be interactive and aesthetically and conceptually engaging to the target audience.

- It is important that it is consistent with the offline execution or at least the tone of the offline brand. The look and feel of the online/viral message needs to match the overall branding strategy so that the consumer makes the connection and a lasting impression is made.

INTERNET, COST AND DESIGN

So what works best when marketing on the Internet? iTunes sells MP3s and Amazon sells MP3s and they are different prices, but they are exactly the same songs. To understand why a consumer would you pay more for a song on iTunes than for a song on Amazon, you have to understand the broader network of offerings that the iTunes store places in front of consumers. iTunes knows that once you are there, it's key that you have a user experience that is really easy to navigate, engaging and friendly. Selling of songs gets you in the door, but after that, it is about the experience—about the design of the user experience.

Price typically has about three different cost components: time, money and psychic costs. In the early days of the Internet, there was a sense that all this vast information would make consumers more sophisticated shoppers. But we are not like a computer and have processing limits. What has emerged are comparison shopping engines which give us the ability to aggregate pricing and quality data that we can manipulate and control in different ways. Since it's easier for a consumer to switch from one retailer to another, marketers and designers must come up with really innovative ways of keeping you engaged because you are just a click away from other retailers online. Creating very engaging and user-focused online experiences for consumers is absolutely paramount. For companies that have a good brand relationship with their consumers, it's also important to carry that over to the online experience.

TRENDS IN ONLINE ADVERTISING

There are some important trends in online advertising, and it's important for designers to be aware of them so they can more effectively work with marketing colleagues and their clients. It's your responsibility as a designer to be familiar with the latest trends and technological developments so you can offer up that knowledge and those skills to your clients. If you are unfamiliar with new alternatives, you will be less than effective in solving problems and in communicating with your client's target audiences, especially if they are a younger target.

Search Advertising

The ads that appear around your search results are termed "search advertising." These ads are based on whatever search term or search phrase you type in. For example, you type a specific CD title and "sponsor links" appear—these music retailers have put out bids on the specific term, in this case a CD title. When marketers bid on certain terms that are relevant to whatever they are selling, they come up with as comprehensive a list as possible. Keep in mind that just because these ads appear, these advertisers aren't paying money unless the links are clicked. There are prime positions and companies bid more for those placements.

Rich Media Advertising

The second trend is the popularity of rich media advertising. Rich media advertising is engaging, interactive and typically it includes video, audio, animation or some combination of the three. Rich media advertising can be especially powerful because it has the ability to tell stories, just like television and radio advertising. It also can be packed with detail and layers of information in a small banner size. Some of the ads can be gamelike, such as typing in commands to cause a change in the action occurring on screen. Most people will engage with this type of interaction several times, which repeatedly reinforces the brand's message.

Behavioral Targeting

The third trend is behavioral targeting, serving up ads based upon online behaviors. For example, imagine that you were at a florist web site, or perhaps you were just Googling "roses." Soon after that, you arrived at CNN. com and an ad that offers you a special deal on a dozen red roses appears on the top of the page. There are even technologies that take into account not just your recent behaviors online, but behaviors from past sessions. These technologies can even consider the items you have looked at from different product sites and what other people have looked at those same sites, and it can do an even better job of targeting advertising to you.

CONNECTING DIFFERENTLY WITH BLOGS

Blogging impacts the marketing world internally, through blogs by CEOs and other employees, and externally, through the blogs of consumers and reviewers. Through blogs, marketers can discover honest feedback and buzz about a company, its products and services. Keeping a finger on that important pulse can be critical to understanding perceptions and reactions.

One service that allows companies to follow the activity in the blogosphere is BlogPulse from Nielsen BuzzMetrics. You can type in a key word or a URL, and it actually searches the blogosphere and lets you know statistics about how much buzz there is about that term, as well as links to specific blogs with mentions. You can also retrieve statistics and find how much buzz there is over a specific period of time. This type of measurement can be critical to demonstrating if a campaign has been successful. For instance, if there's been a lot of activity and discussion during a specific viral campaign, this can be a strong metric for success.

Companies look at things like: What's the volume of buzz about my brand? What's the reach of the blogs that are discussing my company or brand? What specific issues are being discussed? Is it positive or is it negative? What source is it coming from? Is it coming from influential bloggers? From media bloggers? The conversation is out there. It is archived, and it is accessible. The key is how business leaders and marketers tap into that as a source of insight and guidance.

Brands need to listen in a completely different way. All brands do the traditional things, such as focus groups, one-on-one interviews and traditional market research, but they also need to focus on unsolicited, unaided, unvarnished feedback. Sometimes, what the angry or exuberant consumer volunteers without any prompting from the marketer is the greatest source of insight. It's raw. It's emotional. It's important to tap into the conversation about what's driving brand decisions.

This type of information is very important to designers as they are doing research and strategy development for their specific clients. This unvarnished feedback is what you need to get the true brand perceptions of target audiences. Perhaps you are doing a rebranding, including all the identity work, for a business that's been around for many years. Is that business viewed as old, tired and outdated? What specifically about the brand is problematic? How has their previous communication strategy reinforced these negative perceptions? Knowing all this, how can you now reinvent the brand in order to change those perceptions and avoid the problems identified by the bloggers?

MOBILE MARKETING

Through cell phones, marketers can participate in the lives of consumers when they are away from their laptops, desktops or offices. For example, there is a free directory assistance service called 1-800-free411; if you call to get a listing, you have to listen to a message before you get that listing. Bravo's cable channel promoted the third season of their show *Top Chef* by putting a brief message before each restaurant listing. When companies use phones to connect with their target audiences, they can make a strong and consistent statement about their brand.

For designers, there are various challenges with designing for a mobile device. Size is certainly at the top of the list. The screens have gotten larger with better resolution, but they are still small, relatively speaking. How can you design an experience that will effectively play, both aesthetically and functionally, on that restricted format? In addition, there are so many different types and sizes of screens. How can a designer create with various formats in mind? It's key from the beginning to think holistically about the various media a campaign is being produced on and for.

12 TENETS OF DIGITAL MARKETING

FROM *DIGIMARKETING: THE ESSENTIAL GUIDE TO NEW MEDIA & DIGITAL MARKETING* BY KENT WERTIME AND IAN FENWICK

1. Consumers and customers should be engaged as active participants (creators, contributors and commentators) and not viewed as passive targets.

2. Successful digital marketing engages people in a sustained way and is very different from the traditional metrics of reach and frequency. This requires a different sort of planning and strategy.

3. Marketers and designers need to consider the mix of channels that will work for their needs. The personal preferences of the audience should be considered.

4. Relevant content that is high quality and engaging is increasingly important in a world where the delivery mechanisms have become less important.

5. Consumers have more control and will direct more of the conversation. Consumer-generated content has become a critical component and will continue to grow in importance. Designers and marketers should embrace this and reward consumers for content that's relevant to the brand message.

6. Connecting with consumers must be on an opt-in basis, giving them control over when and where they receive messages. In addition, viral marketing will grow in importance.

7. Marketers and designers should understand a wide variety of new media options and the importance of search.

8. It's important to influence—not dictate—the conversation with the consumer.

9. The unification of the consumer experience, both in the digital and physical realms, is of growing importance. The use of customer data will enable a continuous, individualized dialogue.

10. Data has become the lifeblood of marketing because it gives more detailed psychographic and behavioral profiling of consumers.

11. Real-time analysis of data will allow for quick changes to marketing plans and activities.

12. Everything in the marketing mix will be measured and optimized to allow for and ensure continuous improvement.

APPLICATION: THINKING ABOUT DIGITAL MARKETING

- What social networks are you a part of and how are marketing practices integrated into them?

- Do you download any web applications to your cell phone? Have you received any ads?
- How does your digital network influence your day-to-day life and decision-making processes?
- How does your network influence your buying habits?
- How might companies use new and emerging technologies to connect with you?
- Have you forwarded a viral message to your network recently? What were characteristics/elements that persuaded you to forward it?

The questions above relate to you as a consumer. Now think about them again with your designer hat on. Think about the projects you are currently working on. How could you use these new technologies in any of those projects to the benefit of your clients?

Is there a particular medium (web app, blog, etc.) you could use to communicate your client's messages more effectively and persuade consumers about the relevance of what they have to offer?

CHAPTER 25
UNIVERSAL DESIGN

According to the Universal Design Alliance web site (www.universaldesign. org), universal design (UD) is defined as: "The design of products and environments to be usable by all people, to the greatest extent possible, without adaptation or specialized design. A user-friendly approach to design in the living environment where people of any culture, age, size, weight, race, gender and ability can experience an environment that promotes their health, safety and welfare today and in the future."

One of the key misconceptions about universal design is that it is "design for the disabled" as outlined in the ADA (Americans with Disabilities Act) guidelines. This isn't a true interpretation of the intent and philosophy behind universal design. Yes, this approach should result in design solutions of all sorts (architecture, print, web, products) that are more accessible to people with disabilities, but many times designers incorrectly interpret this as a narrow slice of the population. It's important to realize that almost everyone will have a disability of one type or another at some point in his life. Designers should be considering a large audience when approaching design from a universal perspective.

In most instances, when a design is considered from a universal perspective, it improves the design and functionality for everyone. Take doorknobs for instance. A design that doesn't require you to grasp the knob and turn, but just push down, will work for someone without hands, for someone whose hands are injured and for someone who has their hands full of books. This solution has improved functionality for a wide range of needs and situations. Universal design should benefit as many people as possible no matter their age, size or ability.

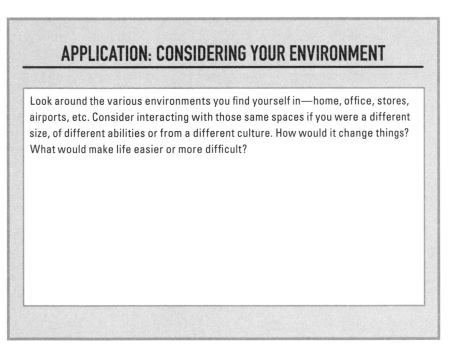

APPLICATION: CONSIDERING YOUR ENVIRONMENT

Look around the various environments you find yourself in—home, office, stores, airports, etc. Consider interacting with those same spaces if you were a different size, of different abilities or from a different culture. How would it change things? What would make life easier or more difficult?

UNIVERSAL DESIGN PRINCIPLES

The Center for Universal Design (CUD) at North Carolina State University's College of Design is a research center that focuses on the promotion, evaluation and development of accessible and universal design products and environments. The center and its web site (www.design.ncsu.edu/cud) are valuable information resources on UD issues. Their mission is "to improve environments and products through design innovation, research, education and design assistance."

THE PRINCIPLES OF UNIVERSAL DESIGN

PRINCIPLE ONE: EQUITABLE USE

The design is useful and marketable to people with diverse abilities.

Guidelines:

1a. Provide the same means of use for all users: identical whenever possible; equivalent when not.

1b. Avoid segregating or stigmatizing any users.

1c. Provisions for privacy, security and safety should be equally available to all users.

1d. Make the design appealing to all users.

Examples:

• powered doors with sensors at entrances that are convenient for all users

• integrated, dispersed and adaptable seating in assembly areas such as sports arenas and theaters

PRINCIPLE TWO: FLEXIBILITY IN USE

The design accommodates a wide range of individual preferences and abilities.

Guidelines:

2a. Provide choice in methods of use.

2b. Accommodate right- or left-handed access and use.

2c. Facilitate the user's accuracy and precision.

2d. Provide adaptability to the user's pace.

Examples:

• scissors designed for right- or left-handed users

• an automated teller machine (ATM) that has visual, tactile and audible feedback, a tampered card opening and a palm rest

PRINCIPLE THREE: SIMPLE AND INTUITIVE USE

Use of the design is easy to understand, regardless of the user's experience, knowledge, language skills or current concentration level.

Guidelines:

  3a. Eliminate unnecessary complexity.

  3b. Be consistent with user expectations and intuition.

  3c. Accommodate a wide range of literacy and language skills.

  3d. Arrange information consistent with its importance.

  3e. Provide effective prompting and feedback during and after task completion.

Examples:

  • a moving sidewalk or escalator in a public space

  • an instruction manual with drawings and no text

PRINCIPLE FOUR: PERCEPTIBLE INFORMATION

The design communicates necessary information effectively to the user, regardless of ambient conditions or the user's sensory abilities.

Guidelines:

  4a. Use different modes (pictorial, verbal, tactile) for redundant presentation of essential information.

  4b. Provide adequate contrast between essential information and its surroundings.

  4c. Maximize "legibility" of essential information.

  4d. Differentiate elements in ways that can be described (i.e., make it easy to give instructions or directions).

  4e. Provide compatibility with a variety of techniques or devices used by people with sensory limitations.

Examples:

  • tactile, visual and audible cues and instructions on a thermostat

- redundant cueing (e.g., voice communications and signage) in airports, train stations and subway cars

PRINCIPLE FIVE: TOLERANCE FOR ERROR

The design minimizes hazards and the adverse consequences of accidental or unintended actions.

Guidelines:

5a. Arrange elements to minimize hazards and errors: most used elements, most accessible; hazardous elements eliminated, isolated or shielded.

5b. Provide warnings of hazards and errors.

5c. Provide fail-safe features.

5d. Discourage unconscious action in tasks that require vigilance.

Examples:

- a double-cut car key easily inserted into a recessed keyhole in either of two ways
- an "undo" feature in computer software that allows the user to correct mistakes without penalty

PRINCIPLE SIX: LOW PHYSICAL EFFORT

The design can be used efficiently and comfortably and with a minimum of fatigue.

Guidelines:

6a. Allow user to maintain a neutral body position.

6b. Use reasonable operating forces.

6c. Minimize repetitive actions.

6d. Minimize sustained physical effort.

Examples:

- lever or loop handles on doors and faucets

• touch lamps operated without a switch

PRINCIPLE SEVEN: SIZE AND SPACE FOR APPROACH AND USE

Appropriate size and space is provided for approach, reach, manipulation and use regardless of user's body size, posture or mobility.

Guidelines:

7a. Provide a clear line of sight to important elements for any seated or standing user.

7b. Make reach to all components comfortable for any seated or standing user.

7c. Accommodate variations in hand and grip size.

7d. Provide adequate space for the use of assistive devices or personal assistance.

Example:

• controls on the front and clear floor space around appliances, mailboxes, Dumpsters and other elements

• wide gates at subway stations that accommodate all users

Please note that the Principles of Universal Design address only universally usable design, while the practice of design involves more than consideration for usability. Designers must also incorporate other considerations such as economic, engineering, cultural, gender and environmental concerns in their design processes. These Principles offer designers guidance to better integrate features that meet the needs of as many users as possible.

Version 2.0, 4/1/97. Compiled by advocates of universal design, listed in alphabetical order: Bettye Rose Connell, Mike Jones, Ron Mace, Jim Mueller, Abir Mullick, Elaine Ostroff, Jon Sanford, Ed Steinfeld, Molly Story and Gregg Vanderheiden.

Major funding provided by: The National Institute on Disability and Rehabilitation Research, U.S. Department of Education.

APPLICATION: APPLYING UNIVERSAL DESIGN PRINCIPLES

Which of the principles could you apply to one of your current or recent projects. How would it benefit the solution and the audience/user?

Now think about a store or museum that you've visited lately. Think through the principles and evaluate/critique the environmental design based upon them.

Lastly, find examples of products that follow the principles of universal design. Why do they work well? What about products that do not follow these principles? What could be changed to strengthen these designs?

DESIGN FOR DEMOCRACY

AIGA Design for Democracy is an excellent example of Universal Design. Starting in 1998, AIGA has focused efforts to apply "design tools and thinking to increase civic participation by making interactions between the U.S. government and its citizens more understandable, efficient and trustworthy." (www.aiga.org/content.cfm/design-for-democracy) Following the 2000 presidential election and the issues surrounding poorly designed ballots that were confusing to voters, Design for Democracy worked to develop ballot redesigns and national election design guidelines. *Design for Democracy: Ballot and Election Design,* authored by Marcia Lausen, AIGA Design for Democracy advisor, outlines the ballot redesign process, which focused on increased readability and clarified typographic hierarchy, and emphasizes the importance of the design profession in this type of endeavor. The ballot redesign makes it possible for all individuals to clearly understand the voting procedure and to freely participate in the election process.

ONLINE RESOURCES ON UNIVERSAL DESIGN:

- Americans with Disabilities Act web site: www.ada.gov
- ADA guidelines for signage: www.access-board.gov/adaag/html/adaag. htm#4.30
- NC State University Center for Universal Design: www.design.ncsu. edu/cud
- CUD's resource page: www.design.ncsu.edu/cud/about_ud/udresourcepage.htm#ADA
- Accessibility in web site and software design: www.usabilityfirst.com/
- Web Accessibility Initiative: www.w3.org/WAI/
- AIGA Design for Democracy: www.aiga.org/content.cfm/design-for-democracy
- Jakob Nielson's web site on usability: www.useit.com
- Universal Design Alliance web site: www.universaldesign.org

USABILITY

Usability is related to Universal Design, as they are both concerned with user-centered design that promotes ease of use and elegance of functionality. Most often, the term usability refers to web site, software or interface design and refers to how easy or difficult it is for the user to perform tasks, such as finding a particular piece of information on a web site. Usability First (www.usabilityfirst.com) notes that, "Usability depends on a number of factors including how well the functionality fits user needs, how well the flow through the application fits user tasks and how well the response of the application fits user expectations. Usability is the quality of a system that makes it easy to learn, easy to use, easy to remember, error tolerant and subjectively pleasing."

PRINCIPLES OF USABILITY

SMASHING MAGAZINE'S "10 PRINCIPLES OF EFFECTIVE WEB DESIGN," 2008

1. Keep it intuitive: A web page should be "obvious and self-explanatory."

2. Don't try the user's patience: The fewer actions required to perform a task, the more likely the user will actually try it out.

3. Focus the user's attention: Use visual hierarchy to point people where you want them to go.

4. Expose the site's features/functions: Clearly communicate what is available/accessible on the site.

5. Watch your writing: Use concise language that is easily scanned and gets to the point.

6. Keep it simple: Clearly present the options and communicate what the site is about.

7. Use white space: If you fill the screen, your user will feel overwhelmed and confused.

8. Build a structure: Keep your visual structure organized, economical and efficient.

9. Use site conventions to your advantage: Using expected conventions doesn't need to be boring.

10. Test early and often: It's very important to user test your site at various points in the process so you can continually improve the design.

In a ZDNet Asia interview on usability ("Usability Make Business Sense" by Isabelle Chan), guru Jakob Nielsen notes the importance of usability to business success: Customers buy products and services from sites that are well-designed, easy to use and navigate. In discussing the similarities and differences between web designers and usability experts, Nielsen notes, "These are two different skills. Sometimes you can be lucky and find one person who can do both well, but that's rare. Most big companies need to hire several people and build an interdisciplinary team for their web site. It is true that there are more web designers than there are usability professionals. My recommendation is to spend 10 percent of a company's web budget on usability. That's what you need to find out what customers want. Then, spend the remaining 90 percent of the budget on building that."

In order to achieve a successful solution, it's critical to test users on the system that's being developed. Through an iterative process of design then test, design then test, overall refinement and continuous improvement will be achieved. It's impossible for an interface designer to anticipate all the users' needs and foretell their reactions to certain types of visual directions and navigation. User testing will reveal interpretations and behavior that the designer could never have predicted on his own.

APPLICATION: LEARNING ABOUT USER TESTING

Choose a web site you visit regularly or one that you've designed yourself. Use the basic steps of user testing to test the site's usability on a person who's not familiar with the site.

What works well?

What needs to be improved?

Is the site navigation effective or confusing? Why?

CHAPTER 26
SUSTAINABILITY

Dr. Gro Harlem Brundtland, in her 1987 report, "Our Common Future," defined sustainable development as the "... development that meets the needs of the present without compromising the ability of future generations to meet their own needs." Richard Grefé, Executive Director for AIGA, notes in his article "2015: A Design Odyssey," "We know that sustainability—cultural sustainability, as well as resource sustainability—is going to be an issue tomorrow, just as it has grown in urgency and importance today. Designers can address this theme and make a positive impact by giving thought to the long-term life span of the products and materials they design. Starting now, designers can make informed choices and be brave enough to ask questions such as, 'Do we need it? Can we live without it?' not only of themselves but of their clients too. Just think how much better positioned we will be to address challenges in just eight years if we start making smarter decisions today."

In answering client needs and developing solutions, designers have a special responsibility to produce work that minimizes adverse consequences to the environment. Because we are involved in the creation of so many types of print and packaging materials, designers play a critical role in supporting businesses in being environmentally responsible because of the effects to both natural and human resources.

It is about advancing important economic activity while simultaneously being responsible about the resources we are consuming and the waste we are creating. Sustainability is good business and can save money, as well as resources. Our activities and choices must be sustainable for our future and the future of our children, economically, socially and environmentally.

AIGA has a downloadable brochure on their website that focuses on "Print Design and Environmental Responsibility" (www.aiga.org/content. cfm/design-business-and-ethics). It presents the standards for our profession regarding our social responsibilities as designers working within a fragile world. As stated in the brochure, "There are many interpretations of the term 'sustainability,' and its definition continues to evolve as global debate on the topic widens. For some, it means maintaining the status quo. For others it is equated with notions of responsibility, conservation and stewardship. However, for a growing number of people, sustainability is a concept associated with 'sustainable development.' The first definition of which was articulated in the United Nations World Conservation Strategy of 1980. 'Development' in this context includes economic growth, human rights and the satisfaction of basic human needs. Regardless of which definition of sustainability resonates with your views, there are several myths and misconceptions about it."

MYTHS ABOUT SUSTAINABILITY

AIGA's brochure on environmental responsibility available at www.aiga. org/content.cfm/design-business-and-ethics discusses five common myths about sustainability related specifically to the graphic design profession. The information below lists these myths and summarizes why they are not true. Use this information to educate your fellow designers and your clients.

Myth 1: Print design isn't an environmental issue.

The production of paper and printing are key environmental issues, and despite predictions that digital media would lessen paper use, print media have grown over time. AIGA notes the following startling statistics:

- Although the United States represents less than 5 percent of the world's population, we consume more than 25 percent of the world's paper and printed products.

- We receive 65 billion pieces of unsolicited mail each year, equal to 230 pieces per person.

- According to the American Forest and Paper Association, the average American uses more than 748 pounds of paper per year.

- It takes approximately 68 million trees per year to produce the catalogs and "junk" mail we receive, and half of it is discarded unopened.

A common perception is that the adverse environmental impact of paper use is most impactful on the consumption of trees, but trees are a renewable resource. Actually, it's the converting of wood to paper that is more problematic—this results in the third largest use of fossil fuels worldwide. Additionally, printing inks can cause environmental issues in production and waste.

Myth 2: There's a limited market demand for environmentally responsible design and print production.

Both business and government are beginning to actively embrace social responsibility and sustainability. Corporations will be starting to ask designers to create Corporate Social Responsibility (CSR) and Global Reporting Initiative (GRI) reports, just like traditional annual reports. Many large corporations such as Procter & Gamble and Toyota are seeing the benefits of incorporating sustainability into their business practices and branding strategies. AIGA notes, "The need for print solutions with improved financial, social and environmental performance is becoming a high priority for companies that rely heavily on print in industries like consumer goods, publishing, retail and banking." Designers are critical advisors to companies regarding their "triple bottom line" of economic, social and environmental perspectives.

Myth 3: Business leaders are concerned only with reducing costs and generating profits.

There is a clear need, given corporate scandals and a sagging economy, for restoring trust in corporate America. Sustainable and socially responsible business practices are seen as ways of demonstrating ethical policies to consumers and investors. Designers have the opportunity to help companies craft their messages by creating effective corporate social responsibility reports that are strong pieces of visual communication modeling sustainable paper and printing practices. It's critical for designers to partner with clients to design solutions that create less waste and more value. William McDonough said, "You don't filter smokestacks or water. Instead, you put the filter in your head and design the problem out of existence."

Myth 4: Using paper with recycled content and soy-based inks will eliminate the negative impacts of print.

Specification of post-consumer recycled paper and the use of inks that are based on renewable resources, such as soy, are good steps forward, but designers need to do more and demand more if we are to make a larger impact. This is a complex problem, and designers need to be careful about oversimplifying the solution. It's critical to educate yourself so that you understand the various facets of this issue. For instance, when we consider recycling, AIGA outlines not one, but four essential aspects:

- the design of products that use less virgin material and that themselves can be recycled

- the manufacture of these materials into new recyclable products
- the collection and processing of recyclable materials
- the specification, purchase and use of recycled-content products

The sustainability of a product is impacted by how it's manufactured, the amount of energy and what type of resources (water, petroleum, etc.) it takes to create the product and the manner in which it is distributed— not just the amount of post-consumer waste in the product. The entire production process should be taken into account. Are there particular companies that use a very efficient process? Are there others whose products have a good recycled content, but whose production and distribution processes are flawed and inefficient? According to AIGA, "Manufacturers can apply for the International Standards Organization (ISO) 14,000 series of standards, an international benchmark for commitment to continuous improvement in environmentally responsible performance; as a consumer or specifier, the designer can ask whether a manufacturer is ISO 14,000 certified. ... Designers have an opportunity to make their interest in environmentally preferable products and services known. To be credible, designers and graphic communication professionals will need to learn to speak the language of sustainability and to engage vendors, suppliers, customers and other stakeholders in this issue. Designers also have an obligation to themselves and to their profession to seek the knowledge and skill required to move sustainable design from the margins to the mainstream of design practice and business communications in print."

Myth 5: There are no resources for information or training to support efforts to design and produce print in a sustainable manner.

There's a wealth of information and training regarding sustainability. As a design professional, you should stay abreast of developments in this area; there are yearly changes in what printers have to offer, for instance. See page 306 for a list of resources on the web and spend some time reading the various blogs. There are also training and continuing education courses at educational institutions, paper and printing companies, and government and community organizations. Take advantage of the educational opportunities available.

AIGA PRINCIPLES FOR ENVIRONMENTALLY RESPONSIBLE PRINT DESIGN

FROM WWW.AIGA.ORG/CONTENT.CFM/ DESIGN-BUSINESS-AND-ETHICS

- Rethink features and functions to use less material and less energy.
- Consider closed-loop lifecycles from design through production, use and recovery.
- Design for recyclability, reusability and recoverability of energy and materials.
- Seek independently verified data about environmental aspects and lifecycle impacts.
- Select materials with less impact and toxicity (via air, water and solid waste streams).
- Increase use of recycled and renewable materials.
- Optimize production techniques to eliminate scrap, error and waste.
- Select lower-impact packaging and distribution systems.
- Design for reduced energy use, water use and waste impacts during use.
- Maximize the length of the product's useful life.
- Recover, reuse and recycle materials at end of the product's life.

ONLINE SUSTAINABILITY RESOURCES

- AIGA Center for Sustainable Design: www.sustainability.aiga.org
- The Centre for Sustainable Design: www.cfsd.org

- Business for Social Responsibility: www.bsr.org
- Green Options network of blogs: www.greenoptions.com
- The Designers Accord global coalition: www.designersaccord.org
- Inhabitat blog on sustainable and design issues: www.inhabitat.com
- Forest Stewardship Council: www.fsc.org
- International Organization for Standardization: www.iso.org
- Institute for Sustainable Communication: www.sustainablecommunication.org
- Sustainable Advertising Partnership: www.sustainableadvertisingpartnership.org
- o2-USA network for green design: www.o2-usa.org
- Renourish articles and resources for the graphic design community: www.re-nourish.com
- Green business information: www.greenbiz.com

GUIDELINES AND QUESTIONS TO ASK

In "Greening Graphic Design: A Step-by-Step Guide," from the blog Inhabitat, Rebecca Silver outlines various ideas and questions to get you started on the road to a more sustainable project.

Guidelines for you:

- Decide early in the project that you will commit to following sustainable principles.

- Calibrate your computer equipment/monitor to facilitate print/color accuracy.

- Pay special attention to your prepress setup to get the job right the first time.

- Try to limit your color so you only need one pass through the press.

- Consider choosing a local printer and supplies that are locally distributed to limit the amount of transportation necessary to get the job done.

- Work efficiently with standard paper sizes and try to limit paper waste as much as possible.

- Specify the most sustainable paper available.

Questions for your printer:

- How does your printer power their equipment?

- Do they do everything in-house or do they outsource portions of the job (binding, for instance)?

- Are they ISO 14,000 certified?

- Does your printer keep Lifecycle Material Data Sheets for their products?

- What processes do they use to minimize waste and toxins?

- What type of inks do they use?

- How do they dispose of their paper, ink and material waste?

APPLICATION: CHANGING YOUR MINDSET

Consider one of your current design projects.

As you conceptualize and create the solution, how could you think differently about it?

What aspects of the problem and solution affect the environment?

Which, if any, of the myths addressed in this chapter is holding your back from creating a sustainable solution?

What could you do to make the design more environmentally friendly and sustainable?

RESOURCES

BOOKS:

100 Habits of Successful Graphic Designers: Insider Secrets on Working Smart and Staying Creative by Plazm

AIGA Professional Practices in Graphic Design, edited by Tad Crawford

A Whole New Mind: Moving from the Information Age into the Conceptual Age by D. H. Pink

Becoming a Graphic Designer: A Guide to Careers in Design, 3rd Edition by Steven Heller and Teresa Fernandes

Design Management: Managing Design Strategy, Process and Implementation by Kathryn Best

DigiMarketing: The Essential Guide to New Media & Digital Marketing by Kent Wertime and Ian Fenwick

Graphic Artist Guild Handbook: Pricing and Ethical Guidelines

The Designer's Guide to Marketing and Pricing: How to Win Clients and What to Charge Them by Ilise Benun and Peleg Top

The Savvy Designer's Guide to Success: Ideas and Tactics for a Killer Career by Jeff Fisher

The 7 Habits of Highly Effective People by Steven Covey

WEB SITES AND BLOGS:

American Institute of Graphic Arts: www.aiga.org
AIGA | Aquent Survey of Design Salaries: www.designsalaries.org/
Business of Design: www.businessofdesignonline.com
Business Week: www.businessweek.com
Color Association: www.colorassociation.com
Color Marketing Group: www.colormarketing.org
Communication Arts: www.commarts.com
Core 77: www.core77.com
Creative Business: www.creativebusiness.com
Creative Hot List: www.creativehotlist.com/
Creative Latitude: www.creativelatitude.com
Design Talkboard: www.designtalkboard.com
Design Observer: www.designobserver.com
Dexigner: www.dexigner.com
Entrepreneur Magazine: www.entrepreneur.com
Fast Company: www.fastcompany.com
HOW Design: www.howdesign.com
Inhabitat: www.inhabitat.com
Mindtools: www.mindtools.com
Monster: www.monster.com
Smashing Magazine: www.smashingmagazine.com
Subtraction: www.subtraction.com

INDEX